HEAVEN *and* HELL

HEAVEN
and HELL

Visions of the Afterlife in the
Western Poetic Tradition

Louis Markos

 CASCADE *Books* · Eugene, Oregon

HEAVEN AND HELL
Visions of the Afterlife in the Western Poetic Tradition

Cascade Books
A Division of Wipf and Stock Publishers
199 W. 8th Ave., Suite 3
Eugene, OR 97401

www.wipfandstock.com

ISBN 13: 978-1-62032-750-0

Cataloging-in-Publication data:

Markos, Louis.

Heaven and hell : visions of the afterlife in the Western poetic tradition / Louis Markos.

xiv + 230 p. ; 23 cm. Includes bibliographical references.

ISBN 13: 978-1-62032-750-0

1. Hell. 2. Heaven. 3. Death in literature. 4. Future life in literature. 5. Hell—Christianity—History of doctrines. 6. Homer—Criticism, interpretation, etc. 7. Virgil—Criticism, interpretation, etc. 8. Dante Alighieri, 1265–1321. 9. Milton, John, 1608–1674. I. Title.

BT846.3 M34 2013

Manufactured in the U.S.A.

For all the wonderful students I have taught in

The Honors College of Houston Baptist University.

Thanks for accompanying me on the Journey.

Contents

Acknowledgments

I would like to thank Houston Baptist University for awarding me the Robert H. Ray Chair in Humanities and the title of Scholar-in Residence, and for inviting me to teach the freshman classical Christian curriculum for HBU's Honors college. These honors have helped make it possible for me to complete this book.

I have dedicated this book to my Honors college students, and I would like to list here a number of those students who not only attended my classes on Greece and Rome but who were active members of my home Bible study. From Spring 2010 to Spring 2013, these students have studied, sung, prayed, and shared with me late into the night. I have also included in this list a number of students who were not in the Honors college but who attended my English classes and were active in the Bible study: Ashley Arnold, Lesleigh Balkum, Brenna Bench, Tyrin Bickham, Beth Bottom, Philip Brewer, Isaac Brocato, Angelica Caamano, Megan Carlisle, Tartan Collier, Matt Davis, Ruth Felder, Jakora Frazier, Andi Garbarino, Jesse Glass, Erin Hallford, Lauren Harter, Brittany Herman, Lupe Hernandez, Chelsea Hill, Lydia Holt, Evan Huegel, Joshua C. Jones, Joshua J. Jones, Lauren Jordan, Milandri Kriel, Ethan Lawrence, Jacquie Lawrence, John Mack, Wil Maestretti, Lauren Manske, Mariah Martinez, David Mathew, Esther Mathew, Jon McIntyre, Rob Oakley, Vince Meyers, Gabe O'Neal, Isha Patel, Morgan St. John, Taylor Suarez, Mason Tabor, Allison Thai, Dustin Thomasy, John Valentine, Joshua Vance, Alesia Voice, and Nicole Yates.

Finally, I would like to say thank you to Dr. Robert Stacey, the Dean of the Honors college, for sharing my love of the classics and of our students, and to Sharon and William Morris for allowing me to use Frans Francken the Younger's *The Last Judgment* as the cover of this book.

Introduction

For thousands of years, philosophers, theologians, and poets have tried to pierce through the veil of death to gaze with wonder, fear, and awe on the final and eternal state of the soul. Indeed, the four great epic poets of the Western world (Homer, Virgil, Dante, and Milton) structured their epics in part around a descent into the underworld that is both spiritual and physical, both allegorical and geographical. In this book, I will not only consider closely these epic journeys to the "other side," but will explore how they were influenced by, and in turn influenced the visions of, such writers as Plato, Cicero, Bunyan, Blake, and C. S. Lewis.

In following these great writers on their heavenly or infernal journeys, I shall attempt to work through a number of questions that are still, I believe, relevant to our modern world: Why is Homer's Hades such a gloomy place? How did Plato supply Virgil and Dante with both an abstract morality and a concrete map for navigating the underworld? How are the Christian visions of Dante and Milton both similar to and different from the pagan ones of Homer and Virgil? How does the notion of divine reward and punishment function in the poetic treatment of Heaven and Hell? What message can the dead give to the living? Are Heaven and Hell real places or merely contrary states of mind? I shall ask these questions as a professor of literature, but I shall also ask them in a way that has fallen out of favor in the modern academy.

As C. S. Lewis points out in *The Screwtape Letters* (#27), when modern academics are presented with works from the past, they do a fine job asking technical questions about the genesis and audience of the work, about the earlier works that influenced it and the later works that it influenced in turn, and about the current scholarly debate over the status of the author, his work, and his age. What they are not good at asking—what, in fact, they rarely bother to even consider asking—is whether or not the work is *true*, whether it draws us closer to that which is Good, True, and Beautiful, or whether it turns us away from the right path. Throughout this book I shall, unashamedly, seek to gain real, honest-to-goodness wisdom from the ancient writers (*both* pagan and Christian), the kind of wisdom that not only leads us to that which is eternal—to what T. S. Eliot called "permanent things"—but which just might encourage us to alter the way we think, speak, and behave.

As for organization, the first half of the book will focus on ancient visions of the underworld, with a view to how these various traditions culminate in Dante's *Inferno*. After an introductory chapter that considers some of the reasons why all people at all times have yearned for information about the afterlife, I shall move into a general overview of the Hebrew concept of sheol and the Greek understanding of Hades. I shall then turn my focus to the first great epic account of the underworld as it is seen through the eyes of Homer's Odysseus. From the sublimities of Homer's epic poetry I shall move into a survey of Plato's numerous speculations of the afterlife as they appear in such works as *Republic*, *Phaedo*, *Apology*, *Gorgias*, and *Phaedrus*. Though it is not often realized, poets have relied as much on Plato as on Homer for their information regarding both the philosophy and the geography of the underworld; indeed, it is Plato more than anyone else who conjures up both the horrors of Hades and the glories of the Elysian Fields (the closest the Greeks came to a vision of Heaven).

Chapter 6 will take us to Rome, and will offer a blow-by-blow description of Aeneas' journey through the underworld (*Aeneid* VI). I will consider how Virgil adapted the Greek visions of Homer and Plato for a Roman audience, and will take a brief look at a second Roman vision of the afterlife: Cicero's "Dream of Scipio." From there, I shall leap into the Christian world of Dante to consider how Dante assimilated the pagan visions of his predecessors into a more Christian understanding of the afterlife. I will begin by surveying Dante's medieval vision of the cosmos and considering why he chose the pagan Virgil as his guide through a Catholic universe, and conclude with a level-by-level tour of Hell that will focus on the arrangement of sins, the punishments meted out, the various monsters that inflict the punishments, and the specific sinners with whom Dante converses.

The second twelve chapters will consider European Christian views of Heaven and Hell. After a brief survey of the New Testament's vision of the afterlife—with a focus on the Resurrection, the Millennium, and the New Jerusalem—I shall offer a level-by-level tour of Dante's *Purgatorio* and *Paradiso*. Here, as in my chapters on the *Inferno*, I shall explore how Dante shaped his pagan material to fit a Catholic Christian worldview, unpack the complex arrangements that he fashioned for his epic look at the state of the blessed, and champion his powerful vision of the true freedom for which we were made.

Chapters 18–20 will carry us forward to late Renaissance Protestant Britain where I shall first consider the last of the great epic visions of Heaven and Hell, *Paradise Lost*, paying particular attention to Milton's unique but influential visions of Hell and its demons and of Heaven and its angels, and then explore John Bunyan's allegorical vision of the Celestial City (*Pilgrim's Progress*) and John Donne's poetic musings on the final resurrection. From there, chapter 21 will discuss how such British Romantic poets as Blake, Shelley, and Byron altered European views of the afterlife and made Milton's Satan into the hero of *Paradise Lost*. Chapters 22 and 23 will offer a fascinating point-counterpoint dialogue between a nineteenth-century Gnostic view of the afterlife (Blake's apocalyptic *The Marriage of Heaven and Hell*) and an orthodox Christian vision (C. S. Lewis's *The Great Divorce*). I will conclude by considering how Victorian thinkers attempted to bring Heaven down to earth, and how their heirs often created Hell on earth instead.

Let me make clear at the outset that I will be limiting myself to the central poetic tradition of the West. I will avoid spiritualist, cultic, and fringe groups, and, though I will have much to say about angels and demons, I shall not plunge into the intricacies of angelology or demonology, or into such practices as witchcraft and voodoo. Further, though I will discuss theology and philosophy when they are relevant, and though I will be treating the theological and philosophical insights of the authors with respect and even reverence, my chief concern will be with the poetic rather than with the theological. Finally, though I will occasionally compare and contrast Western visions of the afterlife with those of Buddhists, Hindus, Muslims, and ancient Egyptians, my focus will remain firmly on the Judeo-Christian, Greco-Roman heritage of Europe. I make no apology for this decision. It is our tradition, it is worth studying and preserving, and it is one that all those born in the West, and all those immigrants who have chosen to identify themselves with the West, should be proud of.

1

Introduction
Piercing the Veil of Death

Long ago, before Achilles fought and died at Troy, the Muse Calliope gave birth to a son whose father, some said, was the god Apollo. The name of the boy was Orpheus, and he grew to be the greatest musician of the ancient world. When he played upon his lyre, the trees danced, the winds sighed, and the very stones moved. Drawn by the beauty of his songs, the dryad Eurydice fell in love with the Thracian singer, and, in the following spring, the two were wed. But sorrow soon befell the young lovers. A serpent bit Eurydice on the heel, robbing her of life and casting her soul into Hades.

Grief stricken by the loss of his wife, Orpheus wandered far and wide in search of the hidden doorway to the world below. Guided by love, he found the secret entrance and began his long, slow descent. With each step, the darkness thickened and an aching sense of despair made his limbs feel heavy and old. As he set his foot on the cold floor of Hell, he heard the sound of three ferocious dogs barking in unison. He peered into the gloom to see the dogs, and found, to his horror, that there were not three, but a single mastiff of enormous size with three heads branching out of its thick and sinewy neck. It was Cerberus, three-headed guardian of the realm of Hades, but the sweet song of Orpheus's lyre overpowered the beast, and he continued safely on his way.

Soon he came to the far bank of that river upon which the gods, having sworn an oath, can never forsake their vow. Knowing that death would carry him away if he tried to wade through the black waters of Styx, he awaited the coming of Charon, the silent, shrouded ferryman of the dead. Charon held out his bony fingers for a coin, and again Orpheus played on his lyre, the same song he had used to overpower the sirens when he had sailed on the Argo with Jason and his men. Charon took him on board, though the weight of the living Orpheus caused the boards to creak and dark water to ooze along the deck.

As the boat glided silently across the Stygian waters, Orpheus saw the souls of the dead massed on the other shore. They looked pale and bloodless, more like shades than men. He could speak with none of them, and so he ventured on alone into the depths of the underworld. Cries of agony soon assaulted his ears, rising upward as from a bottomless pit. Down there, in the depths of Tartarus, the souls of the wicked endured their punishments.

There was Tantalus, suspended in a pool of water while grapes hung in profusion above his head. When he stretched up his hands for the grapes, a wind blew them out of reach; when he bent down his head for a drink, the water rushed out and away from his lips. There was Sisyphus, who must ever push his stone up a hill, knowing that every time he reaches the top, the stone will roll back down. And Tityus, his body stretched out over nine acres while a vulture feeds eternally on his ever-renewed entrails. And Ixion, bound to a wheel that spins without pause. And the sad, sad daughters of Danaus, cursed to carry water in leaky buckets, unable to fulfill the task whose fulfillment alone can win them rest.

And there, with the souls of the damned, lived the Titans, who strove in battle with the Olympian gods and were imprisoned in the lowest pit of Hell by Zeus and his brothers, Poseidon and Hades. There too lived the dreaded Furies, poison dripping from their fangs, their hair a mass of venomous snakes. It is they who drive men mad with guilt and fear and remorse.

In the end, Orpheus found his way to the black throne of Hades. Again and again he begged the Lord of the Underworld to release Eurydice, but the grim monarch refused. For the third time, Orpheus played upon his lyre, but this time he added words to his song. "Lord Hades," he sang, "all the dead belong to you, and soon all that live will come to your dark kingdom. What do you care if Eurydice should live for another forty years? In the end, she will return to you. Think of your wife, Persephone, how love for her beauty drew you to leave your kingdom and seek her hand. Love, my Lord, is stronger than death, stronger even than you. Take pity on me, and send my beloved back to my waiting arms."

As Orpheus sang, the whole world below seemed to change. The mist blew away, the moaning ceased, and marvelous things began to happen. The Furies beat their breasts and wept. Tantalus lay down on the grass with a cluster of grapes in his hand. The vulture sat by the head of Tityus, and the two wept together. Ixion's wheel stopped spinning, and the daughters of Danaus put down their buckets and rested. Sisyphus no longer rolled his stone up the hill but climbed on top of it and sat there listening to Orpheus's song.

But there was a greater marvel! The song of Orpheus touched the cold and stony heart of Hades. It accomplished what a thousand warriors in arms could not do. It, in the words of Milton, "Drew iron tears down Pluto's cheek, / And made Hell grant what love did seek."

"Orpheus," said Hades, his eyes wet with tears, "You may take your Eurydice away with you, back to the world of men. But listen well. Until you and your bride have stepped out of the cave and have felt the sun on your foreheads, you must not look at her. As you climb the stairs, Eurydice will follow behind you. But if you look back at her, even for a moment, she will be lost to you forever."

With joy and hope restored, Orpheus began his long, slow ascent. His face fixed forward, his heart yearning to see the light at the end of the long staircase, he pressed onward in silence. But as he neared the mouth of the cave, fear gripped his heart. What if Hades had tricked him? What if his Eurydice were not walking behind him? As the dead make no sound, Orpheus had heard nothing, not even the smallest footfall, to signal the presence of his wife.

"What could it hurt," he thought, "to take one quick look." And so the foolish lover turned his head and gazed full upon his wife. Eurydice screamed and held out her hands, but a wind blew down the stairs and carried off her phantom form. For a second, Orpheus saw her robe floating on the air, and then she was gone, swallowed by the darkness below.

For weeks on end, Orpheus wandered along the byroads of Greece, playing his lyre and singing of his pain. Wherever he went, the trees bowed before him, and the dew dripped from their branches like human tears. A group of Maenads, who follow in the train of Bacchus and drink of his wine, were moved by the song, and they implored Orpheus to give them his love. But when the singer rejected their advances, rage filled their hearts, and they seized him by his flowing hair. Made strong by the wine of Bacchus, they tore Orpheus to pieces and scattered his limbs along the countryside of Thrace. His hands and his head and his golden lyre they tossed in the river. And as they floated downstream, the severed hands thrummed the lyre and the dead tongue sang its last song of sorrow.

Hopes and Fears

The tale of Orpheus is a tragic one that seems to offer little hope, and yet, do we not, in a way, envy him his wondrous journey? In every age, in every culture, among every nation and tribe, people have been fascinated by tales of the afterlife. Into these tales they have poured their hopes and fears and dreams. And they have passed them on, generation by generation, to their descendants. All people, from the poet to the scientist, the pauper to the prince, the primitive to the PhD, yearn to pierce the veil and see what lies on the other side of death.

True, there are many today, as there have been in all ages, who say that when we die we die, and that is the end of the matter. Nevertheless, even the most doctrinaire Darwinist, the most stubborn materialist, the most confirmed atheist knows, or at least senses, that there is a part of his or her being that cannot be accounted for by physical nature. Our bodies may be like the beasts, and perhaps even the physical synapses in our brains, but can anyone truly doubt that our consciousness sets us apart from the natural world? Is it not self-evident that our mind is not just quantitatively but also qualitatively different from our brain? Is it not clear that there is a part of us that cannot be reduced to physical mechanisms and natural processes? Once the anatomist has catalogued my body parts, the neurosurgeon has dissected my frontal and parietal lobes, and the chemist has unpacked my genetic code, there is still a part of me that escapes completely their surgical knives and chemical formulae. There is the "me" that transcends the physical, that can even touch on eternity (on timelessness) in a way that no mere element of nature can do.

Only humans can perceive, in glimpses, a time that is outside of time and a space that cannot be contained by the physical limits of nature. More to the point, only humans feel hope or fear at the prospect of their own death. Indeed, as C. S. Lewis points out in *The Problem of Pain*, we are the only species on Earth that is afraid of its own dead. Tarzan may feel a numinous sense of awe and dread when he enters the graveyard of the elephants, but the elephant on which he rides feels no such emotion. In one sense, the ubiquitous human fear of ghosts is ridiculous, for how can a mere ghost, a diaphanous shade do us any harm? But then, it is not the fear of physical harm that gives us the gooseflesh and makes our hair stand on end. We fear, rather, the prospect of a soul cut off from its body, a mode of existence that lies outside our experience but which we can nevertheless conceive.

The psychiatrists tell us that no human being can imagine his own death: that is to say, we cannot imagine the extinction or annihilation of our personhood. Every part of our being tells us that we—the inner we, the real we—will persist. The fear of ghosts, I believe, comes from the fear that our soul will be trapped in between this world and the next, forced to wander homeless and displaced. In the religions of the East, the soul either returns in a new form (reincarnation) or joins with a larger One Soul into which it empties itself like a drop in the ocean, but in the major Semitic and European religions of the West, the soul travels to a new home—whether that home be positive (Heaven, Valhalla, Paradise, Elysian Fields), neutral (Hades, Sheol), or negative (Hell, Tartarus). Though the fear of eternal punishment is widespread, the fear of detachment, of being a graveyard ghost who cannot find rest in the world beyond, is often just as strong. The *Iliad*, *Odyssey*, and *Aeneid* all feature souls that beg for proper burial rites that they might find rest, and the play *Antigone* centers on a heroine who sacrifices her life to secure such rites for her brother.

All this is to say that we human beings have always approached death and the afterlife with a certain degree of ambivalence. On the one hand, we, as a species that builds and plans and creates, yearn for assurance that this world and this life are not all there is. On the other hand, we fear we will be asked, in the end, to give an account of what we have built and planned and created. We harbor an unshakable belief that this world should be better than it is, that we too should be better than we are, and so we look forward to an afterlife in which the Paradise we lost is restored. But we harbor, as well, the terrifying prospect that we shall not be welcomed into the heavenly city, but spurned by God, or by spiritual creatures, or by our own ancestors. To express it in the language of the New Testament, we fear that we will not be invited to the Wedding Feast of the Lamb, but instead cast out into utter darkness where there is weeping and gnashing of teeth.

Tales from a Distant Land

The great poets of the Western tradition have all, in their own manner, sought to address our hopes and fears of the afterlife; some have even succeeded in embodying our heavenly dreams and hellish nightmares in visions that continue to challenge and inspire. They speak with enduring relevance to that part of us that transcends the limits of time and space, that reaches out beyond the grave to what lies on the other side of the veil.

On the simplest level, the visions of the poets fulfill the insatiable curiosity of the human race. Who does not enjoy hearing stories of distant lands, and what more distant land can there be than the land of the dead? Tales of the afterlife offer a new and fantastic kind of adventure that may be compared to the science fiction novels and epic fantasies of the nineteenth and twentieth centuries. The poet who writes of Heaven and Hell is like the pilgrim who returns to his village after visiting a far away shrine. No sooner does he reach the village square than he is mobbed by his friends and bombarded with a thousand questions. Some seek mere geographical knowledge, while others hunger for occult ("hidden") knowledge of things beyond the physical. Such wisdom provides both bearer and hearer with a new and heightened perspective from which to view village matters, and, as such, carries with it the promise of insight and power.

On a deeper level, this hidden knowledge from the other side answers to another human need that is as essential as our yearning for food and drink—our need to make sense of the world around us, to discern order, balance, and harmony in the universe. We desire to know the fate of our own individual soul, but we desire as well to know how our soul fits into the greater cosmic scheme. Mankind has always felt in his bones that the cycles of nature, the movements of the planets, and the patterns of the stars were fraught with meaning. That is why poetic and philosophical visions of Heaven and Hell have traditionally included speculation on the deeper rhythms that resonate beneath us and the shape of the Heavens that soar above us.

On the deepest level of all, these speculations have often included a meditation on the justice of the divine, what philosophers refer to as "theodicy." All men, even those who claim to be relativists, fear retribution for their sins and hope for a reward for their virtues. We all yearn to know that we live in a universe of cause and effect, of motive and consequence, of a higher justice that sees all ends and knows all hearts. Perhaps no single issue draws more people away from belief in God than the fear that our universe is radically unjust, that whether we act virtuously or viciously the universe doesn't care. Tales of Heaven and Hell often serve the function of righting the scales of justice—not only theologically but practically as well. For the fact remains that all people in all societies need incentives to keep themselves and their neighbors moral and upright. Concrete images of Heaven and Hell touch us more strongly than abstract principles and strengthen the ethical side of religion. The fear of punishment and the promise of final reward help us resist temptation and remain on the narrow path.

Like the villagers in the illustration above, we naturally gravitate toward those who bring us news from afar, not only because we hope they will supply us with a vision of knowledge, order, and justice, but because there are three other things we most desperately want to be assured of: 1) that we will see our dead family and friends again; 2) that love is eternal and community everlasting; 3) that nothing is finally lost, for all will be redeemed.

2

Sheol and Hades

Hebrew and Greek Visions of the Underworld

Though the New Testament in general, and Jesus in particular, speaks at some length about the afterlife, the Old Testament is all but silent on the subject. The reason for this curious reticence may have to do with the genesis of the nation of Israel. Historically speaking the Jews may be the descendants of Abraham, but the Jews do not really *become* the Jews until they suffer together in Egypt and share in the exodus from bondage. What went into Egypt was an extended family led by Jacob (Israel) the patriarch; what came out was a people chosen by God to worship him alone and to stand as a testimony against the idolatry of the nations.

It is no exaggeration to say that Egypt, the nation out of which they came, was more obsessed with the afterlife than any people before or since. If the Jews were to put down the Book of the Dead and take up the Book of the Law, it may have been necessary for them to separate themselves from speculation about the afterlife and put their focus on this world, the world in which they were to live out God's unique call. In any case, the Jews were to rest in the Lord who provides (Gen 22:14), not in strange burial customs and magic rituals. Obedience to Torah and justice for the widow and orphan, not mummification and incantation, were to be the focus of the twelve tribes.

Judaism, both as it is practiced today and as it was practiced in the ancient world, is fundamentally a this-worldly religion. The promises made to Abraham in Genesis (12:2–3; 15:5; 17:4, etc.) focus not on personal immortality but numerous offspring: not that Abraham will dwell among the stars but that his descendants will be as numerous as the stars. What fills Israel's Patriarchs (Abraham, Isaac, and Jacob), Moses, Joshua, and the Judges with hope is not the promise of heavenly reward but the possession of a physical paradise: the Promised Land, the Land of Canaan. In comparison to the hungered-and-thirsted-for Land of Milk and Honey, the afterlife seemed at best a shadowy business.

The Shifting Face of Sheol

In the Hebrew Bible, the word most often used to designate the underworld, the realm of the dead, is *Sheol*. *Sheol* is generally translated into English as grave or pit, though the King James Version (which I shall be quoting from throughout) sometimes uses hell. In the third century B.C., when the Old Testament was translated into Greek (the Septuagint or LXX), the word *Sheol* was rendered as *Hades*.

Sheol first occurs in Genesis 37:35, when Jacob, seeing the torn robe of Joseph and thinking he is dead, cries out: "I will go down into the grave [*Sheol*] unto my son mourning." Here the grave (*Sheol*) is depicted not as a place of pain or bliss, but of joyless sorrow—a twilight world, more elegiac than tragic, marked by sighs rather than screams, sadness rather than fear. The word is used sixty-five times in the Old Testament, and appears in the Pentateuch, the history books, Job, the Psalms, and the Prophets, with the most appearances in the poetic books. It is used consistently to refer to the place where people go after death, and, though no "geography" of Sheol is given, it is described as being under the earth.

For the Christian reader of the Old Testament, the verses about Sheol are puzzling. On the one hand, they strongly suggest that we will be conscious in Sheol; on the other, this seeming assertion of post-mortem consciousness is rarely allied with any clear notion of an eternal soul. The paradoxical, hard-to-pin-down nature of Sheol is also felt in its relative desirability as a final destination point. In a few cases, Sheol promises true rest. Suffering Job wishes that God would hide him in the grave till his anger is past (14:13), or that he could be like those who "go down to the grave" (21:13), or better, that he had died at birth and could now be at rest "with kings and counselors of the earth" (3:14). In most cases, however, it is a gloomy, sunless place from which no one returns (2 Sam 12:23; Job 7:9; 10:21). It marks the end of all our hopes and plans, a place of futility where one can neither praise God nor grow spiritually (Pss 88:5, 11–12; 146:4): "What profit is there in my blood when I go down to the pit [*Sheol*]? Shall the dust praise thee? Shall it declare thy truth?" (Ps 30:9). Though Sheol does not generally inspire the kind of terror that Hell does, it is clearly not a place that the poet wishes to go.

And yet, even this does not convey the whole story. Dotted throughout the Hebrew Scriptures, we catch glimpses of a far darker side to Sheol—one that suggests an element of retributive punishment. The first such glimpse occurs when the Levite Korah rebels against Moses' authority. In response, Moses calls on the Lord to judge Korah and his gang: "if the lord make a new thing, and the earth open her mouth, and swallow them up, with all that appertain unto them, and they go down quick into the pit [Sheol]; then ye shall understand that these men have provoked the lord" (Num 16:30). In this powerful image, Sheol becomes a hungry Hell-mouth that devours evil-doers. A similar image is used in Isaiah 5:14: "Therefore Hell [Sheol] hath enlarged herself, and opened her mouth without measure: and their glory, and their multitude, and their pomp . . . shall descend into it."

A number of other passages offer similar glimpses of this darker Sheol. As Moses nears the end of his life, he warns the Israelites of God's wrath if they forsake him for idols: "For a fire is kindled in mine anger, and shall burn unto the lowest Hell [Sheol]" (Deut 32:22).

David also, at times, sounds this retributive note: "The wicked shall be turned into Hell [Sheol], and all the nations that forget God" (Ps 9:17), as does Job: "Drought and heat consume the snow waters: so doth the grave [Sheol] those which have sinned" (24:19).

Later in Israel's history, a new, more terrifying word springs up for Sheol: *Gehenna*. The name Gehenna is derived from the Valley of Hinnom (Hebrew, *ge hinnom*), a valley near Jerusalem where idolatrous Jews used to sacrifice children to Moloch (Jer 7:30–34). Also referred to as Topheth, the valley embodied idolatry in it most extreme and vile form. Few acts in the Old Testament provoke greater wrath from God than the murder of innocent children, and few acts better demonstrate Israel's willingness to imitate the evils of her neighbors. Good King Josiah later destroyed the pagan valley (2 Kgs 23:10). The last verse of Isaiah provides a vivid picture of Topheth in all its decay, horror, and stench: "And they shall go forth, and look upon the carcasses of the men that have transgressed against me: for their worm shall not die, neither shall their fire be quenched; and they shall be an abhorring unto all flesh" (66:24).

When Jesus says that anyone who calls his brother a fool "shall be in danger of Hell fire" (Matt 5:22), he uses the word *Gehenna*. When he speaks of sinners going to a place "Where their worm dieth not, and the fire is not quenched" (Mark 9:48), he borrows imagery from the fires of Gehenna (by way of Isa 66:24). Though the Old Testament does not present anything like a doctrine of Hell, it does forge a connection between sin and retribution, hinting at a post-mortem state in which the unrighteous are burned, tormented, devoured, and destroyed (another synonym used for Sheol is *abaddon*, Hebrew for destruction).

Still, amidst the prevailing gloom and occasional terrors of Sheol, the Old Testament does provide some glimmers of hope, and even a few intimations of resurrection. On the simplest level, there are scattered suggestions that God will be with us even in Sheol: "Wither shall I go from thy Spirit? or wither shall I flee from thy presence? If I ascend up into Heaven, thou art there: if I make my bed in Hell [*Sheol*], behold, thou art there" (Ps 139:7–8). David trusts he will see God's face after he wakes from death: "As for me, I will behold thy face in righteousness: I shall be satisfied, when I awake, with thy likeness" (Ps 17:15). In both these passages, Sheol becomes a meeting place between those who have died and the Lord who controls both life and death. Even the deepest pit does not lie beyond God's life-giving presence.

Job, like David, hopes for a post-mortem, face-to-face encounter with God, but this time, God's ability to redeem and restore is highlighted: "For I know that my Redeemer liveth, and that he shall stand at the latter day upon the earth: and though after my skin worms destroy this body, yet in my flesh shall I see God" (19:25–26). David, in a passage that Christians consider a messianic prophecy of Christ's Resurrection (Acts 2:24–28), exults: "For thou wilt not leave my soul in Hell [*Sheol*]; neither wilt thou suffer thine Holy One to see corruption" (Ps 16:10). Sheol, it seems, is not a prison from which there is no escape. As God released the Jews from bondage in Egypt, so he has the power to release the soul from Sheol and to raise it up beyond all decay and corruption.

Perhaps the fullest vision, however, of God's power over the grave is found in a passage that also affirms most fully the retributive aspects of Sheol. In the apocalyptic book of Daniel, we encounter the following description of the final resurrection and judgment of the dead: "And many of them that sleep in the dust of the earth shall awake, some to everlasting life, and some to shame and everlasting contempt" (12:2). It is possible that the reason the Old Testament is so weak on what Plato taught as the immortality of the soul is that the Bible, both Old and New Testaments, is concerned not with the immortality of the *soul* but the resurrection of the *body*. Indeed, Martha embodies precisely this hope in the resurrection of the body when she tells Jesus that she knows that her brother Lazarus "will rise again in the resurrection at the last day" (John 11:24). In light of this final resurrection, Sheol may be viewed more positively as a holding place for the soul, a place whose gloom will one day give way to the uncreated and life-giving light of God.

Close readers of the Gospels and Acts will know that the Pharisees and Sadducees of Jesus' time disagreed quite vehemently over the resurrection of the body, with the former accepting and the latter denying it. In fact, in a memorable scene in the book of Acts (23:6–10), Paul plays on this rivalry between the Pharisees and Sadducees as a way of protecting himself from the animosity that both groups felt toward him and his teaching.

Still, aside from these brief intimations, the Old Testament view of death may fairly be described as dark, shadowy, and essentially pessimistic.

From Tartarus to the Elysian Fields

Like the ancient Hebrews, the ancient Greeks shared a generally gloomy vision of the afterlife. The souls in Hades (also called Erebus) are pale, thin, bloodless ghosts with no real self-consciousness. Hades itself, like its ghostly inhabitants, is a land of mist and shadows hidden deep under the Earth, away from all fecundity and promise of spring. The vivid and passionate song of Orpheus that melts the iron heart of Hades stands in stark contrast to the lifelessness and muted sorrow of the land of the dead.

I mentioned in the previous chapter that the Greeks, like nearly all people, ancient or modern, primitive or urban, put a heavy emphasis on proper burial rites; apart from such rites, they believed, the soul of the departed could not find rest in the afterlife. And yet, despite the importance of this religious duty, and despite the taboos against defiling a corpse (as Achilles does to the body of Hektor in *Iliad* XXII–XXIV), the Greek poets had very few positive things to say of life in Hades. As with Sheol, most of the souls in Hades face misery rather than pain, sorrow rather than punishment; but the Greeks, like the Hebrews, did have a concept of divine retribution, one which they (*unlike* the Hebrews) located geographically in a sub-section of Hades known as Tartarus.

Though Homer, as we will see in the next chapter, sent his hero Odysseus on a tour of Hades, the first Greek poet to attempt anything like a systematic study of Greek religion was Hesiod. In his *Theogeny*, Hesiod not only describes the origins and relationships of all the gods, but the origin and location of Tartarus. According to Hesiod, after Zeus overthrew his father Kronos, a war broke out between the siblings and children of Zeus (the Olympian gods) and the siblings of Kronos (the Titans). Zeus, destined to be a god of justice and civilization, won the battle and locked up the rebellious Titans in a yawning prison wrapped round by bronze and darkest night. As Hesiod describes it, this prison (Tartarus) is so deep that if one were to drop an anvil from the Heavens, it would fall for nine days and on the tenth reach the Earth, and then would fall another nine days before it reached the floor of Tartarus on the tenth.

I find it significant that though the New Testament generally uses Hades to signify Hell, in 2 Peter 2:4 (and *only* here) it uses the word *Tartarus*: "God spared not the angels that sinned, but cast them down to Hell [*Tartarus*], and delivered them into chains of darkness, to be reserved unto judgment." What makes the use here of Tartarus quite stunning is that the rebellious Titans of Greek mythology share much in common with the "sons of God" who mate with the "daughters of men" to produce the nephilim (see Gen 6:1–4) and who are then (according to the pseudepigraphal book of *1 Enoch*) put in prison to await judgment. Could the Greeks have maintained a collective memory of the imprisoned angels alluded to, if somewhat cryptically, in the Bible? In any case, just as Hell in the New Testament is linked both to the angelic rebellion of the "sons of God" and to the punishment of sinners, so Tartarus functions as both the prison of the Titans and the place of suffering for such archetypal sinners as Tantalus, Ixion, and Sisyphus: the sinners, that is, whose cries Orpheus hears rising up from the pit below.

Still, the Greek view of Hades, like the Jewish view of Sheol, was not totally bleak. A more positive, mystical view of Hades was celebrated by an ancient religious cult that met at Eleusis, a city not far from Athens. Their rites, known as the Eleusinian mysteries, were fiercely guarded, but historians have been able to determine that the mysteries centered on the myths of Persephone (daughter of Zeus and his sister Demeter) and Dionysus. In a tale that was told again and again in various forms, Persephone was kidnapped by Hades to be his queen. Overwhelmed by sorrow, Demeter (goddess of the grain) allowed nature around her to die until Zeus promised to bargain with Hades for the return of her daughter. Alas, in the interim, Persephone had been persuaded by Hades to eat three pomegranate seeds, an act that bound her to the underworld forever. In the end, Hades and Demeter agreed to share Persephone; the Lord of the Dead would keep her below for three months of the year, but for the other nine months she would be allowed to live with her mother. The ancient Greeks saw in Persephone's annual journey into Hades on the winter solstice and her return to Earth on the vernal equinox an explanation for the seasonal cycle. For the initiates at Eleusis, whose rites included the presentation of a ripe ear of grain (or corn, as the British call it), the story of Persephone was rich with mystical significance and promised eventual victory over Hades (both the underworld and its ruler).

In contrast to the divine Persephone, Dionysus (or Bacchus) was the son of Zeus by a mortal woman named Semele. Whereas Persephone, like the grain, went below in the winter and returned in the spring, Bacchus (the god of the grape) was believed actually to die and rise each year in tune with the natural cycle of the vine and the more cosmic rhythms of life, death, and rebirth. I believe that Jesus may have had the Eleusinian mysteries in mind when he sent the following cryptic message to a group of Greeks (perhaps from Eleusis?) who wanted to meet him: "Verily, verily, I say unto you, Except a corn of wheat fall into the ground and die, it abideth alone: but if it die, it bringeth forth much fruit" (John 12:24). The promise of rebirth, of redemption from death and Hades, that underlies both myths provided the Greeks with a hope that transcended the gloom and quiet despair of the grave.

And beyond this mystical promise of the annual return, a faint intimation of Heaven. First there was the dwelling place of the gods, the glorious Mount Olympus: "Shaken by no wind, drenched by no showers, and invaded by no snows, it is set in cloudless limpid air with white radiance playing over all" (*Odyssey* VI.44–45).[1] But with the exception of Hercules and Ganymede, both of whom were apotheosized and taken up to Olympus to dwell with the gods, mortals could not enter, or even visit, the divine abode. The deities who dwelt there in eternal ease and dined on nectar and ambrosia were finally above the joys and woes of men, despite their practice of meddling ceaselessly in human affairs.

Olympus, then, was closed to mortals, prompting dreams of a second kind of Eden. The Greeks often dreamed of a race of blessed mortals who lived a utopian existence in the land of Hyperborea ("behind the North wind")—but who could find his way there. The Greek poet Pindar expressed it most poignantly when he wrote: "Never on foot or ship could you find the marvelous road to the feast of the Hyperboreans" (*Pythia* X).[2] Frustrated by their spatial separation from the happy land at the back of the North Wind, the Greek poets sang of a third Eden, the lost Golden Age of peace and harmony. But from that too they were cut off, not by space but by a passage of time that they could not bridge.

With Olympus, Hyperborea, and the Golden Age ultimately out of reach, the Greeks had only one other place to turn, the afterlife. Though the passages are brief and rare, Greek poetry affords us a number of tantalizing glimpses of a final, edenic resting place for the just. The most haunting of these appear in *Odyssey* IV.565–68, when Menelaus is promised

1. All passages from the *Odyssey* will be taken from *The Odyssey of Homer*, translated by E. V. Rieu and revised by D. C. H. Rieu. I will provide book and line numbers in the text; as this is a prose translation, the line numbers will be close approximations of the Greek original.

2. *The Odes of Pindar*, translated by Richmond Lattimore, 88.

that after his death he will go to the Elysian Fields (or Elysium or the Blessed Groves)—to a place "where living is made easy for mankind, where no snow falls, no strong winds blow and there is never any rain, but day after day the West Wind's tuneful breeze comes in from the Ocean to refresh its people."

Though this description sounds a bit like Homer's description of Olympus, Elysium is finally a human place; the ideal of man and God dwelling together that is hinted at in the Old Testament is not a part of the ancient Greek soul. That is why Greek statues of the gods mimic the human perfection of the Olympic athlete, rather than seeking the ineffable qualities of the divine. It may also explain a vital distinction between the Jewish and Greek view of the afterlife. Whereas Israel's God (Yahweh) rules both the Heavens and Sheol, and all that lies between, the Greeks portioned out the Heavens, the sea, and the underworld to three divine brothers, Zeus, Poseidon, and Hades (according to *Iliad* XV.187–93, the division was made by lot). Only in the Old Testament, do we encounter a single God whose presence pervades all aspects of Heaven and Earth, life and death, the Blessed Groves and the gloomy Sheol.

3

Odysseus in the Underworld

The First Great Epic Descent

Books IX–XII of the *Odyssey* recount the fabulous adventures of Odysseus as he crisscrosses the Mediterranean world in search of his island home of Ithaca. At one point in his journeys, the travel-weary Odysseus, his crew dead and all his possessions gone, washes ashore naked on the island of Phaeacia. Fortunately for Odysseus, the hospitable Phaeacians live on an island that combines the beauties of Hyperborea with those of the Elysian Fields. The innocent inhabitants dwell in harmony with one another and with the gods, and their relationship to nature is so intimate, so edenic that the fruit on the trees never fails and the West Wind blows softly and fruitfully all the year round.

In keeping with the rules of hospitality, the Phaeacians bathe and clothe Odysseus and then host a banquet in his honor. Only after he has eaten his fill, do they ask him to share his name and his story. In response Odysseus tells, in first person, of his fairy-tale-like encounters with the Lotus Eaters, the one-eyed Cyclops Polyphemus, Aeolus the wind god, the cannibalistic Laestrygonians, and Circe the enchantress. The Phaeacians are overwhelmed by his tales, but they prove to be only a prelude to the most strange and wondrous part of his travels. As he prepares to leave Circe's isle, Odysseus explains, the enchantress informs him that before he can return to Ithaca, he must travel to Hades and consult the shade of Tiresias, the blind prophet of Thebes. With weary heart, Odysseus sets course for the land of the dead . . . neither Odysseus nor Western literature would ever be the same!

The Purpose of the Descent

The attentive reader of the *Odyssey* will notice something puzzling about Odysseus's journey to Hades: nearly everything Tiresias tells Odysseus in Book XI is repeated by Circe in Book XII. Homer's use of this odd narrative device suggests that Odysseus's purported reason for visiting Hades is in fact a red herring. The true reason, I would submit, that Odysseus must visit the underworld is that he, like all the greatest heroes of Greek mythology (Orpheus, Hercules, and Theseus) must brave the fearsome pit. What better way to test one's mettle, one's courage, one's capacity for despair than to descend bodily into the underworld, to come face-to-face with death itself?

Homer puts his hero through just such a test, and then extends that test in two different directions. When we first meet Odysseus in Book V, we learn that a beautiful nymph named Calypso has fallen in love with him and is keeping him captive on her island. Calypso, who desires to live always with the Greek hero, has promised to make him immortal if he will forget his home and family and remain with her. Odysseus is beguiled by the nymph's beauty and knows that the charms of his wife cannot compare with those of Calypso; nevertheless, his desire to return home to his family is strong, and he gently explains to the doting goddess that he cannot accept her offer.

At this point, readers must remind themselves that although Book V precedes Book XI in the narrative, the events recounted in Book XI (Odysseus's descent) occur *before* his meeting with Calypso. The chronology is significant, for it means that Odysseus's decision to reject Calypso's offer was made *after* he experienced for himself the gloom and sorrow of Hades. Odysseus chooses mortality from a position of knowledge, and, by so doing, stands as a model to all men, whatever their religious beliefs, of the need to accept our status as mortal beings and not seek an immortality for which we were not destined (at least in our current fallen state). Despite their differences, all of the archetypal monsters—from vampires to zombies to mummies to werewolves to Frankenstein-like creatures—share one thing in common: they are "undead." The monsters that haunt the nightmares of every nation and tribe are trapped in a living death, animated corpses that can find neither hope nor rest in this world or the next.

Taken together, Odysseus's encounters with Hades and with Calypso provide us with an object lesson in the nature of mortality, and define the true hero, in part, as someone who has grappled with his own mortality. Homer emphasizes this aspect of Odysseus's adventures in the underworld by factoring in one further narrative detail. I stated earlier that everything Tiresias tells Odysseus is later repeated by Calypso, but that is not fully accurate. There is one thing that Tiresias tells Odysseus that Circe does not, something that Odysseus remembers and tells his wife when he returns home. That something has nothing to do with the *Odyssey* proper, but it has a great deal to do with the kinds of issues raised by poetic journeys to the underworld.

Through the prophetic lips of Tiresias, Odysseus is granted access to a kind of hidden wisdom that is rarely granted to mortals—a glimpse into his own future. A day will come, Tiresias tells the hero, when he will leave Ithaca and journey far over the dry land, carrying a well-cut oar on his shoulder. After long months of walking, he will come upon a people who know nothing of the sea and do not use salt in their food. They will look upon Odysseus's oar and confuse it with a winnowing fan. It is then that Odysseus must plant his oar in the ground and sacrifice to Poseidon, Lord of the Sea, the very god who has hounded him throughout his travels. Having done that, he is to return home and await his own death: a gentle death, far from the sea, with all his family and his people around him.

It seems clear to me that Homer meant Odysseus's journey to mark a spiritual and emotional mid-life crisis for the hero, a moment when his lost past and shadowy future rush to meet each other. As such, Odysseus, like all the heroes after him, stands as an everyman who must endure our mutual fears of death and face our shared anxieties for the future. Is it any wonder that Homer's aesthetic decision to send his epic hero to Hades established a convention that all future epic writers (from Virgil to Dante to Milton to Tolkien) would feel obliged to imitate? The convention came to be known as the *nekuia* (*nekros* in Greek means corpse), a word used to refer both to the descent itself and to the questioning of the dead souls by the hero. Though Virgil, Dante, and Milton all had their own theological and philosophical reasons for including a *nekuia* in their epic, they also felt a strong aesthetic need to fulfill the epic convention laid down by Homer. Indeed, after the *Odyssey*, no hero can truly qualify as an *epic* hero without enduring the awe and terror of the land of the dead.

The Shape of the Descent

Although Orpheus walked to the mouth of Hades in search of his lost Eurydice, Odysseus, we are told, sailed there on his black ship. In his adventure with the Laestrygonians, Odysseus had sailed far to the south, to a land where the days are nearly endless. Now, in sharp contrast to his previous journey, he sails far to the north, to a land of perpetual night, mist, and fog. The ancients believed that all the dry land of the Earth was encircled by a mighty stream that they referred to simply as Ocean. In Homer's geography, Hades, like the land of the Hyperboreans, lies beyond the edge of Ocean, at the point where the rivers of Phlegethon ("burning"), Cocytus ("wailing"), and Styx meet together and flow into Acheron ("sorrowing"). Though Acheron is clearly the main river of Hades, and though both Aeneas and Dante cross it to enter the realm of the dead, tradition has made Styx, the river by which the gods swore, the main one (which is why we use the adjective "Stygian," and not "Acheronian," to refer to the gloom of the underworld). Odysseus, however, crosses no river; indeed, he doesn't even enter Hades itself. Rather, he stands at the mouth of the cave, and the shades of the departed come to him.

To lure Tiresias's ghost, Odysseus sacrifices an animal and drains the blood into a bowl. According to Homer, the shades can only regain true consciousness and memory by drinking the blood, an eerie, memorable detail that seems to be based on an ancient belief that the dead are bloodless. As the pale, specter-thin shades crowd around the bowl, Odysseus holds them back with his sword so that only those whom he wishes to question can drink of the blood. The first spirit he meets is that of Elpenor, one of his sailors who had died on Circe's isle on the morning of their departure for Hades. Odysseus is shocked to see him and asks him a question that lingers hauntingly in the mind of the reader: "Elpenor! How did you come here, to the land of shadows? You have been quicker on foot than I in my black ship" (XI.57–58).

In Book XXIV of the *Odyssey*, where we are given a second glimpse of Hades, Homer explains that it is Hermes, the messenger of the gods, who mesmerizes the dead with his golden wand (his caduceus) and leads them down to Hades. But at this point, Homer is less concerned with the means of Elpenor's transport than with the agony of his situation. In haste to leave Circe's isle for Hades, Odysseus had left the hapless Elpenor unburied; now, with great pathos, the shade of Elpenor begs his captain to give him a proper burial before resuming his journey to Ithaca. Homer the poet captures the two friends in a powerful tableau as they converse over the threshold of life and death: Odysseus with his sword held high to protect the blood; Elpenor pouring out his woes.

Odysseus next speaks with the shades of Tiresias and of his mother, Anticleia, of whose death on Ithaca he was not aware. When Anticleia finishes apprising Odysseus of the situation in Ithaca, her son reaches out to embrace her, but to no avail: "Three times, like a shadow or a dream, she slipped through my hands and left me pierced by an even sharper pain" (XI.208–9). Odysseus, like all of us, must let go of the past and learn to live in the present. As Jesus himself counsels, he must leave the dead to bury the dead. Anticleia assists Odysseus in this by explaining to him that the dead have no sinews to hold together flesh and bone; they are, in a sense, nothing more than shadowy memories.

Up to this point, Odysseus's meetings with Elpenor, Tiresias, and Anticleia are marked by a question-and-answer structure that is common to the *nekuia*; with the disappearance of Anticleia, however, the structure shifts to that of a ghostly pageant. For a hundred lines of verse, Odysseus remains still while a long, slow line of noble women parades by him. Among this catalogue of famous (if tragic) women, Odysseus catches sight of Leda. Though best known for being the mother of Helen of Troy, Leda is introduced in Book XI as the mother of the twins Castor and Pollux (or Polydeuces), each of whom lives on Earth and in Hades on alternate days.

Suddenly, in the midst of the procession, Homer tells us, *in third person*, that Odysseus stopped speaking and that all those in the hall were frozen in awe by the magical power of his words. For a moment, we too (the readers) are held in suspension. The sudden shift from first to third person, from Odysseus to Homer disorients us and leaves us unsure of where we are or what is happening. It is a brilliant narrative move that provides not only a brief intermission to Odysseus's story but conveys to us, directly and powerfully, the wonder that tales of the afterlife inspire in their listeners. Alcinous, King of Phaeacia, exclaims that Odysseus is a true story-teller and not like those false pilgrims, those frauds and impostors who tell made-up tales to extort gifts from their host. Indeed, Odysseus *is* the ultimate pilgrim; he brings news of that most distant of lands, of that "undiscovered country from whose bourn / No traveler returns."

Resuming his tale, Odysseus recounts his conversations with the shades of Agamemnon and Achilles. This episode, in which the hero speaks with the souls of the most famous and influential men of his generation, would also become an epic convention: the necessity for the hero (and the poet) to survey the glories of the past before moving on. Agamemnon, who upon returning home was murdered by his wife and her lover, tells his tragic tale and warns Odysseus not to be too trustful of his wife. These portentous words remain with Odysseus throughout his subsequent journeys, establishing yet another conventional aspect of the *nekuia*: Hades as a place for grim omens that toughen the hero for the challenges he must face in the future.

Then, in what is perhaps the most memorable scene in Book XI, Odysseus meets with the shade of Achilles who sums up in two elegiac lines the essential misery of Hades: "I would rather work the soil as a serf on hire to some landless impoverished peasant than be King of all these lifeless dead" (XI.489–90). Gloomy words, indeed, but Homer quickly lightens them by having Odysseus share with Achilles the news of his son's exploits in battle. This confirmation of his son's prowess cheers the moody Achilles, and, rejoicing in his heart, he passes with great strides down the fields of asphodel.

Odysseus's mention here of asphodel (a Greek plant that sprouts clusters of white or yellow flowers) is an odd one that needs some explanation. In the previous chapter, I spoke of the Elysian Fields as the idyllic resting place of heroes. As Homer describes it in *Odyssey* IV, and as it was generally understood by the ancient Greeks, the Fields lay on the far-off Isle of the Blessed. Here, however, Homer, along with the many poets who imitated him, places the Elysian Fields in Hades itself, describing it as a long, grassy meadow with clusters of asphodel. In the midst of the meadow, Homer places Minos—the legendary King of Crete whom the Greeks revered for his justice—assigning him the role of judge of the dead. (Interestingly, in *Odyssey* IV, when discussing the Elysian Fields, Homer mentions Rhadamanthus, Minos's brother, who was also famed for justice; later poets would include Aeacus as a third noble judge of the dead.) To add to the strangeness of the geography of *Odyssey* XI, Homer places, adjacent to the meadow, the tortured souls of Tityus, Tantalus, and Sisyphus, whose punishments he describes with great poetic relish. These inconsistencies between *Odyssey* IV and XI and between Homer's and Hesiod's placement of the tortured souls should serve to remind the modern reader that Greek mythology is by no means a consistent or systematic thing—each poet alters the myths to suit his own aesthetic or philosophical needs.

Finally, before leaving Hades behind, Odysseus has three strange experiences that also exerted an influence on later depictions of the underworld. First, he meets the soul of Ajax, a Greek warrior who killed himself in wrath after Odysseus tricked him out of the armor of the dead Achilles. The penitent Odysseus begs his forgiveness, but Ajax refuses to speak to him and walks away into the gloom. The epic silence of Ajax was considered by the Greek literary critic Longinus to be more sublime than words. Second, Odysseus meets what he thinks is the soul of Hercules, but learns that it is only his wraith. In what may constitute a pagan glimpse of the uniquely Judeo-Christian teaching of the resurrection of the body, Hercules explains that he himself (the real, embodied Hercules?) now lives on Olympus. Still, even his wraith has the power to strike terror into the shades of Hades. Third, once Hercules leaves, all the dead pour like a wave toward the bowl of blood, and the panic-stricken Odysseus fears Persephone will call up one of the Gorgons and turn him to stone. Pale with dread, Odysseus takes off running, jumps aboard his ship, and commands his men to set sail.

It is a distinctly eerie ending to a distinctly eerie book.

4

Plato and the Geography
of the Underworld

Though most readers look to Homer the poet for information about Hades and the afterlife, Plato the philosopher provides far more information (both geographical and theological) about the state of the soul after death. Plato's wide-ranging thoughts on the subject lie scattered throughout his dialogues; however, one can gain a firm grasp of his views by carefully studying the major passages in *Phaedo*, *Republic*, and *Phaedrus*, and then factoring in minor passages from such dialogues as *Gorgias*, *Apology*, and *Symposium*. Though more systematic than the Greek poets, Plato too shows considerable variety and flexibility in his views, especially when he uses a myth about the afterlife to drive home an ethical or philosophical point.

One of Plato's earliest attempts to visualize the world below can be found in *Phaedo*, a powerful and memorable dialogue that climaxes with the death of Socrates. The dialogue is set just before Socrates must drink the hemlock, and it allows us to eavesdrop on an intimate farewell between the philosopher and his adoring disciples. As the disciples are devastated by the thought of their beloved teacher's death, it is only natural that the dialogue turns toward a discussion of the immortality of the soul. Using his dialectical method, Socrates slowly opens the minds of his disciples, demonstrating as he goes that the soul must be immortal for there is nothing that can kill it. The argument brings some comfort to his disciples, but they continue to feel anxiety concerning the final state of the soul. To calm their fears, Socrates fashions for them an aesthetically rich vision of the Earth, the underworld, and the journey of the soul.

Living in the Hollows

The Earth, Socrates explains, is a sphere and lies suspended and motionless in the center of the Heavens. Despite the fact that grade school teachers and college professors persist in telling their students that all people before Galileo thought the Earth was flat, even a cursory reading of the primary material will reveal that all the educated ancients and medievals (from Plato and Aristotle, to Euclid and Ptolemy, to Cicero and Augustine, to Boethius and Dante) knew that the Earth was round and that it hung in the vast expanse of space. It is true that they thought the Earth hung motionless at the center of the universe, but then they thought that not because they were credulous fools but because they were good scientists—in the absence of telescopes, the geocentric model they constructed best explained the data that they observed with their eyes.

Moving from empirical observation to the world of natural and meta-physical speculation, Socrates references a fifth, heavenly element known as ether that was believed by scientists and philosophers for over 2000 years to be more pure than air or fire. This ether, Socrates explains, swirls continually around the Earth and gives off dregs of water, mist, and air that run down to the Earth and settle into numerous hollows. The Mediterranean world of the Greeks represents but one of many such hollows. Like a good science teacher, Socrates uses the analogy of a leather ball made up of a series of colored patches that have been sewn together to help illustrate his terrestrial model. In the analogy, the ball represents the Earth as a whole, and each individual patch represents a different hollow.

Though we live in these hollows, Socrates argues, we think, in our ignorance, that we live on the surface. We are like fish who think the sea floor is the surface of the Earth, when the actual surface lies far above them. Isolated in our little hollows, we cannot imagine the beauty of the other hollows that lie closer to the surface, most of which are inaccessible to us. With the power of Homer himself, Socrates conjures for his despairing disciples images of what the other hollows are like. In those magical lands above, he says, the colors are brighter and richer, and the precious metals are purer. There is neither corrosion nor decay, and the climate is always perfect. As a result the inhabitants live longer, healthier lives and have heightened senses; indeed, they can gaze directly on the true splendor of the sun and the moon. Better yet, the inhabitants and their land are so pure that the gods actually *dwell* in the temples built for them.

Plato's descriptions of these magical hollows recall Homer and Pindar's descriptions of Olympus, Hyperborea, and the Elysian Fields. In our own day, we still dream of such magical lands, though we refer to them by different names: Eldorado, Shangri-La, Utopia, Camelot, Tir na nÓg, perhaps even Narnia and Middle-Earth. Plato himself wrote in *Timaeus* and *Critias* of just such a land, a lost civilization that was once as perfect in climate and beauty as it was in goodness and truth: Atlantis.

But most of us, sadly, are not able to reach such lands; instead, we live out our lives in the lower hollows, and then sink, in our afterlives, to the even lower hollows of Hades and Tartarus. In *Phaedo*, Plato carefully works out the geographical connections. The hollows, he explains, are connected by a vast series of subterranean tunnels. Rivers flow through many of the tunnels, until they find their way down to Tartarus (the lowest point) and then bubble up again to go their round of the tunnels. Like a living being, the Earth inhales and exhales this liquid, causing tremors as it does. As in Homer, the outermost stream is Ocean; opposite to it, flowing in a different direction and eventually swirling down under the Earth is the mighty Acheron. Between the two, lies Phlegethon (or Pyriphlegethon, a lava stream that empties into Tartarus), and opposite to this, Styx, which, when it runs into Tartarus, changes its name to become Cocytus.

Plato's geographical and theological theories of the underworld were influenced not only by Homer but by the Eleusinians, the Pythagoreans, and the devotees of Orphism. From the first group he learned to perceive and respect the cycles of nature, while from the second he learned the importance of attuning the soul to the greater cosmic harmonies. From the third group, from those who traced their beliefs back to the earliest visitor of Hades (Orpheus), he learned the most vital lesson of all: that the soul can only be purified through punishment.

Guided by these three mystery religions, Plato (through Socrates) describes how the soul is led by its guardian spirit through the network of tunnels to Hades and the river Acheron. Neutral souls, those which are neither good nor evil, cross Acheron and undergo a regimen of purification. Evil souls, in contrast, are cast into Tartarus. Even in Tartarus, however, there are gradations of justice. Whereas souls that are incurably evil are cast into Tartarus forever, those that have committed lesser sins for which a remedy is possible are only punished in Tartarus for a limited time. Interestingly, Plato here makes a distinction between incurable and curable sins that parallels (and most likely influenced, via Aristotle) the Catholic distinction between mortal sins that lead to eternal suffering in Hell and venial sins that lead to temporal suffering in Purgatory.

After they have completed their time in Tartarus, Plato's venial sinners are cast either into Cocytus (if guilty of manslaughter) or Phlegethon (if they abused their parents but repented of it). Their souls are then carried by the twin rivers past Acheron, where they cry out to the souls of those whom they have wronged and seek their forgiveness. If they are forgiven, they are released from the river; if not, they are cast back down into Tartarus to await a second chance to ride the river back up.

Such is the fate of evil souls. Not so those who have lived lives of goodness and justice. The souls of the just, chief of whom are philosophers, are set free from the confinements both of their bodies and of the underworld and are sent to live in bliss on the true surface of the Earth. These are they who dwell in Elysium, in those golden lands which modern man still yearns for, even as he ridicules such yearnings as naïve and idealistic.

Judgment Day

Plato recounts a similar myth of the underworld at the close of *Gorgias*, but this time he adds a number of memorable details that would exert an influence on later poets of the afterlife. First, we learn that the souls brought to judgment are naked and cannot hide their true nature. Second, the mortal sinners are distinguished from the venial by a mark, with the former group being composed mostly of powerful public figures (tyrants, kings, politicians), and the latter mostly of private men who fell into error. Third, the three judges of the underworld, Aeacus, Rhadamanthus, and Minos, are each assigned a specific duty. The first two judge, respectively, the souls of Europeans and Asians; the third acts as the appeals judge. Fourth, Plato makes it clear that the terrible, eternal punishments of those in Tartarus are meant to act as dire warnings and object lessons for other souls. As in *Phaedo*, Plato counsels that it is best to be a philosopher, for it is they, and not the great politicians, who go directly to the Blessed Isles. Plato ends both myths by saying that though the details may be shaky, something *like* these myths must be true, and that we should prepare appropriately.

The fact that Plato adds this caveat to both myths of the afterlife should warn the reader away from interpreting them in too literal a fashion. The reason, for example, that Plato describes in such haunting detail the golden lands that lie above our dark hollows is not to encourage sailors to dash off on an adventure. The hollows he describes (both low and high) are as much geographical as they are ethical: what holds us back from reaching the purer lands is not lack of resolve but lack of knowledge. We are ignorant of the true nature of our world, for we trust only to our bodily senses. As for the scenes of judgment he describes, they are meant to warn us that our choices bring consequences and that the immortal nature of our souls means that we will not be able to escape those consequences, either in this life or the next.

This is the method used in nearly all of Plato's best and most memorable dialogues: he guides us through a logical, reasoned, dialectical argument, usually one that calls for virtue, and then loses himself in a carefully-crafted myth. The myth not only helps drive home the moral, but embodies it in the flesh of allegory. In the case of *Phaedo*, the myth of the hollows allows Plato to emphasize that while the body decays, the soul is immortal, and he advises his friends to let go the passions, sins, and errors of the body and seek the way of the soul. Just before turning to the myth of the hollows, Socrates explains that what we call a ghost is actually a departed soul that still yearns so much for the things of the body that it is dragged earthward to hover about the grave where its body lies. If we focus too much on the physical body, we shall never see the truth about ourselves or our world; neither shall we yearn for the higher realities that lie waiting for us in all their purity and beauty in the distant hollows.

Out of the Cave

Plato's allegorical myth of the hollows succeeds powerfully in embodying the more abstract philosophical teachings of the *Phaedo*, but it is eclipsed by what is surely his finest and best known myth, the Allegory of the Cave (*Republic* VII). According to the allegory, we are all like prisoners born and raised in a deep cave cut off from the light of the sun. To add to our wretched plight, we have all been tied down from childhood to chairs that face the back wall of the cave. Behind us a fire rages, and between us and the fire, puppeteers parade, in an endless circle, their life-like marionettes. The fire casts the shadows of the puppets on to the cave wall, and we, who have spent our lives staring at the wall, think that the shadows of the puppets are reality.

Now imagine, says Plato, that one man should break his chains, turn around, and discover that what he has watched all his life is not, in fact, reality but merely a parade of shadows: really shadows of shadows, since the puppets themselves are imitations of real men. It would take his eyes a long time to adjust to the direct light of the fire, but if he persisted, he would eventually be able to move on and even to exit the cave. Once outside, his eyes would again be blinded by the true light of the sun. At first he would only be able to look at shapes reflected in ponds, but eventually he would raise his eyes to the sun itself.

For Plato, our world, like the cave, is a world of shadows; true reality is to be found only in the world of Being, where the Forms (or originals) of all earthly objects and ideas dwell in unchanging perfection. Since the objects of our world are only pale imitations of the Real, we must not trust only to our senses; rather, we must learn to perceive the Forms themselves with the eyes of our psyche (a Greek word that means both mind and soul). The man who escapes from the cave is the philosopher who realizes the errors of his senses and, by a strict regimen of philosophical study, learns to see instead with his psyche.

As we saw in the *Phaedo*, Plato links the senses to the body and reason to the soul. That is why in all his musings on death and the afterlife, he exhorts his disciples to privilege soul over body and to perceive the eternal things not through bodily senses but through a philosophically-trained psyche. Those who put all their focus on the body and its five senses will be dragged downward (into the lower hollows of Hades and Tartarus, back into the cave), while those who trust the soul and its perceptions will ascend (toward the higher hollows, out of the cave, and into the light of the sun).

Both *Phaedo* and *Gorgias* lay out clearly the choice between ascending and descending, and both offer glimpses of the final abode of the just, but neither provides a clear description of the Elysian Fields. For that we must turn to Plato's *Apology*, to his account of the defense made by Socrates before the assembly of Athens in 399 B.C. Near the end of the *Apology*, just after he has been condemned to death, Socrates turns to those jurymen who acquitted him and assures them that all will be well. He tells them with great surprise and elation that his oracle (or daimon) that had always, in the past, prevented him from making the wrong decision had not once, during the entire trial, tried to stop him. On account of the silence of his oracle, Socrates concludes that death must not be a bad thing, a conclusion that, in any case, seems logical to him. For surely death must be one of two things: either a kind of psychic annihilation akin to a long, peaceful sleep, or a migration to a better and more wonderful place. That better place is the Elysian Fields (apparently the same place where the just go in the *Phaedo* myth), and Socrates describes it in simple but lovely words that have not lost their power to enchant and inspire. Indeed, it is here, in the closing lines of Socrates' *Apology*, that Plato offers the fullest and most compelling description of "heaven" to come out of the ancient Greek world.

Oddly, the description is wholly bereft of physical details. Socrates chooses to focus instead on moral/spiritual details. He paints Elysium as a world free of the injustice and error that have just condemned him to death. There he hopes to meet the true judges of the Earth: Minos, Rhadamanthus, Aeacus, and (Plato adds) Triptolemus. There too he hopes to meet all the great poets and philosophers (Orpheus, Musaeus, Hesiod, Homer) and converse with those great heroes (Ajax, Palamedes) who, like him, were victims of injustice. Above all, he hopes to spend his time there, as he did here on Earth, questioning and examining people to discern who is truly wise and who merely thinks that he is. What a great thing it would be, he exclaims, to mingle, talk, and debate with the great heroes of old. For Plato, "heaven" is not a place of stasis, of fixed, unending perfection, but a dynamic place of growth and development and learning: a true philosopher's paradise. It is, as we saw at the end of chapter 2, a finally human place where we tell old tales and ask new questions. For surely, concludes Socrates, in that better world they do not put people to death for asking questions.

5

Plato and the Theology of the Afterlife

In the previous chapter, I made frequent use of a word that is too often misused by modern people: myth. Living as we do in a post-Enlightenment world that makes a sharp, finally artificial distinction between reason and emotion, logic and intuition, science and religion, fact and fiction, we are apt to use the word myth as a synonym for falsehood and set it in direct opposition to history. We are wrong to do so. A myth, at least as it was used in the pre-modern world, was not the same thing as a lie. Rather, it was a story used to explain abstract ideas, teach virtues, and/or embody deeply felt beliefs.

Both creation and evolution are myths in the sense that they seek to explain, and make sense of, a certain view of God, man, and the universe. Arguments have been made, and continue to be made, as to the factual truth or untruth of Genesis 1–2 and Darwinian natural selection; nevertheless, the relative historical and scientific accuracy of these two competing origin theories does not take away from their status as foundational myths upon which a host of assumptions and presuppositions rest. I myself believe that Adam, Eve, and Noah were actual people, but that does not prevent me from making reference to the myth of the fall or the myth of the flood—the mythic power of both stories exists alongside their status as historical fact or literary fiction. The parables of Jesus are clearly fictional in their context, but that does not take away from their mythic-allegorical truth. C. S. Lewis and J. R. R. Tolkien were fond of referring to the sacred Christian narrative of the incarnation, atonement, and resurrection of Christ as a *true myth*—for it happened in real time and space while *simultaneously* paralleling a key mythic archetype (what Sir James Frazer dubbed the Corn King) that is common to all ancient civilizations.

I myself would locate Plato's myths of the afterlife midway between the true myth of Christ and the fictional parables of Jesus. Neither Plato nor those who were influenced by him considered his allegories of the afterlife to be simple falsehoods; yet they also understood that his ultimate goal was, as we saw in the previous chapter, more spiritual than physical. With this in mind, let us consider several other Platonic myths that, while maintaining Plato's aesthetic flair for vivid imagery and geographical detail, develop more fully the theological ramifications of his theories of the afterlife, divine judgment, and Heaven and Hell.

The Journey of the Winged Soul

In his beloved *Just so Stories*, Rudyard Kipling offers his readers fanciful etiological tales to explain how the leopard got his spots, the elephant his trunk, and the camel its hump. In *Phaedrus*, one of two dialogues that include an encomium to the god of love, Socrates spins an equally fanciful etiological myth to explain why it is that when we fall in love and gaze into our beloved's eyes, we get goose pimples. The answer to such a question might seem simple enough, but not as Socrates tells it. Indeed, to answer it fully, he weaves one of his most beautiful and elaborate allegories, one that provides a fascinating glimpse into the relationship between soul and body and between our world and the Heavens beyond.

Our soul, Plato explains, was not created at the same moment as our body; on the contrary, in the long ages before it was weighted down to Earth by a body, our soul had wings and flew through the Heavens. In those days (or, better, eons) when it existed in a disembodied state, our soul followed in the regal procession of the gods as they made their way through the cosmos. For a thousand years we flew in company with that procession along the back rim of the great arch of the sky. Far removed from the shadows and falsehoods of our earthly World of Becoming, where all things change, decay, and die, our soul communed with the Forms, with Reality. It participated joyously in the heavenly World of Being, where all is perfect, unchanging, and eternal.

To help us understand the true nature of the winged soul, and of the choices it makes even when it is apart from the body, Plato compares it to a charioteer whose chariot is pulled by two very different horses. One of the horses is noble, just, and moderate, and does its best to keep the chariot on course. The other is stubborn and recalcitrant and possesses a vicious nature. As long as the charioteer gives reign to the good horse and checks the bad, he will follow the gods beyond our changing world of shadows into the ethereal regions beyond the skies. Better yet, he will gaze directly on the immortal, the indestructible, and the uncreated, and will, by so doing, gain the ultimate form of philosophical understanding. Unfortunately, such a state of pure communion with the Forms cannot last forever. When the winged soul comes to the end of its thousand-year circuit, an impulse from the bad horse inevitably pulls it earthward, dragging and tearing its wings, and causing it to become dense and heavy. If the impulse is strong enough, the soul will literally fall into physicality.

The modern reader who encounters Plato's allegorical theory of the tri-partite soul (a theory that is also central to the *Republic*) cannot help but be reminded of a Freudian myth that continues to resonate in the twenty-first century, despite the fact that the theories of Freud as a whole have been discredited. I speak of Freud's myth/theory of the Ego, Superego, and Id. Our Ego (Greek for "I") is the charioteer; if it is to attain emotional and psychological health, it must balance the claims of the Superego (the good horse) and the Id (the bad horse). The Id insists on having its desires met immediately and will brook no restrictions or interference; if the Ego capitulates to it, it will be drawn off course and face ruin. The Superego embodies the moral standards of the community and of our own individual conscience, and it resists the siren song of the Id. The Ego, which is strongest when it is firmly tied to reality (a reality that for Freud is physical but for Plato is metaphysical), must heed the warnings of the Superego while not fully squelching the instinctual desires of the Id. Only thus can it stay on course.

To return to Plato's myth, when the charioteer (Ego) loses control of the horses, the bad horse (Id) takes control and drags the soul downward. Its wings crumpled, the soul quickly becomes imprisoned in a body of flesh, thus losing its freedom of movement and its ability to perceive the true nature of reality. But all is not lost forever; intimations of the glory it once knew remain dormant within the soul—intimations that are normally awakened by the study of philosophy but which also can be awakened by the experience of love. For, on rare occasions, when the soul stares into the eyes of the beloved, it catches a glimpse of that immortal Beauty it saw in its journey through the Heavens and with which it once communed. In response to this glimpse of the Form of Beauty, the feathers of the soul begin to grow again, tickling and pricking the inside of the flesh with a thousand tiny bristles; the result: goose pimples.

Plato's myth is a moving and richly satisfying one that can be enjoyed fully on aesthetic terms But if we have the patience and courage to look more deeply, we will find that the myth also illustrates and embodies a major tenet of Plato's theory of knowledge: namely, that all true wisdom comes not through logic but recollection. Though modern readers of the dialogues often overlook it, the true, metaphysical purpose of Plato's question-and-answer dialectic is to rip away all false illusions and to spur in us a memory of what our soul saw when it communed with the Forms during its thousand-year journey. The true wisdom already resides deep within our soul; the goal of the dialectic (of philosophy) is to help us re-access that pre-natal wisdom.

This key Platonic belief, that our soul existed in Heaven and thus participated in Goodness, Truth, and Beauty before entering our body, is generally referred to as the theory or doctrine of the pre-existence. Both in its philosophical-theological and aesthetic forms, the doctrine of the pre-existence has had much play in European Christian thought. Though the Bible nowhere embraces such a doctrine, it nowhere directly condemns it. Indeed, one of the church fathers, Origen, played with the notion in his (at times, heterodox) writings. Origen found the doctrine helpful for it seemed to offer a solution to the mystery of why some are born with more advantages than others. Origen—committed to a strong, many would say radical, free-will theodicy—suggested (in the guise of philosopher rather than theologian) that perhaps our lot in life is dependent in part on our actions in the pre-existence.

In the aesthetic realm, the most famous use of the doctrine is found in Wordsworth's "Ode: Intimations of Immortality from Recollections of Early Childhood," a poem in which he struggles with an unshakable sense that he has lost the directness, spontaneity, and wonder he once had as a child. When he was young, the poet muses, the world seemed bathed in an ethereal light, but now he searches in vain to perceive that heavenly glow in the natural world. His poetic (not theological) answer for this disparity is that children, being closer to the pre-existence, still retain some of the glory of Heaven, a glory that slowly fades as the child grows to adulthood. However, as in Plato's myth, the adult will often catch a glimpse that will call back up in his soul a recollection of his former state: "Hence in a season of calm weather / Though inland far we be, / Our Souls have sight of that immortal sea / Which brought us hither, / Can in a moment travel thither, / And see the Children sport upon the shore, / And hear the mighty waters rolling evermore" (lines 161–67).

Just as the soul, which gazes upon the face of its beloved, feels a stirring within as the feathers grow anew, so the adult who casts a backward glance toward that faint, distant shore that gave him birth will experience, in fleeting moments of calm, intimations of the freshness, intimacy, and connectedness that he once knew.

A recent, more popular expression of the pre-existence of the soul appears in Betty Eadie's book *Embraced by the Light* (1992), where she gives a first-person account of her lengthy and complex life-after-life (or near-death) experience. According to Eadie, one of the things she learned (and witnessed) during her journey to the other side was that all of our souls pre-exist in Heaven and that they choose what bodies they will inhabit on Earth, often for the good of other souls. It should be noted that Eadie is a member of the Mormons (or Latter-Day Saints), a sect that believes strongly in the pre-existence of the soul. In Mormon theology, however, it is taught that our souls not only pre-existed in Heaven, but that they have *always* existed. This more radical understanding of the pre-existence is inconsistent with orthodox Christian teaching, for it puts us, ontologically, on a level-playing field with God himself! It is also inconsistent with Plato, who, in *Timaeus* (the only Platonic dialogue that was available in the Middle Ages), makes it clear that God, the Demiurge, created all souls at the beginning and, at first, assigned them all equal lots.

The Rising Path

The Platonic doctrine of the pre-existence is what we may call an abiblical doctrine, for it is neither clearly affirmed nor categorically rejected in the Bible. The same cannot be said for a corollary doctrine that also appears in several of Plato's myths: reincarnation. In the *Phaedrus* myth, Plato explains that the soul dragged to Earth must go through 10,000 years and numerous incarnations before it can return to its original state of freedom. As in Hinduism, those incarnations may take the form not only of various human beings but of higher and lower animals as well (Plato says the same in *Timaeus*). Given that Christian doctrine clearly teaches that we are not souls inhabiting bodies but enfleshed souls, that each person will be subjected to one judgment, and that our final destiny is to dwell not as disembodied souls but in resurrection bodies, there is no possibility of reconciling the Christian view of the afterlife with Plato's embrace of reincarnation.

But did Plato actually embrace it? Though, again, reincarnation appears with some frequency in the dialogues, it could be argued that Plato's use of the doctrine was more metaphorical than literal—that he used it as a (fictional) myth through which to illustrate and embody a deeper philosophical-theological concept. The concept to which I refer, one that is as central to Plato as the pre-existence, might best be termed "the rising path" or "the education of the philosopher."

In *Phaedrus*, and especially in *Symposium* (a drinking party in which Socrates and his companions each celebrate love), Plato lays out a program by which the soul can reach enlightenment. Oddly, both love and philosophy are equal partners in this program, no doubt because both have the capacity to afford direct recollections of the Forms. In *Phaedrus* we are told that if the soul can incarnate as a philosopher three times, its stay on Earth will be shortened from 10,000 to 3000 years! In *Symposium*, the one who would achieve true wisdom is instructed to pursue the following path: begin by loving one individual, then move upward to love all physical beauty, and then move yet higher to love more abstract things (like institutions and the sciences). If this program of gradual ascension is followed, it will lead the philosopher, in the end, to a love and perception of the Forms themselves.

To be a Platonic philosopher means not only to turn one's eyes from the physical and the temporal to the spiritual and the eternal, but to live one's life in perpetual preparation for death. It is a good thing to be a philosopher in life, for knowledge of the Forms provides one with the best standards for healthy and virtuous living, but it is an even better thing to be a philosopher in death, for it is the philosopher who has the best chance of escaping further imprisonment to the world of becoming and journeying in the divine procession through the world of Being.

Again, as I read Plato's myths of the afterlife, I think his philosophical and theological views can be separated from a literal belief in reincarnation. Still, it must be admitted that many of Plato's teachings, though they lie at the foundation of Western philosophy, share remarkable similarities with Eastern teachings of the afterlife. For most Hindus and Buddhists, the ultimate goal is to break free from the wheel of reincarnation (*samsara*), a wheel to which we are bound by our own bad choices (*karma*). It is finally the holy man (or lama or monk) who separates himself from the demands and delusions of the body who has the best chance of escaping from samsara and ascending to a state of passionless and personless bliss (*moksha* or *nirvana*). Though Plato, like his teacher, Socrates, was hardly a passionless man, he does seem at times to advocate an Eastern kind of stoicism that would remove itself from all feeling and seek ultimate release from both pleasure and pain. Where Plato differs, however, from the philosophies of the East is in his rejection of monism: a predominately Eastern worldview (though it was taught by the Western Parmenides) that holds that everything is one and that physical matter, which we wrongly see as possessing a separate reality, is an illusion (*maya*). Though Plato (like his neoplatonic and gnostic heirs) viewed the flesh and the physical world as inherently negative and fallen when compared to the greater reality of the soul and the spiritual realms, he nevertheless (unlike the Hindus and Buddhists) granted them a real existence.

The Myth of Er

Plato's myths of the afterlife are many and diverse, but there is one myth in which Plato conveniently draws together all of his musings on Hades, Elysium, and the judgment of the soul. After devoting some 300 pages to fashioning a perfectly just state, Plato climaxes his *Republic* with a tale about a warrior named Er who has a near-death experience that allows him to observe firsthand how divine justice is meted out to human souls. Like Dante after him, Er is chosen by the gods to be their messenger to the living of the state of the dead.

As the myth begins, Er is led to a mysterious place where he sees two openings in the Earth and two in the Heavens. Through the first two openings, the souls of sinners depart and return from judgment; through the second two, the souls of the just ascend and descend. The former group, who appear dirty and ragged, journey downward and to the left to face their punishments; the latter, who are clean and bright, journey upward and to the right to embrace their reward. Plato is quite specific in setting forth these directional binaries (up vs. down; right vs. left), as if he wished (in the manner of Pythagoras) to ascribe a moral dimension to the four quadrants of the Cartesian coordinate system. In the Western tradition, poets and philosophers who write on the afterlife frequently highlight the mystical meanings of numbers and shapes. They seem to grasp, intuitively if not logically, that a truly just deity would manifest his justice both in the proper assignment of souls and in the harmonious balance of the cosmos.

Er learns that the punishments and blessings of the evil and virtuous souls last a thousand years, with each soul receiving penalties or rewards in accordance with a tenfold ratio. For each vice committed, a penalty is meted out once each century; for every virtue a similar program of rewards is assigned. As in the later Catholic Church, greater punishments are assigned to those who commit suicide, as well as to those who are impious to the gods or to their parents.

When the thousand years are over, the sinners exit the cave—unless they were guilty of tyranny in their previous life. If that is the case, the cave mouth shakes, and the soul of the tyrant is chained, flayed, pierced, and cast into Tartarus. The rest of the souls, whether they came from Heaven or from Hades, proceed to a meadow where they receive a vision of eight heavenly spheres. As the souls watch in awe, the spheres rotate in perfect concentric circles around the Earth. On each sphere a siren sits, singing endlessly a heavenly song. The songs of the eight sirens combine to produce a celestial music that Europeans for 2000 years would refer to as the music of the spheres. To this day, critics dispute how exactly the astrological details of the Myth of Er (many of which are repeated in *Timaeus*) should be interpreted, but whatever exact meaning we ascribe to them, the fact remains that these details had a profound influence on classical, medieval, and renaissance thinkers.

After the eyes and ears of the souls have been purified by the rotation and music of the spheres, the souls are brought face-to-face with the three Fates: Lachesis, Clotho, and Atropos. It is these fates who will be responsible for aiding the souls as they chose their next life. Lachesis, who represents the past, assigns the lot (that is, the new life into which the soul will enter); Clotho, who represents the present, spins the thread of life; and Atropos, who represents the future, cuts the thread at death.

Plato works here with ancient religious teachings and symbols, but he adds to the process a vital element of choice. It is the souls themselves, and not Lachesis, who choose their next lot in life. If they choose foolishly, they must not put the blame on the gods or the workings of destiny. For Plato, all of our education and philosophical training (or lack thereof!) leads up to this terrifying moment of choice. It is, he warns, our greatest moment of peril, for the choice we make in that moment will determine the arc of our lives and beyond.

As Er watches in wonder, a soul fresh from Heaven impulsively chooses the lot of a tyrant, only to find that he will have a ghastly end. He, of course, blames fate for his choice, but it was his own folly that seduced him to choose the wrong lot. Some souls switch their sex (Atalanta chooses to be a male athlete, Epeius a female artisan); others choose to be animals (Orpheus chooses to be a swan, Ajax a lion, and Agamemnon an eagle). Odysseus, reputed for his wisdom and his craftiness, chooses best of all: the lot of an ordinary man who minds his own business. The wise man, Plato uses his myth to explain, is the one who chooses a life that lies in the mean between the extremes: neither rich nor poor, beautiful nor ugly, powerful nor weak.

Once it has chosen its lot, the soul is forced to drink from Lethe, the river of forgetfulness: Washed clean of the memory of its past life, the soul is now ready to assume a new form and return to the land of the living.

6

Aeneas in the Underworld
The Shape of the Journey

When the Roman Virgil wrote his epic, the *Aeneid*, he knew it would have to include a *nekuia*—and not just any *nekuia*, but one patterned closely on Odysseus' descent into the underworld. It should come as no surprise then that all the elements that make up *Odyssey* XI are echoed, in one form or another, in *Aeneid* VI. But Virgil, one of the greatest aesthetic craftsmen in the history of literature, was not content merely to imitate. While paying full tribute to Homer (and Plato), Virgil reinterprets and reinvents earlier Greek visions of the afterlife to suit the greater purposes of his epic and the wider scope of the Roman Empire, whose birth he witnessed and whose glory he celebrated.

The changes Virgil makes to the epic convention of the *nekuia* begin with the changes he makes to his epic hero, Aeneas. Unlike Odysseus, whose simple goal is to return home, Aeneas is chosen by the gods to leave Troy and find a new land (Italy), where he will give birth to a new civilization that will, in the fullness of time, become Rome. This means that his descent is not only set in a wider historical perspective—the eventual founding and rise to power of the Roman Empire—but has a fuller personal significance as well. Whereas Odysseus is, and must remain, the same from beginning to end, Aeneas, during his long journey from Asia Minor to Italy, must slowly transform from a Trojan into a Roman. In an almost ruthless fashion, Virgil rips away all of Aeneas' links to his past: at the end of Books II, III, IV, and V, he loses, respectively, his wife (Creusa), his father (Anchises), his lover (Dido), and his close friend and companion (Palinurus). Then, in Book VI, having been robbed of all his links to the past (except his son, who represents the future), he descends into Hades, marking the symbolic death of the old self (Aeneas the Homeric Trojan) and the rebirth of the new (Aeneas the Virgilian Proto-Roman).

The journey Aeneas takes into the underworld represents more than a generic test of his courage, more even than a source of wisdom. Everything he sees and hears in Hades is meant to prepare him for his task: laying the foundation for the future glory of Rome.

The Sibyl and the Bough

Virgil begins his adaptation of Homer by setting his *nekuia* in a real, historical place. Whereas Odysseus' descent into the underworld is set in a shadowy, indistinct region unidentifiable on any map, the entrance to Virgil's Hades is housed in the ancient Greek city of Cumae: a very real city that has been well excavated by archeologists and is located near modern-day Naples. By Virgil's time (first century B.C.), the city had already been abandoned, but wealthy Greek and Roman tourists—Virgil almost certainly among them—flocked to the site, eager to visit the ruins and underground tunnels of Cumae. During their guided tour, they would be told eerie tales about the Sibyl, a prophetess who was as honored by the Roman people as the oracle of Delphi was by the Greeks.

The Sibyl, Virgil explains in *Aeneid* III, would write her riddling prophecies on leaves, but the wind would blow into her cave and scatter them. Even if a seeker could manage to gather them all back together, he would likely lack the wisdom to reassemble the sibylline leaves in their proper order. According to legend, the Sibyl once tried to sell nine scrolls of prophecy to a Roman tyrant, but he, in his arrogance, refused to pay the price. In response, the Sibyl burned three of the scrolls. Still, the tyrant refused, and she burned three more. Finally, awed by the numinous presence of the Sibyl and terrified by her prophetic powers, he purchased the three remaining scrolls for the original price demanded by the Sibyl. In Virgil's time, these legendary three scrolls where supposedly hidden away by priests—few, if any, knew their dark secrets, though many believed that men like Caesar Augustus made their decisions based partly on the secret scrolls.

It is significant that Virgil chose the Sibyl to be Aeneas's guide through the underworld. By doing so, Virgil establishes an indigenous Italian source of inspiration, one that can compete on an equal footing with the Greek oracle of Delphi, whose prophetic words not only echo throughout the best Greek literature (especially the tragedies) but proved decisive in many of the key political decisions made by the ancient Greeks. Using the Sibyl as guide further allowed Virgil to link his epic hero to Rome's prophetic past. Virgil's reasons were not lost on the Renaissance Italian artist Michelangelo. A millennium-and-a-half later, Michelangelo would include the Cumaean Sibyl on the Sistine chapel—thus placing Virgil's pagan Rome within the orbit of the grander historical scheme of the Christian God.

As Aeneas and his men await the arrival of the Sibyl, they stare at a massive gate, on which Daedalus, the great artificer, had long ago inscribed the tale of King Minos of Crete, Theseus and the Minotaur, and the death of his son, Icarus. This opening image of tragedy and personal loss haunts Aeneas's entire journey through the dark regions and gives Book VI its distinctive elegiac tone. Aeneas desires to stare longer at Daedalus' handiwork, but the Sibyl rushes him on, as indeed she does throughout the descent. Hades is not a place to linger; a sense of urgency drives Aeneas (and Virgil) on, as it will one day drive Dante.

Aeneas is next led to the prophetic cave of the Sibyl—a honeycombed cavern with a hundred mouths whose voices carry her prophecies on the wind. Here and throughout Book VI, Aeneas, in a manner typical of the epic *nekuia*, engages in a series of questions and answers with the Sibyl. Knowing how even the wisest man can be befuddled by the sibylline leaves, Aeneas asks the Sibyl to speak her prophecies rather than write them on leaves: a request that may be interpreted as a homage to the oral tradition out of which the *Iliad* and *Odyssey* emerged. In response, the Sibyl falls into a prophetic trance and warns Aeneas of the civil war that he will initiate when he arrives in Italy, and how he will be forced to beg assistance from a Greek city. Unlike the calmly-spoken prophecies of Tiresias (*Odyssey* XI), the Sibyl's prophecies are not only frantic in nature but are quite literally ripped out of her by Apollo in a sort-of mystical rape. Virgil, the poet of empire, is well aware of the institutionalized violence upon which empires often rest, and his depiction of the Sibyl's agony adds a political dimension to the *nekuia*.

The Sibyl instructs Aeneas to pray, and, in his prayer, he carefully establishes epic precedent for the feat he is about to attempt—namely, exploring Hades while yet in his mortal body. Aeneas (and behind him, Virgil) references in his prayer the journeys of Orpheus, Pollux, Hercules, and Theseus. He does not mention Odysseus's journey, for, at this point in the narrative, there is no way for Aeneas to know that Odysseus has visited the same place only four years earlier. (Aeneas's *nekuia* occurs seven years after the fall of Troy; Odysseus's occurs roughly three years after the war.)

After Aeneas (and Virgil) makes his prayer, the Sibyl tells him that before he can enter Hades (known to the Romans as Dis or Orcus), he must pluck the Golden Bough. The Bough grows on a tree in a thick wood and can only be found by those who are guided to it. Aeneas must find the tree and pluck the Bough from it: if he is truly chosen for the journey, it will come away easily in his hands; if not, he will not be able to remove it. Once the bough is plucked, she tells him, another will grow in its place.

The image of the Golden Bough has fascinated writers for ages. Sir James Frazer's famous work of cultural anthropology (*The Golden Bough*) begins as a search to identify the Bough. Frazer, following Virgil, identifies it as the mistletoe, a plant sacred to the Druids. Other critics identify the Bough as a talismanic border figure that lies on the margin of life and death, mineral and vegetable, art and nature, sky and Earth, upper world and lower. Virgil seems to use it for another, more subtle purpose. After finding the Bough, Aeneas is able to pluck it, but, Virgil tells us, he does so with great difficulty. By including this detail, Virgil forces his reader to ask a question that has wider historical and political ramifications: is Aeneas *really* the chosen one? And therefore by extension: has Rome *truly* been chosen to rule? This riddling and somewhat contentious note, one that balances praise of Caesar Augustus with criticism, is sounded again at the end of Book VI. After explaining—in imitation of Homer—that there are two Gates of Sleep in Dis, a Gate of Horn out of which issue true dreams and a Gate of Ivory out of which issue false dreams, Virgil has Aeneas exit the underworld by the latter gate. Is Rome destined for eternal rule, or is the whole march of Roman history a false dream? Virgil allows the question to remain hovering on the winds of time.

Into the Dark

Aeneas and the Sibyl enter the underworld proper through a volcanic cavern near Lake Avernus. Huddled about the entrance to the cave, he sees countless horrific forms: not only monsters like Scylla, Hydra, Gorgons, Harpies, and Centaurs but the bestial embodiments of Disease, Hunger, and Age. He sees too an ancient elm under whose leaves cling numberless false dreams. In fear, Aeneas raises his sword to fight the monsters, but the Sibyl laughs and tells him they are only shadows. Aeneas must learn new strategies, new virtues if he is to fulfill his mission. Hades tests far more than our physical strength and courage; it tests our patience, our vision, and our capacity to endure.

As Aeneas descends, he comes upon a bank where a throng of souls beg passage across the river Acheron so that they may find rest within. The recipient of their petitions is Charon, the foul-bearded, fiery-eyed ferryman of the dead. In ancient times coins would be placed on the tongues of corpses as payment for Charon. Even in some isolated villages along the Mediterranean, the locals still speak of warding off Charon from their family.

As he watches the souls flock to Charon, Virgil compares them to falling leaves and migrating birds. Among this group, he sees Palinurus who had been washed overboard at the end of Book V. Palinurus, like Elpenor in *Odyssey* XI, begs Aeneas to find his body and give it proper burial that he might find rest. But that is not to be. The Sibyl tells the shade of Palinurus that he will not receive the burial he seeks, but that, in compensation for his pain, an Italian port will be named in his honor. Like Aeneas, Palinurus must learn to be patient: his reward will come far in the future.

Though Charon resists ferrying the living Aeneas across Acheron, when he is shown the Bough, he grudgingly relents. Aeneas enters the raft, and his living weight causes it to groan and take on water. Once on the other shore, Cerberus, the three-headed guardian of Hell, barks ferociously, but the Sibyl throws him a honeyed sop that drugs him into silence. As Aeneas's eyes adjust to the gloom, he begins to see various souls, many of them grouped in accordance with their sins—sins that have been judged by the legendary King Minos. The first such group Aeneas comes upon are those whose deaths were sad and bitter: infants who died young, those who were falsely accused, suicides, and those who died for love.

Amongst the latter group, he sees his lover Dido, the Carthaginian Queen whom he had first loved and then abandoned to continue his mission to Italy. In sorrow and anger, Dido had killed herself and been judged by Minos a suicide for love. When Aeneas sees her, he weeps and asks her forgiveness, but she, like Ajax in *Odyssey* XI, remains silent. She spurns Aeneas and is reunited with her former husband, leaving us a Virgilean contrast between the one who sacrifices love for empire and the one who sacrifices empire for love—as Marc Antony would one day do for the love of Cleopatra.

Aeneas next speaks with the tragic soul of Deiphobus, a Trojan who took Helen as his wife after the death of Paris, but whom she betrayed to the Greeks to curry favor with Menelaus. In his tale, he curses Odysseus the schemer, reminding us that we are now seeing Hades from the viewpoint, not of the Greeks (as in Homer), but of the Trojans and their Roman heirs.

Aeneas desires to talk further with his kinsman, but the Sibyl again rushes him on. The hour is late, she warns, and they must not tarry. Soon, they come to a great fork in the road: one path leads upward to Elysium; the other lead downward to Tartarus. As in Plato's Myth of Er, the upward path bends to the right, while the downward bends left. Tartarus, we learn, lies within the City of Dis, which is guarded by a triple wall and a massive gate. Aeneas yearns to see what lies within, but the Sibyl tells him that no pure soul may cross into Dis, though she, as the caretaker of Avernus, was allowed a full tour of Hell by Hecatë.

Though there are some similarities between Hecatë, an ancient goddess of the underworld, and Persephone, Hades' queen whom he kidnapped from her mother Demeter, the two should not be confused. Hecatë was, in fact, worshipped in the form of a triple goddess (often allegorized as mother, maid, and crone): Hecatë, who dwelt below in the underworld; Diana, the virgin goddess of the Crossroads who dwelt on the Earth; and Selene, the goddess of the moon who dwelt in the sky. Diana, the sister of Apollo (known as Artemis to the Greeks), was served by the King of the Wood, who won his title by plucking the Golden Bough and killing his predecessor. Frazer tells the tale in full in *The Golden Bough*, emphasizing the continued archetypal power of such scapegoat rituals that unite human sacrifice with divinely-chosen kingship. We catch a glimpse of this archetype in *Aeneid* VI, when Virgil tells us that at the very moment Aeneas plucks the Bough, one of his comrades, Misenus, dies.

Though Aeneas cannot enter Tartarus (that task will be completed by Hell's greatest explorer: Dante), the Sibyl agrees to give him an overview of Dis. Rhadamanthus, the brother of Minos, is the judge of Tartarus, and he has the power to force the souls to confess their sins. The gatekeepers of Tartarus are the Furies (led by Tisiphone, who lashes the guilty with her whip of writhing snakes) and the Hydra (who roars out of her fifty throats). Tartarus itself is a yawning pit twice as deep as Heaven is high (Virgil doubles Hesiod). It was originally intended as a prison for the Titans, whose rebellious attempt to seize Olympus the law-abiding Virgil rebukes.

In keeping with traditions laid down by Hesiod, Homer, and Plato, Virgil offers, through the mouth of the Sibyl, a traditional catalogue of sinners and punishments, emphasizing sinners who fell through arrogance, blasphemy, greed, and treachery. In a strongly Platonic moment, he even has one of the sinners (Phlegyas) call out in the dark, warning all to show justice to men and piety to the gods.

And with that, Aeneas and the Sibyl turn right along the forking path and make their way to the Elysian Fields.

7

Virgil & Cicero

Roman Visions of the Afterlife

Having made his way through the shadowy realms of Hades and glimpsed the hellish pit of Tartarus, Aeneas is now led by the Sibyl to the final resting place of the blessed. He has come to the underworld not merely to test his courage and his capacity to endure but to fulfill a rendezvous with the spirit of his father Anchises. Along with the other inhabitants of Elysium, Anchises has earned his place through the practice of virtue and *pietas*, whose meaning in Latin is closer to "duty" than "piety." Though Virgil's Blessed Groves are patterned after the Elysian Fields of Homer (and Plato), Virgil's vision of the pagan Paradise is inflected in a distinctly Roman way.

In sharp contrast to the perpetual gloom that shrouds the sad Elysium of *Odyssey* XI, Virgil's Elysium, though located underground, abounds with life and color and possesses its own sun and stars. On the eternally green fields of grass, the souls of the righteous play athletic games, sing, dance, and feast. Orpheus, wearing a long robe, leads the music, playing on his seven-stringed lyre. Far from a place of sad indolence, Virgil's Roman Heaven is a place of robust, healthy activity. Many of the souls have brought their chariots and horses with them, and they still engage in the joys of war; others have brought their oxen and plows, and continue, as was their wont, to practice the art of husbandry. Though it is hard to say for sure, it is possible that Virgil was influenced here by Egyptian views of the afterlife, which, unlike those of the Greeks, imagined a post-mortem state not wholly unlike the one that preceded it.

Among the righteous souls in Elysium are all those in the royal line of Troy (and therefore Rome), as well as all those who died fighting for their country. Though goodness and clean living are honored in Virgil's Heaven, the Roman poet also places a heavy emphasis on the virtue of patriotism. These souls have not only *been* good; they have *done* good things. Indeed, all in Elysium have gained some kind of fame (*fama*), whether through holy lives, prophetic songs, the use of new skills, or the discovery of new truths. In one way or another, they have all done something to be remembered, and it is through the memory of their great deeds that they gain immortality.

A Glimpse of Glory

Once Aeneas has taken his fill of the Blessed Groves, the Sibyl approaches Musaeus and asks him where they may find Anchises. The mythical singer and poet, who, together with Orpheus, is mentioned in Socrates' description of Elysium (*Apology*), answers that no one in that blessed place has a fixed dwelling. Rather, they are left free to wander over the meadows, through shady groves, and by the rivers and streams. Aeneas and the Sibyl find Anchises in a lush valley where he is surveying a group of souls who are destined one day to become his own descendants: that is to say, the future makers of Rome.

In a burst of creative genius that raises aesthetic imitation to a new level, Virgil borrows Plato's doctrine of the pre-existence of the soul and finds a stunning and original use for it. By effecting a grand fusion of the mythic and the historical, Virgil suggests that the future glory of Rome is not only written prophetically in the stars but is spiritually "stored up" in the underworld. The seeds of the Roman harvest to come are already present, literally, in a mythic Hades. In a startling inversion, Hades is transformed from the endpoint of all human vanity to the starting point of all earthly glory and *fama*.

When Aeneas realizes that it is Anchises who is surveying the souls, he rushes to his father and attempts three times to hug him. Alas, as Odysseus found when he tried to embrace his mother in *Odyssey* XI, this is no longer possible. Aeneas's hands pass through the shade of his father as if he were made of wind, or only a dream. Perhaps to distract himself from the sorrow he feels, Aeneas gazes at the landscape around him and catches sight of Lethe, the river of forgetfulness. And that is when he sees the vast multitudes of shades. Like a swarm of bees, the souls of a thousand nations hover around Lethe; each soul waits to drink from the river and thus forget his past life before taking on his new. Here, as in Plato (and the Pre-Socratic

Pythagoras), Virgil's meditation on the pre-existence of the soul expands to include the possibility of reincarnation. For some of these souls, it appears, have already sojourned upon the Earth and are now awaiting a second chance to breathe the air of the upper world.

When Aeneas learns from Anchises that the souls beside Lethe *desire* to return to Earth, he responds with shock and dismay: "'Must we imagine, / Father, there are souls that go from here / Aloft to upper Heaven, and once more / Return to bodies' weight? The poor souls, / How can they crave our daylight so?" (965–69).[1] Aeneas's world-weary, almost life-denying response is distinctly un-Homeric (remember the shade of Achilles who would prefer to be the slave of a slave on Earth than king of all the dead!), but then Odysseus's journey promises a happy return home, whereas Aeneas' promises only pain and civil war. We must also remember that when Aeneas dies, he will get to remain permanently in Elysium for he will have gained *fama*. The souls that gather around Lethe, on the other hand, have yet to perform deeds that will be remembered.

Anchises, seeing that his son is puzzled and disturbed by this apocalyptic vision of the transmigration of souls, responds by reciting, in the manner of a Roman orator, two explanatory speeches. Anchises' first, somewhat longwinded speech is spiritual and philosophical in focus, and blends together various theories from Pythagoreanism, Orphism, Platonism, Epicureanism, and Stoicism. Behind all nature and the cosmos, he explains, there lies a pervading Spirit or Mind that infuses all things. Out of this heavenly Spirit comes a fiery energy that is the source of all animal life. In its original form, man's soul is pure and free, but, when imprisoned in "deathly flesh," it becomes poisoned and clogged and falls prey to the extremes of human emotion and desire. So strong is the body's impact that even when it dies it leaves its imprint on the soul. Often these imprints are so deep-rooted that the soul can only rid itself of them through punishments, which, we are told, include exposure to winds, floods, and fires. After the souls have completed their penance, those who have gained *fama* proceed to Elysium, where, over a long period of time, their stains slowly erode away, leaving them once again as pure heavenly fire. The unremembered, in contrast, must wait a full thousand year cycle before they can drink from Lethe. These long cycles, which hearken back to Plato, are also quite Eastern in tone and suggest a cyclic, rather than linear, view of history.

1. All passages from the *Aeneid* VI will be taken from Robert Fitzgerald's translation of Virgil's *Aeneid*. I will provide line numbers in the text. Fitzgerald's line numbers do not correspond with those of the original Latin; however, he does provide the cumulative Latin line numbers at the bottom of each page.

Anchises' second speech is more ethical and rhetorical in focus, and consists of the kind of advice a Roman father might give his son. As the souls of his descendants parade by, Anchises tells the history of Rome to come, beginning with the grandsons and great-grandsons of Aeneas and proceeding through Romulus, the early kings of Rome, the heroes of the Republic and the Punic Wars, and the key players in the civil wars of the first century B.C. He saves his greatest praise, however for Rome's first Emperor and the patron of the *Aeneid*: Caesar Augustus. Though Anchises' review of souls is organized chronologically and genealogically, the real thrust of his speech is to celebrate the virtues of patriotism and pietas, and to warn against the dangers of greed, pride, and civil war.

As his speech rises to a mighty crescendo, he reminds all future Romans (that is, Virgil's contemporaries) that their true art is not to be sculpture or rhetoric or astrology, but the art of just rule. The arts of Rome, he concludes, are to be these: "'To pacify, to impose the rule of law, / To spare the conquered, battle down the proud'" (1154–55). Through words that eerily foreshadow the Magnificat of Mary (Luke 1:46–55), Anchises instructs the Romans of Augustus' day that if they are to achieve greatness and everlasting fame, they must learn to crush the belligerent but show mercy to the defeated. Or, to quote Mary's prayer, to "put down the mighty from their seats and [exalt] them of low degree" (verse 52).

His "secular sermon" over, Anchises points out the future soul of the one who will be Marcellus, the son of Augustus' sister Octavia and husband of his daughter Julia. Augustus, together with all of Rome, had hoped that the noble and charismatic Marcellus would succeed him as emperor, but he died in his early manhood without achieving the glory due him. Speaking over a thousand years before the event, Anchises prophesies the tragic death, and laments how that death will dash the hopes of Rome. He then offers his own tender eulogy: "Let me scatter lilies, / All I can hold, and scarlet flowers as well" (1199–1200). Tradition has it that Virgil read Book VI of the *Aeneid* aloud to Caesar Augustus and his court; when he read these mournful words, it is said that Octavia fainted in grief.

And so, in what is perhaps the most ambiguous moment in the *Aeneid*, Virgil transforms the great march of Roman history and glory into a funeral procession for Marcellus. That Virgil meant to do so is corroborated by one of the unique funeral rituals practiced in his day. During the first century B.C., wealthy senators who could afford elaborate funerals processions would include in the line of mourners people wearing masks representing the ancestors of the deceased.

Even more ambiguously, Virgil suggests in Book VI that the price of Roman history may be too great. In Homer, Odysseus's descent is "paid for" by the single death of Elpenor; in Virgil, no less than four young men must suffer to ensure Aeneas' passage and, by extension, Rome's greatness: one past (Icarus), two present (Misenus, Palinurus), and one future (Marcellus).

As with Aeneas' exit through the Gate of Ivory and his difficult plucking of the Golden Bough, the death of these four young men leaves a single question hovering on the winds of time. Not "am I the chosen one?" but "What price glory?"

Plato for Romans

A generation before Virgil, another great Roman (Cicero) wrote his own account of the afterlife. The account (or, better, vision) occurs at the end of *On the Republic*, a more Roman, more practical, reworking of Plato's *Republic* that retains Plato's rhetorically-rich prose and dialogue form and ends with its own Roman Myth of Er. Referred to by critics as "The Dream of Scipio," Cicero's myth is told through the mouth of Scipio the Younger, who, in 146 B.C. (almost a century before Cicero wrote *On the Republic*), helped to defeat and utterly destroy Carthage and her empire. Scipio was himself the adopted grandson of Scipio Africanus, who had ended the Second Punic War by defeating Rome's greatest nemesis (Hannibal) at the Battle of Zama in 202 B.C.

In the dream, which is meant, as in Plato, to embody the political and moral values expressed in the dialogue, the ghost of Africanus appears to Scipio with a message. He begins by prophesying the political future of his grandson—which will include both a rise to power and a betrayal—and then inspires him with a vision of the afterlife. The vision is relatively brief but it would go on to inspire not only Virgil but all subsequent authors who would take upon themselves the task of describing the afterlife, the judgment of the soul, and the starry heavens.

Before lifting the eyes of Scipio to the stars, Africanus steps aside and reunites Scipio with the soul of his father, Paulus. Like Odysseus before him and Aeneas after him, Scipio reaches out to embrace his dead parent, but Scipio, alone of the three heroes, is able actually to do so! Then, in good Roman patriarchal fashion, Paulus (as Anchises will later do in *Aeneid* VI) gives his son a lesson in ethical behavior. He promises Scipio that all those who have helped to preserve and grow their fatherland will be ensured a place in Heaven where they will experience both eternal life and eternal bliss. In fact, he assures him that God, the ruler of the cosmos, values law and political justice above all things, and that the greatest rulers have both come from and will return to Heaven. Though Cicero lived before the days when Christian theologians would teach that man's highest end is to glorify God, Cicero *did* understand that man was born with a purpose and that God gave us our lives and beings that we might fulfill that purpose. And that purpose is to assist the Creator in bringing peace and order to the Earth. Anticipating, and perhaps influencing, the strong Catholic prohibition against suicide, Cicero condemns those who take their own lives—for to do so is to desert the post to which God assigned them.

Having warned Scipio away from all thoughts of suicide, Paulus challenges his son to live a life of virtue and pietas and to honor his parents, his ancestors, and their beloved country. He admonishes him to resist the pleasures of the body and to train his soul, reminding him that the soul is but a spark of the divine mind held for a time in the custody of the body. From a Christian point of view, we might say that Paulus instructs his son in the rigors of a "works religion," and yet, though it is true that Paulus presents the practice of pietas as the way to Heaven, his advice to his son transcends the narrow confines of legalism. Cicero's concern here is not with behavior per se, but with the shaping of the soul. Indeed, it was precisely because Cicero's understanding of ethics and morality was focused more on the soul than the body that many of the early and medieval church fathers considered him to be (along with Plato and Virgil) a proto-Christian whom God used to prepare the pagan world for the coming of Christ.

The ethical lecture at an end, Paulus steps aside and yields the podium back to Africanus. What Cicero *really* wants to say surpasses even the expansive vision that Virgil would later embody in *Aeneid* VI. To set all in its proper perspective, Cicero must, through the mouth of Rome's supreme hero and savior, present Scipio with a God's-eye view of greater cosmic order: one that would inspire Dante's *Divine Comedy*, and that I will slowly unfold in all its glory over the course of subsequent chapters.

In a flash, Africanus lifts Scipio above our changeful World of Becoming and exhorts him to gaze upon the might of the heavens. Then, in a vision based on Plato but surpassing even Cicero's Greek master, Scipio's eyes are opened that he may gaze with wonder on the full majesty of the Ptolemaic universe. In rapid succession, Scipio's eyes take in the nine ascending spheres (Earth, Moon, Mercury, Venus, Sun, Mars, Jupiter, Saturn, Fixed Stars), and he is instructed by Africanus in the different traits and influences that accompany each planet. The Earth, he is told, is heavy and motionless and draws all weight to itself, but the eight upper spheres revolve eternally, their varying motions and intervals producing the celestial music of the spheres. All our lives, we have heard that heavenly harmony, but our very familiarity with the music has caused us to grow deaf to its beauty. Like the people who live beside the roaring waterfalls of the Nile, our dull hearing and eyesight have been overwhelmed by the sound and glory of the cosmos, causing us to lose sight of that which should draw our soul upward.

Indeed, despite the power of the vision, the distracted Scipio keeps looking down, and he must be reminded that earthly fame is meaningless, that on the cosmic map our noble cities are like blisters. Even the mighty Roman Empire is like a small island in a vast sea; and as for time, the history of Rome is but a second in terms of the greater cosmic cycles. Therefore, he counsels Scipio, focus your soul not on Rome but on your eternal home; care nothing for the petty rewards of men, but let a higher virtue guide you to the stars.

Sic transit gloria mundi. So goes the glory of the world.

8

The Shape of Dante's Universe

The fullest poetic account of the afterlife, the one that embodies and surpasses all that came before, is Dante's *Commedia*. Composed of three separate parts—*Inferno*, *Purgatorio*, and *Paradiso*—Dante's *Comedy* (later critics added the word "divine") takes as its theme nothing less than the universe of the Christian God and man's temporal and eternal place in it and in Him. And yet, despite its grand scheme, the *Comedy* begins humbly, quietly, with little epic fanfare and with little sense of the cosmic journey to come: "Midway in our life's journey, I went astray / from the straight road and woke to find myself / alone in a dark wood" (*Inferno* I.1–3).[1]

Here is no larger-than-life warrior (like Achilles), no city-sacking wanderer (like Odysseus), no founder of an empire (like Aeneas), but an ordinary man who, in the midst of his ordinary life, has lost his way. As happens to so many of us, Dante experiences a mid-life crisis. He feels cut off, estranged, isolated; all those things that once seemed so clear to him have lost their clarity.

As long as Peter kept his eyes focused on Christ, he was able to walk, with effortless ease, on the tumultuous waters of the Sea of Galilee. But the moment he took his eyes off of Christ and let the waves and winds distract him, he began to sink. Just so, when the *Comedy* begins, Dante has lost his focus on the True Way and has strayed from the narrow path. Not only terror but helpless confusion assault the dazed poet, for it all happened so suddenly, with no signposts and little warning. One wrong turn, and he finds that he is lost, alone, and afraid.

---

1. All passages from the *Commedia* will be taken from John Ciardi's masterful translations of *Inferno*, *Purgatorio*, and *Paradiso*. I will provide book and line numbers in the text.

Divine Conjunction

The opening of the *Comedy* is dark indeed; nevertheless, two factors quickly emerge that extend hope to the wandering poet (and to the reader) that though the beginning is bad, the ending will be good. First, there is the simple fact that Dante called his work the *Comedy*. To call one's poem a "comedy" is not necessarily to imply that it is funny. Dante himself, in a letter he wrote to one of his patrons, explains that the generic category of comedy suggests a poem that, unlike a tragedy (which begins well but ends terribly), is harsh at the outset but happy in its resolution. He also explains that a comedy, rather than being written in a sublime and elevated style, is more loose and mixed in its diction. The *Comedy* will be a poem of highs and lows, sublimities and crudities, darkness and light—but it *will* have a happy ending.

Second, and more important, the inevitable happy ending is signaled from the outset by the special day that Dante chooses—or, rather, *constructs*—for the beginning of his journey. In the Psalms (90:10), our life is measured out poetically as "three score and ten" (seventy years). By announcing in the first line of his poem that he is in the middle of his life's pilgrimage, Dante identifies his age as thirty-five. Since Dante was born in 1265, that sets the year of his journey as 1300, an auspicious year that carries with it the promise of new life.

But Dante is not finished. To increase the promise of renewal symbolized by the beginning of a new century, Dante adds four further details that embody, on a cosmic scale, the theme of rebirth: it is dawn, during a full moon, on the vernal equinox, and the sun is in the position of Aries. If we recall that the vernal equinox is the first day of spring and that after it the days grow increasingly longer, and if we bear in mind that medieval theologians believed the sun was in Aries on the day of Creation, we will see that Dante is concerned not so much with the physical as with the spiritual meaning of the heavenly conjunction that signals the start of his epic pilgrimage. Indeed, Dante presents the heavens themselves as conspiring together to provide him with an auspicious beginning for his journey.

But Dante is still not finished. At the Council of Nicea in 325, the church adopted a method for determining the date of Easter that is still used today by Catholic and Protestant (though not Eastern Orthodox) Christians—an odd and somewhat complicated method that explains why the date of Easter varies widely from year to year. Easter, the church decided, was to be celebrated on the first Sunday after the first full moon of the vernal equinox. Though many today think that the only people who are interested in the movements and conjunctions of the sun, the moon, and the stars are neo-pagans, the church—which worships a Savior whose birth was signaled by the Star of Bethlehem and whose death was marked by a noontime eclipse of the sun—has always shown a deep concern with astrological phenomena. Even today, we cannot determine the date of the most holy day in the Christian calendar without consulting the position of the sun and the phases of the moon.

Dante's journey begins on the vernal equinox under a full moon, a conjunction that signals to the reader that we are in the midst of Holy Week and that the Sunday to come will be Easter. That this conjunction did not, in fact, occur in 1300 gives support to the argument that Dante consciously constructed a perfect Easter to drive home his thematic and spiritual message of rebirth. At this point, I trust it will come as no surprise that Dante further identifies the day of his beginning as Good Friday. Just as the vernal equinox stands as a firm pledge that spring will soon be here, so Good Friday carries within it the seed of the resurrection that is to follow. Both the heavens and the church calendar testify together: pain and terror will give way to life and joy. The ending *will* be good; though Dante will enter Hell on Good Friday, he will emerge from the pit, strengthened and renewed, on Easter morning.

Dante, along with his fellow medievals, lived in a sympathetic universe that was fraught with meaning and purpose. The stars were not dead and cold, cut off from the lives of men; their positions and movements rained down influence on the Earth, even as great upheavals in the earthly realm were reflected and broadcast in the heavenly. The medievals, like the ancients before them, referred to the universe by the Greek word *kosmos*— a word whose root meaning is "ornament" (as in our modern word, cosmetics). The cosmos was considered by ancients and medievals alike to be ordered and harmonious, because it was created by a God of order and harmony. It was, in fact, God's ornament. Both humanity and nature were part of God's cosmic order and harmony, and thus it was only natural that the two should exist in sympathy with one another. Dante's universe did not simply exist; it *meant*, and it meant intensely. The universe was less a thing to be studied than a poem to be loved and enjoyed.

Ascending and Descending

No sooner does Dante find himself alone in the dark wood than he begins to look for a way of escape. As he wanders through the woods, his eyes are drawn toward a small hill upon which the sun is shining. Buoyed up by the hope of reaching the light and escaping the darkness around him,

Dante begins to ascend the hill. Alas for the hopeful poet, his way is quickly blocked by three beasts (a lion, a she-wolf, and a leopard) whose threatening advances cause him to retreat backward into the woods.

Like the earlier *Romance of the Rose* and the later *Pilgrim's Progress*, Dante's *Comedy* is, in part at least, an allegory. As such, many of the images, figures, and events that occur in the *Comedy* stand for something else or point to a second, higher meaning. Throughout Dante's three-part epic, the sun always represents God's love, grace, and salvation. Once we realize this, it becomes clear what the three beasts represent. According to Christian theology, there is one thing that prevents us from attaining (on our own power) God's salvation and finding union with him: and that thing is sin. Barred from reaching the sun (God's grace) by the beasts (sin), Dante sinks back into darkness and gives way to despair.

And that is when God intervenes. As Dante loses all hope, suddenly, on the mist, the shade of Virgil appears to him and promises to be his guide. In the next chapter, I will survey the many reasons why Dante chose Virgil as his guide. Let it suffice here to say that Virgil explains to the bewildered Dante that if he wishes to reach the sun (that is, God), he must go by a longer route. He must first descend through the nine levels of Hell and climb the nine ledges of Purgatory before he can ascend through the nine spheres of Paradise to God—an itinerary that establishes the *Comedy's* tri-partite division into *Inferno*, *Purgatorio*, and *Paradiso*.

This key Dantean notion, that we must descend before we can ascend, is not only implicit in *Odyssey* XI and the Myth of Er, but functions as a main theme in both Virgil's *Aeneid* and the Bible. Just as Aeneas must die to his old Trojan self before he can be reborn as the Father of Rome, so the city of Troy must be destroyed in order that, in the fullness of time, Rome may appear. In the Bible, the heirs of Abraham cannot possess the Promised Land until they first descend into Egypt and slavery. Only after their literal and spiritual descent into bondage can they return and possess the Land of Canaan. On an even grander scale, the human race had to fall through Adam and lose the joys of Eden before it could be reborn through the Second Adam (Christ) and attain the greater joys of the New Jerusalem. In the Catholic Church, this paradoxical teaching is expressed in two Latin words: *felix culpa* ("happy fault"). Though the fall of man was certainly the worst event in human history, when that event is viewed eschatologically (from the end rather than from the beginning), it is transformed into a *felix culpa*, for it leads to Christ's incarnation. In the same way, Christians refer to the day of Christ's crucifixion as Good Friday, not because it was good in itself but because it led to the greater joy and victory of Easter.

For Dante, this central theme—that we must descend before we can ascend—has not only spiritual dimensions, but geographical ones as well: a statement that can only be understood in full by surveying the shape of Dante's universe.

Heaven and Earth

As he lived before Copernicus and Galileo, Dante shared Cicero's Ptolemaic view of the cosmos. That is to say, he lived in a geocentric ("Earth-centered") rather than a heliocentric ("sun-centered") universe. Were I to make a map of Dante's universe I would therefore begin by drawing a circle at the center and labeling it "Earth." Most of you who read the last sentence were perhaps shocked that I spoke of drawing a circle to represent the Earth. Should I not have said a line? Did not all the medievals believe they lived on a flat Earth? Well, no. As I explained in chapter 4, all the ancient and medieval authorities, from Ptolemy to Aquinas, knew that the Earth was spherical. The long-cherished belief that the medievals believed the Earth was flat is based not on historical fact but on Enlightenment propaganda invented to make the medievals (particularly all those "superstitious" Catholics) look foolish and backward.

In America, the myth was propagated through a widely-read biography of Christopher Columbus written by Washington Irving (of "Rip Van Winkle" and "The Legend of Sleepy Hollow"). According to Irving, and to the tens of thousands of grade school teachers who have unknowingly passed on his fabrication, Columbus thought the world was round while his opponents insisted it was flat. In matter of fact, they all knew the world was round. It was Columbus who was in error, for he insisted that the Earth was half as big as it actually is (to the day he died, he continued to believe he had landed in India!).

"Very well," says the cynical modern, "I will concede that the medievals *did* know the Earth was spherical, but that does not take away from the fact that they placed the Earth at the center. Surely that proves that they were deluded by arrogance and overestimated their own importance in the universe." Well, no again. As we saw in the previous chapter, Cicero considered the Earth to be insignificant in comparison to the cosmos, a sentiment that was championed by the Christian Boethius (who wrote around 500) and which was shared by nearly all medievals, Dante included. As we shall see in the chapters to come, there is nothing noteworthy about being at the center. Whereas the heavenly spheres spin, dance, and sing as they bask in God's glorious light, the Earth is motionless, dark, heavy, and silent. Indeed, the medievals did not even consider the Earth to be a planet, for *planet* in Greek means "wanderer," and the Earth is the one heavenly body that does not move.

In many ways, Dante's Earth/Heaven distinction parallels Plato's distinction between the body and the soul, the world of becoming and the world of Being. Like Plato's transitory world of becoming, everything that lay beneath the moon (sub-lunar) was, so Dante and the medievals thought, prey to constant change, decay, and death. Above the moon, however, in the realm of the heavenly spheres, all was, like Plato's world of Being, perfect, pure, and unchanging. Like Cicero, Dante's Heaven consists of nine ascending spheres, but with one difference. Whereas Cicero counted the Earth as the first sphere, Dante, following Aristotle and Aquinas, left out the Earth and replaced it with a ninth sphere known as the *Primum Mobile*: the "prime mover" that sets the others eight spheres in motion. For Dante, then, the nine spheres that made up the heavens were as follows: Moon, Mercury, Venus, Sun, Mars, Jupiter, Saturn, fixed stars, *Primum Mobile*. And, in keeping with the absolute beauty and harmony of God's cosmic ornament, the spheres rotated in perfect concentric circles, producing as they spun that same celestial music of the spheres described by Plato and Cicero.

But let us return to Dante's view of the Earth, which is quite different from our own. Living before the discovery of the New World, Dante believed that all the land on the Earth was concentrated in the Northern Hemisphere in an arc sweeping from Spain in the West to Jerusalem in the center to India in the East. In contrast, the entire Southern Hemisphere, the pre-Columbian Dante believed, was covered with water—with one single exception. Directly opposite to Jerusalem (the "North Pole") stood the mountain of Purgatory (the "South Pole"). Using a little poetic license, Dante informs his reader (in *Inferno* XXXIV) that when God cast Satan out of Heaven, he smashed into the "South Pole" and was driven to the center of the Earth. In fear all the land in the Southern Hemisphere fled north—all except one piece that fled upward instead and became the peak of Purgatory.

In Dante's cosmic scheme, Hell stretches under the northern part of the Earth, spiraling downward in an enormous, slowly tapering funnel. At the bottom of this funnel—in the center of the Earth—Satan lies trapped forever in a block of ice. In their journey, Dante and Virgil proceed level-by-level down the nine circles of Hell till they reach Satan, at which point they grab on to Satan's shaggy hide and climb down to his waist. A few moments later, they find themselves on a river bank and see Satan's feet sticking up behind them. Dante is bewildered for a moment until Virgil explains to him that they have reached the center of gravity and now must climb out to the southern pole. Virgil, of course, does not use the word "gravity," but that is what he means. As moderns, we sometimes imagine that Newton "discovered" gravity, when in fact he only labeled it and discerned its mathematical laws.

As Dante struggles his way up the river bank, he asks Virgil how such a bank was formed in Hell. It was formed, Virgil explains, by the ceaseless flow of the river Lethe, which Dante locates on the top of Purgatory. After the souls in Purgatory have purged away their sins, they must drink from Lethe (the classical river of forgetfulness) to erase even the memory of sin. The river, heavy with the memory of sin, winds its way down Purgatory and then flows under the Earth until it reaches the ice sheet that imprisons the rebellious Satan. In Dante's universe, *all* sin that exists in the universe eventually finds its way down the cosmic sewer of Hell.

The poets climb up the bank formed by the flow of Lethe and emerge, on Easter Sunday, on the mountain of Purgatory. They then begin their slow ascent up the nine levels of Purgatory until they reach the Garden of Eden, which Dante places on the apex of the mountain. From Eden, Dante then begins his ascent, level by level, through the nine spheres of Paradise. At the top (really outside) of the universe, he has a vision of God and his journey ends.

Both literally and geographically, Dante must go down before he can go up, and, in so doing, he follows in the footsteps of another pilgrim whose journey also lasted from Good Friday to Easter. According to some versions of the Creed, after his crucifixion, Christ descended into Hell where he broke down the doors and rescued the souls of the righteous people of the Old Testament: an event known as the harrowing of Hell. Then on Easter he rose from the grave and ascended to Heaven and the throne of God. This fall and rise of the Christ is perhaps best illustrated by a poetic passage in Paul's epistle to the church at Philippi:

> Let this mind be in you, which was also in Christ Jesus: Who, being in the form of God, thought it not robbery to be equal with God: But made himself of no reputation, and took upon him the form of a servant, and was made in the likeness of men: And being found in fashion as a man, he humbled himself, and became obedient unto death, even the death of the cross. Wherefore God also hath highly exalted him, and given him a name which is above every name: That at the name of Jesus every knee should bow, of things in heaven, and things in earth, and things under the earth; And that every tongue should confess that Jesus Christ is Lord, to the glory of God the Father. (Phil 2:5–11)

Though Christ begins in Heaven and is equal with God, his descent into humanity and humiliation leads him to rise up to an even higher level. If even God himself must descend in order that he may ascend, then surely we as his creatures must do the same.

Yet even this powerful passage from the Epistles does not exhaust the full meaning of Dante's descend-in-order-to-ascend theme. Morally speaking, Dante must descend into an awareness of his own sins and the punishments those sins deserve before he can seek after the grace that alone can save us from our sins. Just so, John the Baptist's message of repentance preceded Christ's gospel of grace: for no one seeks a Savior unless he thinks he needs to be saved from something.

The medieval model that undergirds Dante's *Comedy* is indeed a rich and fertile one. For Dante, the universe was not a cold, dead place—as it is, finally, for us moderns—but a living embodiment of that order, balance, and harmony that exists in the mind of its Creator. In *The Discarded Image*, C. S. Lewis admonishes those moderns who would disparage the medieval model and conclude smugly that their view was all wrong and ours is all right. We laugh at the medieval notion that heavenly bodies move through celestial influence, but is such a view any more metaphorical than our notion that all objects must obey the laws of gravity? Yes, Lewis admits, it is true that the medievals saw in the heavens the pageantry and hierarchy that they so highly valued; yet is it not equally true that we have found in *our* heavens the rational laws that we so love. When it comes to models, Lewis concludes, we find what we're looking for; just so in court, the lawyer's questions often determine the shape of the testimony.

Dante's vision of the afterlife, of Heaven and Hell, differs from our own, not only because his conception of the cosmos was medieval rather than modern, but because he was bold and honest enough to ask the kinds of questions about God, man, and the universe that we no longer ask—possibly because we are not willing to accept or even consider the answers!

9

Christian Humanism
Why Dante Chose Virgil as his Guide

If I were Dante, and I were planning to take an epic journey through the length and breadth of the medieval Catholic universe, Virgil would not have been my first choice as guide. Surely such a journey would demand a Christian guide. Perhaps not Jesus himself, but if not him than surely one of his disciples (Peter or John) or one of the early missionaries (Paul or Silas) or one of the great theologians (Augustine or Aquinas). But Dante does not choose any of these likely candidates. He turns instead to a pagan poet who died in 19 B.C., who never journeyed to the Holy Land, and who had no knowledge of the Old Testament. Why?

Passing the Epic Baton

In Dante's day, Virgil was considered the greatest of poets, the true epic heir to Homer. Indeed, throughout the Middle Ages and Renaissance, it was Virgil, rather than Homer, who was hailed as the supreme epic poet—so much so that it is impossible to understand the history of European literature without reference to the *Aeneid*. In pre-Enlightenment (if not pre-twentieth-century) Europe, to be educated was to know and love the *Aeneid*. Even if one had little interest in literature, one was expected to know Latin, and to know Latin meant to know Virgil (and Cicero). It is no exaggeration to say that university-educated Europeans for some 1500 years knew the *Aeneid* almost as well as they knew the Bible.

In constructing the *Comedy*, Dante, like Virgil (but *unlike* Homer), self-consciously set out to write the next great epic. He knew, or at least hoped, when he wrote it that it would be profusely annotated and studied by critics and schoolboys alike. And he succeeded! The *Comedy* is the second-most annotated book after the Bible and is on every scholar's list of the essential Great Books of the Western canon. No less a poet and critic, T. S. Eliot once asserted that Dante and Shakespeare divided the world between them.

Could Dante have known these things as he worked on his epic, he would have been overjoyed, but he had no such assurances at the time. In fact, Dante wrote his *Comedy* during the second half of a twenty-year exile from his beloved Florence, an exile that ended with the poet's death in 1321. If Dante was to realize his high poetic aspirations, he would have to find a way to authorize his ambitions—and what better way than to associate himself with the most universally hailed poet in the Western world. Virgil's presence as Dante's guide through Hell and Purgatory drives home the message that just as Virgil was Homer's heir in the lofty genre of the epic, so Dante is now ready to take up the epic baton from Virgil.

Indeed, Dante makes this passing of the baton explicit in a memorable passage from the *Inferno*. As we shall see in the next chapter, the first level of Hell holds the souls of the virtuous pagans—people who led lives of virtue but lacked the grace of Christ to save them. Among these souls Dante places all the greatest poets and philosophers of ancient Greece and Rome; among the poets, he specifically identifies five as representing the supreme epic poets: Homer, Virgil, Horace, Ovid, and Lucan. Dante converses joyously with the five poets, and then has his joy ratcheted up an additional notch when the five welcome him as sixth in their number. Few poets in the history of literature have ever constructed for themselves such a weighty and sublime authorization of their own literary status!

Dante makes clear the literary progression from Homer to Virgil to himself, a progression he further emphasizes by the very subject matter he chose for the *Inferno*. Just as Virgil modeled his account of Aeneas' descent into Hades on that of Odysseus—with Homer himself mimicking the earlier journeys of Orpheus, Hercules, and Theseus—so Dante, *both* as author and pilgrim, carefully patterned his descent on that of Aeneas. Virgil offers a vital precedent for the would-be explorer of the underworld, and that precedent functions both aesthetically (as an epic convention) and practically (as author of *Aeneid* VI, Virgil knows what's down there). But Dante goes Virgil one better. Whereas the pagan Aeneas was only authorized by the Sibyl to travel through Hades and the Blessed Groves, the Christian Dante is commissioned by God to travel through the dark depths of Tartarus, where the great sinners endure the most terrible of punishments. Travel . . . and return to tell the tale.

Finally, Virgil the epic poet proved an ideal guide, for he succeeded in a role that Dante himself hoped to excel in: molder of the national language. In Virgil's day, the Romans still suffered from something of an inferiority complex. Though they had proven themselves to be the greatest builders, soldiers, civilizers, and lawgivers of the ancient world, they lived aesthetically in the shadow of Greece. Not only did they look to Greece as the exemplar of poetry, philosophy, and statuary; they considered the Greek language to be far nobler than their own. That is, until Cicero (in prose) and Virgil (in verse) so purified and perfected Latin as to give it a linguistic prestige comparable to Greek. What Virgil did for Latin, Dante would do for the Italian vernacular of Florence. Before Dante, every region (city-state) in Italy spoke its own distinct vernacular; after Dante, all that changed. Though the regions would retain their "accents" and local vocabulary, Dante's poetic prestige ensured that the Florentine tongue would *become* the Italian language. Two centuries later, influential Renaissance writers like Luther, Cervantes, and Shakespeare would play a major role in shaping the languages that would become modern German, Spanish, and English, but they were all preceded in that role by Dante—just as Dante was himself preceded by Virgil.

Virgil as Proto-Christian

As well as being hailed as the premier poet of the classical world, Virgil was also considered by many of the key Christian poets and philosophers of late antiquity and the Middle Ages to be the greatest exponent of classical humanistic knowledge. On this point, Dante concurred and that is why Virgil, in addition to being the ideal guide, serves a second, more vital function in the *Comedy*. Within the complex allegorical structure of Dante's epic, Virgil represents human reason in its most enlightened form: a living embodiment of the farthest natural man, unaided by divine grace, can hope to achieve.

As a Catholic, Dante believed in original sin rather than in total depravity. Although it is true that the Calvinist doctrine of total depravity is "supposed to" infer only that every aspect of man's nature—from his desires to his reason to his imagination—was subjected to the fall, the doctrine has often been used to paint a much darker picture of unregenerate humanity. Too often in the history of Protestantism total depravity has deteriorated into a view of man's wretchedness that is so profound it comes close to effacing the image of God in which we were created. Yes, man is fallen and possesses a sinful nature, and yes, unregenerate man cannot find salvation apart from grace, but that does not take away from the fact that the divine spark of the Creator remains in us. Our conscience, though broken, remains operative (hence the strong Catholic belief in natural law), and we, as creatures made in God' image, retain the capacity to strive after God's truth and light. Again, we cannot find the truth of God on our own—that takes both grace and the special revelation of Christ and the Bible—but we can yearn and we can perform genuine deeds of virtue.

Along with Aquinas, Dante believed that human reason was the greatest of God's gifts. Indeed, together with our self-consciousness and our ability to make moral and ethical choices, our reason was the mark that we were made in God's image, and that our nature was therefore qualitatively (and not just quantitatively) different from that of the lower animals. Likewise, our natural, in-bred yearning to seek after the higher things—after those unchanging Forms and celestial truths that are the goal of the Platonic philosopher—was considered a direct gift of God that was marred, but not lost, when we rebelliously and disobediently partook of the fruit of the knowledge of good and of evil.

The distinctions I am making here are not just academic; they are vital for any reader who would understand why the pagan Virgil had such a high reputation during the Christian Middle Ages. For most of the finest Christian poets and philosophers, one thing was abundantly clear: though Virgil lived before Christ and did not know the Torah, he, like Plato and Aristotle and Cicero before him, nevertheless strove for virtue: not the higher Christian virtues of faith, hope, and charity (or love), but the slightly lower, though no less noble, classical virtues of fortitude (or courage), prudence (or wisdom), temperance (or self control), and justice. For Dante, Aquinas, and others, knowledge and practice of the four classical (or cardinal) virtues were within the grasp of the higher pagans, for they were available via general revelation (through our reason and conscience and through nature) and did not require the kind of special revelation through which the fullness of the three Christian virtues entered the world (see 1 Cor 13).

It is, in fact, precisely by aid of the four classical virtues that Virgil is able to lead Dante through the levels of Hell (Virgil, like Plato, understood the nature of human sin), up to Purgatory (both also understood the need for the soul to seek purification), and to the very gates of Eden (meant to be man's natural state of perfection). This, however, is as far as Virgil can go; to continue to Paradise and the presence of God, Dante will require a second guide, one who represents not human reason, but divine grace. That guide will be Beatrice, embodiment of the Christian virtues of faith, hope, and love.

Along with Plato, Aristotle, and Cicero, Virgil's reputation as a man of almost-Christian virtue was secure. Indeed, his reputation was even higher than that. As odd as it may sound to modern ears, Virgil was considered by many to be nothing less than a proto-Christian. To the medievals, Virgil was a white magician, a pagan poet-prophet whom God used to prepare the classical world for the coming of Christ. Though Virgil should be properly spelled with an "e" (Vergil), it came to be spelled Virgil as a pun on his name and the Latin word for wand (*virga*): that is, the wand of the proto-Christian white magician Virgil. So high, in fact, was Virgil's status as a pagan prophet, that many medievals and not a few Renaissance figures (most notably, Rabelais and Charles I) who were in search of God's direction in their lives would open up the *Aeneid* at random and seek revelation in the first verse that their eyes fell upon. The practice was known as the *sortes Virgilianae* and may be compared to the practice of opening the Bible at random as a vehicle for discerning God's will: a semi-superstitious practice that carries neither biblical nor ecclesiastical sanction, but which is nevertheless practiced widely today by Christians of all denominations.

Virgil's status as proto-Christian rests in part on the *Aeneid*, a work whose hero, like St. Paul, is forced by the gods to learn new strategies that border on the Christian virtues of hope, faith, and long-suffering. When Paul recounts his road-to-Damascus conversion before Festus and Agrippa II (Acts 26), he adds one detail that is not in Luke's third-person account of Paul's conversion (Acts 9). In addition to asking Paul why he is persecuting him, the risen Christ shares the following bit of advice with the reluctant convert: "it is hard for thee to kick against the pricks" (26:14). A prick, or goad, is a long pointed stick used to prod recalcitrant animals. When a stubborn donkey gets mad and kicks against the pricks, it only succeeds in cutting open its hooves, making its inescapable burden more difficult than it might have been. Aeneas, like Saul the Pharisee, is just such a donkey; both men must be prodded along by divine forces intent on shaping them into very different kinds of heroes, and both must suffer much before they are molded into usable vessels.

However, despite the links between Aeneas and Paul, and despite the fact that Christians of Dante's day would study the *Aeneid* to instruct them in virtue, the real source of Virgil's status as proto-Christian and pagan prophet was a short lyric poem he wrote around 40 BC. Before attempting the *Aeneid*, Virgil wrote two shorter works of poetry, the first of which consisted of ten pastoral poems known as the *Bucolics* or *Eclogues*. Although the *Bucolics* are mainly devoted to celebrating the life of the Sicilian countryside, in his Fourth Eclogue, Virgil suddenly leaves behind his shepherds and fields to chant a sublime and stirring prophecy. Here are some scattered lines from this remarkable poem:

> Sicilian Muse, I would try now a somewhat grander theme. . . .
> Ours is the crowning era foretold in prophecy:
> Born of Time, a great new cycle of centuries
> Begins. Justice returns to earth, the Golden Age
> Returns, and its first-born comes down from Heaven above. . . .
> This child shall enter into the life of the gods . . .
> And rule a world made peaceful by his father's virtuous acts. . . .
> Goats shall walk home, their udders taut with milk, and nobody
> Herding them: the ox will have no fear of the lion . . .
> Come soon, dear child of the gods, Jupiter's great viceroy!
> Come soon—the time is near—to begin your life illustrious!
> Look how the round and ponderous globe bows to salute you,
> The lands, the stretching leagues of sea, the unplumbed sky!
> Look how the whole creation exults in the age to come![1]

Critics still disagree as to whom Virgil is speaking of in this poem, though he is most likely referring to the young Octavian: the adopted son of Julius Caesar who would one day become Caesar Augustus, the first emperor of the Roman Empire and one of Virgil's chief patrons.

Still, whatever historical figure Virgil had in mind, it was clear to the medieval Christians that Virgil, without knowing it, was foretelling the birth of Christ. Indeed, apart from the mythological references to the muses and Jupiter, the poem reads like a passage out of Isaiah: a prophecy of the long-awaited Messiah who will bring peace and justice to Earth. *Messiah* is a Hebrew word that means "anointed one," a word that, when translated into Greek, yields *Christos*, Christ (as in our English words, "chrism" and "christening"). To be anointed or christened with oil is to be set apart for some high purpose or calling, and therefore the word can be taken in either a political or spiritual sense. A close reading of the Old Testament yields two types of messianic imagery: some passages (like Isa 9 and Ps 2) suggest a reigning king who will save his people from their oppressors and establish a righteous kingdom; others (like Isa 53 and Ps 22) suggest a priestly suffering servant who will intercede for the sins of his people. It should come as no surprise that many Jews at the time of Jesus were hoping for a political Messiah (like David) who would overthrow Rome. When Jesus turned

1. *The Eclogues and Georgics of Virgil*, translated by C. Day Lewis, 30–35. The lines quoted are 1, 4–7, 15, 17, 21–22, 48–52.

out to be the other kind of Messiah (a priestly suffering servant), both the religious leaders and the fickle crowd turned away from him, choosing instead to release a political revolutionary named Barabbas (his name means "son of the father") who hoped to regain the Holy Land from the Romans by military force.

Dante's contemporaries, like all orthodox Christians, interpreted the messianic riddle of the Old Testament to refer to two separate comings of the Christ: only when Christ returns again at the end of the age (an event known as the second coming) will he reveal himself as a reigning monarch and establish a glorious kingdom that will have no end. It is surely significant that at the time of Jesus' first coming, the Mediterranean world was ruled by just such a (secular) Messiah: Virgil's patron and the real (though hidden) hero of the *Aeneid*, Caesar Augustus.

Athens and Jerusalem

For Dante, it was clear that the Messiah foretold in the Fourth Eclogue was Christ, a belief that strengthened his Christian humanist faith that the classical and Christian worlds need not be incompatible. Just as the pagan astrological wisdom of the Gentile Magi led them to the full revelation of the Christ child (Matt 2), so Dante, and all those who share his Christian humanist faith, believed strongly that human wisdom *can* point the way to divine grace. Paul's speech before the Stoics and Epicureans of Athens (Acts 17), in which he proclaims that he will reveal the "true identity" of the unknown God they long have worshipped in ignorance and backs up his proclamation by quoting their own pagan poets ("in him we live and move and have our being"), offers further proof that pre-Christians can glimpse divine truths and that Christians can (and must) learn from the wisdom of the ancients. There is a road that leads from the Greco-Roman wisdom of Athens to the Judeo-Christian fullness of Jerusalem, and that road is best embodied in the person and work of the proto-Christian Virgil.

To drive home this Christian humanist vision, Dante introduces a character in his *Purgatorio* (a lesser pagan poet named Statius) who claims he was led to Christ not by the Bible but by Virgil himself. In his testimony, Statius tells Dante and Virgil that his eyes were first opened to Christ when he realized that what the Christians were preaching squared with the prophecy of the Fourth Eclogue:

> When you [Virgil] declared, "A new birth has been given.
>> Justice returns to earth, and the first age of man.
>> And a new progeny descends from Heaven"—
> you were as one who leads through a dark track,
>> holding the light behind—useless to you,
>> precious to those who followed at your back.
>
> (*Purgatorio* XXII.67–72)

Here, in addition to being a proto-Christian, Virgil becomes almost a Christ-figure, a scapegoat who suffers so that others may benefit, who prophesies a joy in which he himself cannot share.

Dante even extends this role to Aeneas, who, though he neither knew it nor took any profit from it, was the real founder of the Roman Catholic Church. Rather than deny Virgil's eschatological belief that the establishment of the Roman Empire would mark the end of history, Dante moved that event to the middle of history, saving the climax for the establishment, not of the Roman Empire, but of the Roman Catholic Church. By so doing, Dante makes Aeneas, the legendary founder of Rome, one of the chief founders of the church. Just so, the great Renaissance Christian artist Michelangelo includes on the ceiling of the Sistine Chapel five sibyls (that is, pagan prophetesses) who, like Virgil and Aeneas, were used by God to prepare the ancient world for the coming of Christ and the church.

The purpose of this chapter has been to explain why Dante chose Virgil as his guide, but I feel the need here to answer a second question: why have I digressed at such length on Dante's (and his fellow medievals') Christian humanist beliefs? It was, I believe, necessary to do so, for it was precisely these beliefs that led Dante to construct not only a Hell but a Purgatory and Paradise that combines the very best of both classical and Christian learning. Dante's guide books include not just the Bible and the church fathers; but the epic poetry of Homer and Virgil, the myths of Plato and Cicero, and the philosophy of Aristotle. Dante's epic, like few works before or since, draws together into one monumental fusion the spiritual yearnings of all those in the West (pagan, Jewish, and Christian) who have sought to understand the nature and purpose of the afterlife. Dante is one of the chief formulators and referees of that Great Dialogue that lies at the core of Western culture, and, in fulfilling that dual responsibility, Dante refused to leave any voices out.

True, Virgil may not have seen as clearly as Moses or Paul, but he did, nonetheless, *see*.

10

Dante's *Inferno* I
Yearning for What We Fear

At first glance, Dante's *Comedy* may seem an archaic work that can only speak to Christians, if not indeed only to Roman Catholics of a medieval bent. The last seven centuries have given the lie to any such fear. Not only Christians of all denominations, but readers with different religious and cultural backgrounds, and even readers who have no religious beliefs at all, have found the *Comedy* to be a nearly inexhaustible source of goodness, truth, and beauty. Even those who deny the existence of Hell have found themselves challenged and chastened by the *Inferno*. Dante's portrait of what sin does to the soul of the human person has an emotional and psychological force that is as strong as its theological and philosophical value. One need not accept all of Dante's doctrinal beliefs to concede that terrible consequences ensue when we either waste away our gifts and talents or misuse them for selfish and nefarious ends. One need not accept a literal Hell to realize in a moment of clarity that we are capable of making our own hell on Earth. One need not believe in a literal devil to see that there is something dark and sinister within us that drives us off course and leads us to make a shambles of our lives.

Let us begin our journey into Hell by laying down five Dantean ground rules whose truth applies as much to this world as to the next.

Evil is a Negation

The first thing the attentive reader should notice about Dante's Hell is that everything in it is a perversion of something in Heaven or on Earth. Among the great theological and philosophical triumphs of St. Augustine was his success at defining evil as an absence rather than a presence, a privation rather than a creation. Too often today people think of goodness in negative terms, as an absence of evil, when in fact the truth is exactly the opposite. Good is primary and positive; evil represents a lack or loss of that primary goodness. Evil is incapable of creating anything; it can only take what God has made good and destroy or corrupt it. Evil can neither act nor build up; it can only react and tear down. It was God who made the good pleasures of sex, food, and sleep; it was Satan who perverted those good pleasures into the sins of lust, gluttony, and sloth.

The essentially negative nature of evil greets Dante and Virgil on the very threshold of their journey into Hell. As they pass through the gate to the underworld—a gate left permanently open by the harrowing of Hell—they read these words inscribed above it: "I am the way into the city of woe. / I am the way to a forsaken people. / I am the way into eternal sorrow" (*Inferno* III.1–3). The triple repetition of "I am the way" calls up Jesus' central claim that he is the way, the truth, and the life and no one comes to the Father except through him (John 14:6). The Gospel of John records a number of other such "I am" claims, claims by which Jesus identified himself with the Old Testament God who revealed to Moses that his name was "I am that I am." Among these claims, Dante seems to have had the following particularly in mind: "I am the door: by me if any man enter in, he shall be saved, and shall go in and out, and find pasture" (John 10:9).

In John's Gospel, Jesus is presented as the doorway through which the chosen ones will pass into a place of bliss. In the inscription above the gate of Hell, however, Jesus' claim—and Jesus himself—is twisted and perverted. Through *this* door shall issue a forsaken people on their way to endless sorrow. Hell has neither life nor joy to offer; it can only take the True Life and Joy offered by the True I AM and twist it into death and woe. As Jesus explains in the next verse: "The thief cometh not, but for to steal, and to kill, and to destroy: I am come that they might have life, and that they might have it more abundantly" (John 10:10).

As Dante and Virgil proceed through Hell, they encounter dozens of things that ape divine truths. The most blatant of these perverse imitations of holy things is Satan himself, whom Dante depicts as having three heads—a clear parody of the Triune God of Christian orthodoxy. At the top of Purgatory, Dante sees the Griffin, a magnificent beast, half lion and half eagle, that embodies the dual, incarnate nature of Christ. In Hell, Dante sees a number of mixed creatures—most notably, the Minotaur (half man and half bull) and the centaurs (half man and half horse)—but there, in the twisted funhouse of Hell, their dual nature points not upward to the incarnate Christ but downward to what happens when man turns away from God and his nature becomes half bestial. In Paradise, Dante perceives God in the form of three interlocking circles, for the circle represents both perfection and eternity. In Hell, he witnesses a number of punishments that involve the sinners going round in a perpetual circle. The infernal circle, however, though it promises eternity, embodies not glory and perfection but dishonor and futility.

We Must Take Sides

After passing through the gate, the poets arrive in the vestibule of Hell (not to be confused with limbo) where they gaze on the eternal punishment of the opportunists (or neutrals). Here are housed those sinners who in life refused to take sides, preferring rather to watch things unfold without any risk to themselves. They include not only human beings who were content to play both sides against the middle (had Dante lived today, he likely would have placed the gun-running Rhett Butler in the vestibule), but those angels who refused to swear allegiance to either side when Satan rebelled against God.

These sinners, who are refused a place either in Heaven or Hell, must chase forever an elusive, circling flag. As they run naked in their endless circle of futility, they are stung mercilessly by wasps and hornets. In a ceaseless flow, the pus from the sores, mixed with their tears, runs down to their feet where it is devoured by maggots. For Dante, opportunists are not slick politicians or charismatic survivors; they are the moral refuse of the universe. Even Hell scorns to give them shelter.

Given the fact that Dante spent the last twenty years of his life in exile on account of fierce partisan politics, one might have expected him to celebrate opportunism. After all, if everyone refused to take sides, there could be no factions or civil wars. But Dante does not do so, for the God he worshipped was very much a God of history. Unlike the watchmaker God of Deism, who creates the laws of nature and then lets things run on their own without divine "interference," the God of the Bible is intimately involved in the lives of nations and of men. Indeed, one of the most fruitful ways to the read the Bible, a way that helps give it a unity that it often seems to lack, is to read it as a chronicle or record of God's actions and interactions in human history. And not just the history of the Jews, but of the Egyptians, Assyrians, Babylonians, Greeks, and Romans: nations through which God works, mostly invisibly, to steer the course of his greater plan of salvation and redemption.

I would suggest that one of the reasons Dante chose to fill his epic with hundreds of allusions to history is that he *wanted* his readers to look up the references. One of Dante's goals in constructing his *Comedy* was to inspire his readers to study and to discern the true shape of that complex human and divine drama that has been unfolding for thousands of years on the proscenium stage we call the Earth. One of the messages that the *Comedy* teaches believers and unbelievers alike is that we must make choices, that we must participate in the drama of history. Only thus can we fulfill God's plan for us and our world.

We Must Not Squander Our Gifts

Having passed through the vestibule, the poets come to the first river of Hell. Like Homer, Plato, and Virgil before him, Dante identifies the four rivers of Hell as Acheron, Styx, Phlegethon, and Cocytus. But Dante adds a new twist to these rivers by fashioning for them a unique and original source. Out on the island of Crete, Dante tells us in Canto XIV of the *Inferno*, stands a giant statue made of four metals: gold, silver, bronze, and iron. This image, of course, was not invented by Dante. He borrows it from Nebuchadnezzar's dream (Dan 2) and uses it to signify the same four empires: Babylon, Persia, Greece, and Rome. For Dante, however, the statue represents not only those mighty empires, but, by extension, all the plans and strivings of humanity. Dante also adds one vital detail not found in Daniel: the statue is weeping. In a slow but persistent trickle, the tears flow down the body of the giant and drop into the Earth, where they become the four rivers of Hell. For Dante, that is to say, the source of the rivers of Hell is the tears of humanity.

Hell, as Dante depicts it, is a sad, sad place, a place of broken dreams and wasted potential. Hell is the sewer of the universe; it is the place where all go who have thrown away the light God gave them, who have abdicated their calling and purpose. If there is one biblical passage that undergirds the *Inferno*, it is the parable of the Talents (Matt 25:14–30).

As in so many of Jesus' parables, this one begins with a master going away on a far journey. Before departing, he calls to his side his three chief stewards and leaves in their care five talents, two talents, and one talent, respectively. After many years, the master returns unannounced and demands an accounting from his servants. The first replies: "Lord, thou deliveredst unto me five talents: behold, I have gained beside them five talents more." In reply, the master speaks the words that every Christian hopes someday to hear: "Well done, thou good and faithful servant: thou hast been faithful over a few things, I will make thee ruler over many things:

enter thou into the joy of thy lord." The second servant approaches next and exclaims that from the two talents he was given, he has made two more. In reply, the master gives him the exact same blessing. Although this may at first seem unfair—why should the one who made two talents receive the same blessing as the one who made five—the identical blessing acknowledges the fact that both servants made full use of what they were given. God is fair and just and does not expect us to make bricks without straw. We are expected only to make full use of the gifts given to us.

The third servant, alas, makes no use of his single talent; afraid that his lord is a harsh taskmaster, he buries it in the ground instead. When the master learns of this, he becomes angry and tells the wicked and lazy servant that he should at least have put the talent in the bank so that it could have gained interest. The master then seizes the single talent of the third servant and gives it to the one with ten, saying: "For unto every one that hath shall be given, and he shall have abundance: but from him that hath not shall be taken away even that which he hath." In this strongly un-American verse, Jesus reminds us that we are all stewards to whom God has entrusted great wealth. If we do not make use of this wealth, it will be taken from us, and we, like the wicked servant in the parable, will be cast, like refuse, into "outer darkness" where "there shall be weeping and gnashing of teeth." The talents referred to in the story were large units of money; however, Jesus uses them to symbolize not just money but all those gifts and talents that we are endowed with by our Creator. In fact, our modern word "talent" owes its origin to the parable.

When teaching the *Inferno* to college students, I drive this point home with considerable urgency. Dante's message is one that carries equal weight for believers and unbelievers alike, but especially for those who have been afforded special opportunities to nurture and develop their skills and talents. I believe, as both a Christian and an educator, that much is, or at least should be, expected of young people who have the chance to attend college. To waste away such a precious opportunity is to cut oneself off from the source of one's strength: whether one believes those strengths come from God or from nature.

In the fifth circle of Hell lie the sullen, those who wasted away their gifts through sloth and apathy. Again and again, they sing the same sad song: "Sullen were we in the air made sweet by the Sun; / in the glory of his shining our hearts poured / a bitter smoke. Sullen were we begun; / sullen we lie forever in this ditch" (*Inferno* VII.121–24). Let us all beware lest we end up like these poor sinners. No, we may not be heroes (like Odysseus and Aeneas) or philosophers (like Plato and Aristotle) or poets (like Virgil and Dante), but we all have gifts for which we are accountable.

Sin is Self-Destructive

Charon ferries Dante and Virgil, as he does the dead, across the first river of Hell (Acheron), but he is far fiercer and wilder than the Charon of Virgil (*Aeneid* VI). As pitiless as he is splenetic, the demon Charon inspires fear in the sinners, whose teeth chatter in terror as they await their chance to cross the river into Hell. Their terror, however, does not lead them to repentance. Instead, as they wait on the shore, they begin, in a chorus, to blame everyone and everything for their sorry state: from their genes to their environment to the very womb that bore them. They blame everyone, that is, but themselves. Dante's sinners no longer have the power to confess their sins or even to feel shame.

How did they get this way? Because, Dante tells us, somewhere along the course of their lives they lost the fear of God. According to numerous verses in the Bible, the fear of the Lord is the beginning of wisdom. By "fear of the Lord," the biblical writers do not mean we should cower in abject terror before the Lord (as the sinners do before Charon), but we should feel a sense of reverence and numinous awe before the presence of the Lord God of Hosts. It is this proper kind of fear that keeps us focused and on track, that allows us to measure and judge our lives and our actions. The fear of the Lord is at once a boundary and a yardstick, a signpost and a touchstone. When we lose the fear of the Lord, we lose all sense of proportion and fall off the narrow path, as Dante does in the opening canto of the *Comedy*.

As Dante describes the sinners who stream over the banks toward Charon, he uses the same two similes that Virgil uses (in *Aeneid* VI) to describe the souls in Hades: they are like the falling leaves of autumn or like migrating birds. Here, however, the interpretation is richer. Dante uses the same Virgilean similes to show that when we lose the fear of God, we sacrifice our human rationality and volition and become driven by our animal instincts. Indeed, Virgil tells Dante that the sinners pass *eagerly* into Hell, for here, "Divine Justice transforms and spurs them so / their dread turns wish: they yearn for what they fear" (*Inferno* III.122–23).

This statement may at first sound absurd: who could possibly yearn for something that causes him harm? And yet, is this not precisely the case with a drug addict or a woman caught in a series of abusive relationships? Again, Dante's psychological truths are as acute as his spiritual ones. In one way or another, each of Dante's sinners is fixed forever in what we today would call a self-destructive lifestyle. Hell is one eternal repetition compulsion: a circle of futility with no hope of escape or even of self-knowledge. Everyone in the inferno is tied up in knots, unable to break free from, or even admit to, the very sin that causes them pain. Dante's understanding of human psychology, I would argue, is deeper than that of the ancients, who believed (after Plato) that no one willingly and knowingly chooses what will harm him. Dante knew better.

Hell is a Place We Choose

On the gate of Hell (III.1–9), Dante reads that four things created the inferno: sacred justice, divine omnipotence, ultimate intellect, and primordial love. It is the fourth item, of course, that sticks out; yet it is also the fourth item that lies behind the most often asked question about Hell: how can a loving God condemn someone to Hell? Dante's answer is a simple one: Hell is a place we choose, for Hell promises us what Heaven does not—to allow us to hold on forever to ourselves and our sins. We sometimes forget that Heaven and Hell are not the equivalents of getting an "A" or an "F" in a college class. Heaven means being in the presence of God for eternity, just as Hell means being cast out from the presence of God for all eternity. The sinners in Dante's *Inferno* have no desire to spend eternity with God; they want to spend it instead with themselves and their sin. And God, out of love, allows them to do just that.

As we shall see in the next chapter, all the sinners in Hell are both profoundly narcissistic (they love themselves more than others or God) and unashamedly idolatrous (they have made their sin into an idol that takes the place of God). This key Dantean notion helps us understand the oft-misunderstood first level of Hell (limbo), where dwell the virtuous pagans: those who, like Virgil, lived virtuous lives but lacked the grace of Christ. Among the virtuous pagans are not only the five epic poets mentioned in the previous chapter, but the great philosophers and the heroes who made Rome.

Those who dwell in limbo do not suffer any active pain; rather, their punishment is that they lack all hope of Heaven. Many have criticized this as unfair, but a close reading reveals that Dante's description of limbo is modeled after Plato and Virgil's Elysium: that lovely meadow on which souls converse for eternity. In other words, Dante gives the virtuous pagans what they most desired from the afterlife, enshrines them forever in a classical paradise that represents the limits of their imaginative yearnings. In fact, many of the souls that Dante sees in limbo are those very souls Aeneas saw waiting in Elysium for their future bodies: from Elysium they came and to Elysium they have returned!

Limbo, like Virgil, represents the highest man can reach apart from God's grace. The virtuous pagans, like all the sinners, get exactly what they desired: neither more nor less.

11

Dante's *Inferno* II
Idolatry, Narcissism, and Poetic Justice

The episodes described in the previous chapter represent but the ante-chamber of Hell. Only after Dante and Virgil leave behind the virtu-ous pagans do they enter the inferno proper. Technically speaking, limbo should have been closed off after Christ's resurrection; however, Dante does allow for at least three Muslims to join the great Greco-Roman poets, philosophers, and soldiers. Two of them are philosophers who helped bring the fullness of Aristotelian thought back to the West and who exerted a profound influence on Dante's master, Thomas Aquinas: Avicenna and Averroes. The third is the Saladin, the great warrior who took Jerusalem back from the Crusaders, but who was nevertheless considered by many in the West to be a noble enemy—rather the way the North felt about Robert E. Lee. Still, for all intents and purposes, limbo is full. For the rest of humanity, a spot either in Hell proper or Heaven (after sufficient time in Purgatory) is reserved. It is to the former group that I shall now turn my attention.

Love is God

As they exit limbo, the poets come upon King Minos, he who was con-sidered by Plato, Virgil, and most of the other writers of antiquity to be the judge of Hell. One by one, the sinners come before him and are forced, as they are in *Aeneid* VI, to confess their sins (though in Dante, they feel no remorse when they do so). Minos judges which of the remaining eight levels they belong in, and then, coiling his tail once for each level, sends the sinners flying down to that level of Hell. The decision to give Minos a tail was Dante's alone, a clever detail that Dante most likely adapted—as he did nearly all his mythological details—from Ovid's *Metamorphoses*. In keeping with Greek mythology, the Roman Ovid identifies Minos as the son of Zeus, who, in the form of a magnificent bull, seduced and raped the lovely Europa.

Once past Minos, Dante is given the opportunity to gaze on the damned souls of the carnal, of those who, on Earth, gave themselves over to lust. In Dante's infernal architecture, the further down one goes in Hell, the worse the sins and their punishments become. For the typical American Christian, who, like his Puritan forefathers, tends to rate sexual sins as the worst possible sins, it should come as something of a shock that Dante considered carnality to be the least bad sin. Or perhaps it shouldn't come as a shock, since Jesus himself counted the sins of the soul far worse than the sins of the flesh. Let us not forget that during his earthly ministry, Jesus was accepted by prostitutes and rejected by Pharisees! All of this is not to say that Dante turned a blind eye to lust. Sin is sin, and those guilty of carnality are punished for misusing their God-given sexuality, but their sin, as it contains some element of love, is far less grave than the sins encountered in the deeper regions of Hell.

The punishment Dante constructs for the carnal is, like all of the punishments in the *Inferno*, appropriate to the crime that prompted it. In the case of the carnal, their souls are blown around forever in a violent wind. Just as, on Earth, they allowed their passions to control them, so here, they are left at the mercy of the winds. Like nearly all the souls in Hell, the carnal are naked; they can no longer hide their sin. Indeed, the true nature of their sin—that they, to paraphrase a line from Shakespeare's *Antony and Cleopatra*, made their passion lord of their reason—is made plain in the nature of the punishment. Among the sinners who soar without pause through the rough air, Dante spies Dido, Aeneas's lover, who, in *Aeneid* IV, killed herself in despair when Aeneas abandoned her to continue his journey to Rome. Though we would expect to find Dido's soul with the suicides, Dante places her here, it seems, because the true sin that drove her to suicide was not pride or despair but lust: a lust that drove her to subordinate her reason to her passion. Lust, not suicide, was Dido's *defining* sin, the sin that kept her from letting go of herself and embracing the love and mercy of God.

In addition to Dido, Dante also recognizes the souls of two historical lovers who are wrapped together in a perpetual embrace. Their names are Paolo and Francesca, and they were killed in the late thirteenth century—when Dante himself was roughly twenty years old—by Paulo's brother (Francesca's husband), who caught the two lovers in adultery. Dante calls out to the shade of Francesca in the name of love, and she responds by telling her tragic tale.

> Love, which in gentlest hearts will soonest bloom
>> seized my lover with passion for that sweet body
>> from which I was torn unshriven to my doom.
> Love, which permits no loved one not to love,
>> took me so strongly with delight in him
>> that we are one in Hell, as we were above.
> Love led us to one death. (*Inferno* V.97–103)

Most readers, especially modern ones, feel great sympathy for the lovers; indeed, Dante himself, not yet able to harden his heart against sin, faints after he hears her tale. Some readers even envy the lovers their chance to spend eternity in a perpetual embrace, viewing it more as reward than punishment.

But Francesca is not as innocent as she seems, nor is the fate of the lovers as romantic as appearances might suggest. Francesca herself admits that her sweet body that so inflamed Paolo with lust is gone; all that remains is her soul, the part Paolo neither knew nor cared for. As for her love for him, it is significant that Francesca never once refers to her lover by name. It is, in fact, love itself, and not Paolo, that Francesca loves. The fact that she begins three succeeding stanzas with the word love suggests that she has made love an idol, one that has taken the place of the Trinity. The lovely Francesca tries to convince Dante (and us) that her actions were motivated by the biblical teaching that God is Love (1 John 4:8); in reality, she was motivated by her unbiblical belief that Love is God. Rather than serve the God who is love, she worships the love she has made into a god. Her allegiance is not to the Giver of all good gifts, but to one of those gifts, which she has perverted into a surrogate deity. And that deity, Francesca makes clear, is one that cannot be resisted. Like all sinners in Hell, Francesca accepts no responsibility or blame for her actions.

Later in the canto, Francesca tells (but does not confess) how her affair with her brother-in-law began. It happened on one fateful day while the two as-yet-innocent lovers were reading together a romance about Lancelot and Guinevere, the adulterous lovers whose affair brought down King Arthur and Camelot. As Paolo and Francesca read the tale, their eyes drew together, then their hands, then their lips . . . and then they stopped reading. This too sounds romantic, but Francesca's narrative makes it clear that the real lover she desires is not Paolo but Lancelot. Or, better, what she really loves is the idea of being in love. Or, better yet, what she *really* loves and desires is herself. Like all the souls in Hell, Francesca is utterly narcissistic. Whereas God's love manifests itself in a movement out of narcissism—seen first in his creation of the world as a thing separate from himself and then supremely in his loving choice to live and die as one of his own creatures—Francesca's love is essentially a movement toward the self.

Dante's Hell is a place of terrible tension, for all the sinners are tied up in knots; they cling so tightly to themselves and their sins that they are unable to open their arms and receive God's grace.

Gaining and Losing Perspective

Once Dante recovers from his swoon, the poets proceed to level three, which punishes the sin of gluttony. Here, in a pit of dirty, icy, putrid slush, lie the damned souls of the gluttons. Among these miserable souls, Dante places as well Cerberus, the three-headed dog of Hell, who appears in every Greco-Roman description of the underworld. As Cerberus tears at the sinners with his triple mouth, Dante's readers are invited to perceive the tragic irony of the situation: that those who lived for food are now food themselves!

It is here that Dante meets Ciacco the hog, and hears the first of many prophesies of his coming exile. Though readers of the *Inferno* need (surprisingly) little background information to be able to follow the narrative, a few details from Dante's biography are necessary to make clear the highly personal nature of his fantastic journey through the medieval Catholic universe. In the Florence of Dante's day two bitterly divided factions, known as the White Guelphs and the Black Guelphs, fought for control of the city. In 1300, the year in which the *Comedy* is set, the Whites (Dante's party) seized the city and ousted the Blacks. As a result, the thirty-five-year-old Dante quickly rose to power and was given an important government position. Better yet, in 1301, he was hand picked by his party to go to Rome and petition the help of the Pope. Unfortunately for Dante, while he was away on his commission, the Blacks retook Florence, accused Dante of graft (the charge was false), and forbade him, on pain of death, from returning to the city. It is for this reason that Dante spent the last twenty years of his life separated from his beloved Florence.

Though Dante wrote the *Comedy* during his long and bitter exile, he set it in 1300, during the height of his political career. This narrative device allowed the poet to fill his epic with predictions and prophecies about himself and Italy that had already transpired before the writing of the *Comedy*. As a result, Dante's journey, like those of Odysseus, Aeneas, and Scipio, becomes, in part, a prophetic experience, one meant to prepare him, and Italy, for the hardships to come. It also helps raise his perspective beyond Florence and remind him that though he will lose his citizenship in

Florence, his citizenship in Heaven will be secure. Finally, the eschatological structure that Dante builds into his *Comedy*, a structure that explains the past and present by looking toward the future, lends his epic a sense of wider historical patterns that puts it on par with Virgil's *Aeneid*.

The perspective that Dante gains through his epic pilgrimage is completely lost on the misers and spendthrifts who populate level four. Here are punished sinners whose misuse of money—whether through hoarding or wasting—has not only cut them off from God, but from all human companionship and life itself. In an endless, futile war, they push enormous boulders back and forth, with one side yelling, "why do you hoard?" and the other yelling back, "why do you waste?" So wrapped up are they in their sick game that it is impossible to distinguish one from the other. In fact, this is the only level where Dante does not recognize a single sinner. Greed and prodigality have totally effaced their personalities.

Level five, like level four, punishes two extremes of the same sin: wrath and sloth. These sinners are actually punished in the second river of Hell, the stagnant swamp of Styx. Here, for all eternity, the wrathful thrash around in the muddy water while the sullen lie fixed in the slime. These, like all the sinners, receive a punishment that exactly fits their crime; however, that is not to say that Dante's chief concern is to provide his readers with a series of dramatic object lessons in poetic justice.

The sinners in Dante's *Inferno* don't merely suffer their "just deserts." In Hell, they get what they truly desired, to live in a tiny microcosm of self and sin. As always in Dante, the psychological truth is pointed and exact: it is *we* who create our own hells by losing our perspective, by cutting ourselves off from love and community, by stagnating, by shrinking our human potential. Most of the sinners in Hell engage in some kind of futile game, a game not all that removed from our own earthly rat race or our own obsession with keeping up with the Joneses. Even those who deny the afterlife can sympathize, I believe, with Dante's grief and anger over the mockery that we make of ourselves and our lives. As I explained in the previous chapter, Hell is a sad, sad place, a place of broken dreams and wasted potential.

As the poets cross Styx on the boat of Phlegyas, a bloodthirsty ghoul who clearly enjoys his job of ferrying sinners to their doom, one of the wrathful (Filippo Argenti) grabs on to the boat. Dante has political and personal reasons to hate this sinner and requests that he be scrubbed down by demons. The "kind-hearted" Christian who reads this scene will be shocked to find that Dante's request is not only granted but *celebrated*. How can this be? Did not Jesus instruct his followers to hate the sin but love the sinner? He did, but his teaching no longer applies in Hell. One can only love the sinner and hate the sin if there is a distinction between the two. In Hell, that earthly distinction is lost. The souls in the inferno have ceded their God-given humanity; as terrible as it sounds, they have *become* their sins.

No Friendship in Hell

On the far shore of Styx, there rises a huge gate blocking the way to the City of Dis: Dante's name for the lower part of Hell that houses the greater sinners. Unlike the gate to upper Hell, this one is locked, bolted, and guarded day and night by the rebellious angels who followed Satan in his coup against God. When Jesus harrowed Hell, he had no reason to break down the gate of the City of Dis. He came only for those righteous Jews who awaited him in limbo. For a moment, terror grips the poets as they lose all hope of entering the infernal City. But then, miraculously, a divine messenger appears, walks over the muddy surface of Styx, and forces open the gate with his wand. From his presence, sinners and demons flee, and Dante and Virgil proceed unharmed into lower Hell.

Level six, which punishes the sin of heresy, lies on the outskirts of the City proper and appears at first to be a vast cemetery. Coffins lie scattered everywhere, their lids opened to the murky air. As Dante's eyes adjust to the gloom, he notices two ghastly details: that hundreds of souls are stuffed together in each coffin and that a series of roaring fires perpetually heat each coffin to a burning red. Though the church has faced numerous heresies over the last 2000 years, Dante seems here to have in mind heretics who denied the afterlife: on Earth, they believed that their souls would die with their bodies; in Hell, their souls are literally buried alive.

As Dante stares at one of the coffins, the damned soul of Farinata rises upward, causing his body to be visible from the waist up. On his face, Farinata wears a look of dignified scorn and refuses to speak with Dante until he is assured that Dante possesses noble blood. Though both poets treat Farinata with respect, Dante does not hide the fact that this "great" soul is actually terribly pathetic, stuffed as he is in a burning coffin. This dissonance between the dignity shown to Farinata and the clear indignity of his condition highlights a key aspect of Hell: that the sinners are not only unable to hide (Farinata, like almost all the sinners, is naked), but that they cannot fool anyone, except themselves, as to the true inner nature of their souls.

Traditional Christian doctrine teaches that all souls, whether in Heaven or Hell, will not receive their resurrection bodies until after the second coming of Christ and the final judgment. And yet, the souls that

Dante meets all seem to have bodies, many of which Dante is able to recognize. The answer to this mystery is not revealed to Dante until Canto XXV of *Purgatorio*. Here Dante is told that the "bodies" worn by the dead are actually made of air. As the dead soul moves through the air, it acquires around it an airy body; but that body, rather than shaping itself in an exact copy of the original body, shapes itself in accordance with the soul's inner nature. What that means in practical terms is that the damned receive the form their soul merits; no amount of rosy flesh can hide the greed or vanity within.

I have often warned my students that the process Dante describes is one that begins while we are still on the Earth. If, I ask my students, I were to bring into this classroom two twenty-year-old girls—one sweet and gentle, the other vain and manipulative—and instruct them to assume the same pose and facial expression, could you tell which was the good one and which was the bad one? The right answer, of course, is "no." But what if I were to bring in two sixty-five-year-old women—one charitable and the other avaricious—and instruct them to adopt a neutral pose and expression: could you tell the difference now? The answer this time is a clear "yes." As George Orwell once quipped, by the age of fifty, everyone gets the face he deserves. Even on this Earth, we will, if we live long enough, become on the outside what we are on the inside. Lacking a picture of Dorian Gray to hide in our closet, it is our own faces that will eventually bear the marks of our virtue or vice, greed or charity, kindness or bitterness.

As Dante and Farinata speak together, a second soul (Cavalcanti) rises up out of the coffin to inquire after his son. Mistaking Dante's reply, Cavalcanti thinks, falsely, that his son is dead, and, in grief and despair, sinks back down into the coffin. As he sinks, Farinata, who had paused while Cavalcanti spoke, picks up exactly where he left off, as if Cavalcanti and his problems did not exist. Like Francesca, Farinata is wholly narcissistic. Although he is destined to spend all eternity in the same narrow coffin with Cavalcanti, and although Cavalcanti's son was married to Farinata's daughter, the proud and self-absorbed Farinata shows no concern whatsoever for Cavalcanti's grief. The two men might as well be strangers.

Many joke that they want to go to Hell because that is where all their friends will be. Dante gives the lie to this joke: in Hell, there is neither friendship nor community. There may be honor among thieves, but there is no friendship among the damned.

12

Dante's *Inferno* III
Violence and Fraud

Having entered the City of Dis and passed the cemetery of level six, the poets are now ready to venture into the Tartarean depths of lower Hell. As they prepare to do so, however, they are stopped by the overpowering stench that rises up from the last three levels. The value system that Dante constructs for the *Inferno* is exact: the farther down one goes into the pit of Hell, the darker, heavier, colder, and smellier it becomes. Before they can proceed, Dante and Virgil are forced to pause for some time while they become accustomed to the stench. Dante, perhaps remembering the punishment of the slothful, asks Virgil what they can do to best make use of the time; Virgil responds by explaining to Dante (and us) the precise arrangements of the sins in Hell.

Taking his cue from another virtuous pagan, Aristotle, Virgil explains that though there are nine levels of sin, those sins can be broken into two general types: incontinence and malice. Malice can be further broken into violence and fraud, yielding three general categories that most critics identify with the three animals that prevent Dante (in Canto I) from ascending the hill toward the sun: incontinence (she-wolf), violence (lion), and fraud (leopard). Incontinence, the sub-categories of which are punished in upper Hell (levels 1–5), is less bad than malice, for it only injures the sinner and because it is an excess of something that is otherwise good: sex, eating, saving, and zeal are good things, but when taken to an improper excess, they become carnality, gluttony, hoarding, and wrath. Violence (level 7) is less bad than fraud (levels 8 and 9), because while animals can commit violence, only human beings—who were endowed with reason by God—can commit fraud. Though all fraud constitutes a perversion of reason, there are some versions of fraud, those in which we deceive a victim whom we should otherwise love, that are particularly heinous. Accordingly, Dante places those guilty of simple fraud in level eight and those guilty of treachery in level nine. Though Dante never clearly categorizes heresy (level 6), it is likely that he meant it to mark a transition between incontinence (heresy may be interpreted as an excess or misuse of human intellect) and violence (heresy may also be interpreted as a form of violence against church doctrine).

River, Forest, and Desert

As Cerberus stands guard over level three, so level seven has its own bestial guardian, one whose twisted form embodies the exact nature of the sin of violence. That guardian is the Minotaur, and his dual nature (half man and half bull) stands as both a reminder and a warning that when human beings give way to their violent instincts, they become more animal than man. The level over which the Minotaur presides is itself sub-divided into violence against neighbors (murder), self (suicide), and God. Violence against God is further divided into violence against God proper (blasphemy), violence against God's natural order (sodomy), and violence against those skills or arts with which God gifted us (usury).

If a medieval Italian were to be magically transported to twenty-first-century America, the one thing that would likely shock him the most is that our entire capitalistic system is founded upon something that his age considered a grievous sin: usury, or the lending of money at high rates of interest. For medieval Catholics (and for Muslims, then and now), usury was considered a sin, for it violated (or did violence to) God's desire that we should use our skills to work and to create. Even pre-fallen Adam had a job to do in Eden; the curse upon him was not that he would work, but that he would now work by the sweat of his brow. The modern stereotype that all banker are Jews (a stereotype that continues to fuel anti-Semitism around the world) is actually based on something that was once true. In the Middle Ages, Jews alone were allowed to engage in usury, particularly after the Templars (the real "inventors" of banking) were violently suppressed: an event that occurred in between 1300 and the writing of the *Comedy*.

The punishment for the first sub-category of level seven (violence against neighbors) is carried out in the third river of Hell (Phlegethon), which Dante terrifyingly transforms into a river of boiling blood. Depending upon the severity of their violence, the murderers stand at different depths of the river; if they try to move higher than their sin allows, vicious centaurs shoot them with fiery arrows. Here, up to their eyebrows in boiling blood, are punished not only Attila the Hun but Alexander the Great, both of whom Dante clearly considered to be butchers.

As the poets make their way down the bank of Phlegethon, the river narrows and runs through a dark forest populated by grotesque trees which hold imprisoned within their twisted bark the souls of the suicides. When a suicide is judged by Minos, Dante is told, his soul is cast at random into the forest of level seven; the soul immediately takes root and grows quickly, but soon the tree grows bent and deformed. As the suicides wasted their potential, so their trees ever twist away from beauty and perfection; as they so thanklessly cast away their bodies, so in Hell they are denied a human form. Even when the final judgment comes and the suicides leave their trees to receive their resurrection bodies, they will not be allowed to wear them. Upon their return to level seven, they will be forced to hang their new bodies on one of the thorns of their tree and then reenter its twisted bark. Not until the end of the world, Dante explains, will the punishments of Hell, and the blessings of Heaven, reach their fulfillment. When that day comes, for example, a mighty angel will go to level six and nail lids on each of the coffins.

But Dante adds one further gruesome detail to the plight of the suicides that makes this punishment the most memorable and frightening. When Dante arrives in the forest and gazes here and there for signs of the sinners, he is instructed by Virgil to break off one of the branches. The moment he does so, a mixture of blood and sap flows out of the snapped branch, making a sputtering sound as it does. The sound slowly morphs into human speech, and Dante is able to converse briefly with the suicide who is incased in the tree. Indeed, we soon learn, this is the only way that any of the suicides can speak. Just as, on Earth, their ultimate form of self-expression was to spill their own blood, so here, in Hell, the only way they can speak is through the renewed flowing of their blood. Only through further pain and sorrow can they now express their grief and torment.

As river gave way to forest, forest now gives way to a desert of burning sand. Lying forever prostrate on the sand, the souls of the blasphemers endure a searing to match their own fiery violence against God, a searing that is intensified by burning flakes of sand that fall upon them in a flaming perversion of winter snow. The homosexuals, whose crime is slightly less than that of the blasphemers, are forced to walk in an endless weary circle on the sand; if they stop, even for a moment, they are forced to lie prostrate for a hundred years. The usurers, whose crime is slightly less again, squat like baboons on the burning sand and weep forever into their money bags. The burning, infertile sand of level seven offers a powerful metaphor for the utter barrenness of blasphemy (which isolates the sinner from his Creator), sodomy (which produces no offspring), and usury (which creates nothing to better or beautify the Earth).

Interestingly, Dante sees only male sodomites (he does not identify any lesbians) and learns that many of them were "men of letters" and "scholars of renown" (*Inferno* XV.107). Among them, he meets and converses with his poetic mentor, Ser Brunetto Latino. With great love and concern, Ser Brunetto instructs Dante to always follow his star (his genius and his calling) and issues a third prophesy of his exile to come. As he did Farinata, from whom he received the second prophecy of his exile, Dante treats Ser Brunetto with great respect and compassion; nevertheless, he does not shy away from what this once great poet and teacher has made of himself. But for his bondage to the sin of sodomy, Ser Brunetto might have reached out of himself to embrace God's freeing mercy and transforming love.

Both the *Aeneid* and the *Inferno* are epics of profound sadness, but the nature of the sadness is radically different. Whereas the Virgilean sadness rests upon the stoic realization that we have no free will and that we cannot finally escape our fate, the Dantean sadness is based upon the fact that we do have free will given to us by a loving Creator . . . but look what we do with it!

Country-Club Prisons

As the desert ends, Phlegethon rages forward, becoming a waterfall that plunges down into level eight. In order to get down the waterfall, the poets are forced to ride on the back of Geryon, a winged beast that from the neck up looks like an honest man, but from the neck down is reptilian and sports a scorpion's tail. Just as the Minotaur embodies the true nature of violence, so Geryon embodies the true nature of deceit, which boasts a clean front while hiding within a serpent's heart. After a vertiginous ride, Geryon deposits the poets on the edge of level eight, a level to which Dante gives a sinister name: Malebolge. Malebolge (Italian for "evil ditches") is thus named for it is formed of a descending series of ten ditches, each of which punishes a separate sub-category of deceit.

Bolgia One holds the damned souls of the panderers and seducers; in an endless double file, they parade back and forth while an army of horned demons beats them on with fiery whips. The flatterers who populate Bolgia Two are similar in their sin but radically unique in their punishment. Rather than march back and forth with demons at their heels, they are doomed to spend all of eternity bobbing up and down in a river of human excrement. As the former group are driven on with the same ferocity with which they drove others, so the latter are hurled into the same substance which they, on Earth, hurled at others. Imagine, Dante says, if all the latrines of the world could be emptied into a single stinking ditch—for that is what Bolgia Two is most like. Of course, this should come as no surprise since the inferno is essentially a giant cosmic sewer of sin, perversion, and despair.

Bolgia Three punishes a sin that, like usury, is little heard of today. In the Middle Ages, when the Roman Catholic Church owned vast tracts of land and many of its cardinals, bishops, and priests were rich in wealth, power, and prestige, important parishes and bishoprics were coveted and bartered. The name given to this immoral and unethical practice of buying and selling church office was simony, a word derived from Simon Magus, who, in Acts 8, tried to purchase the Holy Spirit from the apostles and was soundly rebuked (verse 20). For these traffickers in holy orders, Dante fashions a punishment that reminds us again that everything in Hell is a corruption of something in Heaven or on Earth. The simoniacs are buried head first in stone while their exposed feet are scorched by burning oil, a double perversion of two of the church's seven sacraments: baptism and extreme unction. As Dante gazes on the jerking feet of the simoniacs, several of whom are popes, he launches into an attack on the corrupt papacy that includes a warning that if she does not cease her ungodly ways, she will become the Whore of Babylon described in Revelation. Though Dante was a committed Catholic, he was horrified by the corruption of Rome and by church leaders who sought political and military power. He prophesies that the church will receive her comeuppance, a prophecy that was fulfilled when (between 1300 and the writing of the *Comedy*), Phillip IV of France, who orchestrated the destruction of the Templars, kidnapped the Pope and dragged him (along with the papacy) to Avignon, France.

In Bolgia Four, we meet the damned souls of the fortune tellers, whose punishment is to circle their ditch forever with their heads turned backwards. As they cry, their tears run down their backs and through the clefts of their buttocks. For Dante, they are a perfect example of what a mockery we make of ourselves when we yield control of our lives to sin. At first, Dante weeps for their deformity, but he is halted by Virgil, who admonishes him for feeling pity for those whom God has justly condemned.

Those guilty of the sin of graft are punished in Bolgia Five in a steaming vat of pitch: a reminder, perhaps, that embezzlers have sticky fingers. Whenever one of the sinners tries to pull himself out of the pitch, a demonic gargoyle—patterned on the gargoyles that hung from the sides of medieval cathedrals—grabs him with a pitchfork and rakes his skin off with a grappling hook. Interestingly, Bolgia Five marks one of the few places in the *Inferno* where Dante faces real danger from one of the sinister administrators of Hell. With the help of Virgil, he tricks the gargoyles and escapes their wrath, but the reader is left to infer that the gargoyles eventually got their revenge on Dante by instigating the Black Guelphs to invent the trumped up charge of graft which legitimized his banishment from Florence.

Two other aspects of Bolgia Five are also worth noting. First, the gargoyle scenes are particularly graphic and crude in their content and language. I mentioned in chapter 8 that one of the reasons Dante called his epic the *Commedia* was because in composing it he abandoned the elevated style of tragedy in favor of the loose, mixed style of comedy. When Dante reaches Heaven, his diction will soar and his imagery will flower into sublime beauty; when dealing with grafters and gargoyles, his language sinks to the level of fart jokes and four-letter words. Second, Dante's depiction of Bolgia Five counteracts modern charges that the *Inferno* is an "ultra-conservative," "politically-incorrect" book. On the contrary, those who hold politically liberal views will be delighted to find that Dante punishes white-collar criminals far worse than blue-collar criminals. It is not the poor man who steals a loaf of bread, the inner-city orphan who has never been taught to control his libido, the abused prostitute who sells her body for room and board, and the gang member who is drawn into a life of wrath and prodigality who merit Dante's greatest scorn. On the contrary, it is the wily manager who cheats his company, the scheming bishop who fleeces his flock, and the rich, bored, amoral rake who uses his smooth tongue to ruin innocent girls who merit the sterner condemnation and the harsher punishment.

Dante's upbraiding of the white-collar criminal is made even clearer in Bolgia Six, where we are introduced to the wretched souls of the hypocrites. Around and around their evil ditch they circle dressed in cowls that look beautiful and white on the outside but are made of a heavy lead that weighs them down painfully. Jesus, who showed far more patience with blue-collar prostitutes than with white-collar Pharisees, referred to the latter group as whitened sepulchers, white-washed tombs that look clean on the outside, but inside are full of dead men's bones and all corruption (Matt 23:27). Like Jesus' whitened sepulchers, Dante's punishment identifies the true nature of hypocrisy as residing in the disparity between outward claims of piety and holiness and an inner state of sin and depravity.

Eternal Cycles of Pain

Among the hypocrites, Dante sees Caiaphas, the high priest who condemned Christ and who claimed that it would be better for one man to die than that the whole nation should perish. In a provocative visual tableau that is not soon forgotten, Dante depicts Caiaphas as crucified on the floor on wooden spikes. As the hypocrites walk over him, they press him down further and increase his agony. This is Dante's crowning image of the perversions that reign in Hell. Caiaphas functions here as a grotesque parody of Christ: as Christ bore our sins on the cross, so Caiaphas bears the full weight of hypocrisy on himself. However, whereas Christ died once for all, Caiaphas' sacrifice is as eternal as it is futile. A time will come when the foot of every hypocrite in creation will have pressed Caiaphas down on the spikes. But when that time comes, it will mark neither the end of his pain nor the end of the sin of hypocrisy; on the contrary, the circle of pain will repeat itself again and again and again.

Bolgia Seven imprisons the souls of the great and cunning thieves. Their punishment, guaranteed to make the skin of every "reptiliphobe" crawl, is to dwell in a pit full of vipers that have the power, literally, to steal the bodies of the sinners. If they want their body back, they must steal another from someone else. Dante relishes the chance to outdo Ovid in the art of describing strange and disturbing metamorphoses!

Evil counselors fill the ditch of Bolgia Eight, their punishment illustrating yet again the perverse nature of Hell. Acts 2 records the miracle of Pentecost, when the Holy Spirit descended on the apostles in the form of tongues of fire and granted them the temporary gift to speak in different languages. Dante's evil counselors, in a direct parody of Pentecost, are encased forever in tongue-shaped flames. Among them is Ulysses (Latin for Odysseus), he who devised the ruse of the Trojan Horse that led to the destruction of Troy: an evil act for Virgil and thus for Dante. In one of the most exciting and memorable narratives of the *Inferno*—one that Dante himself invented—Ulysses tells the poets of how he yearned to go on a final voyage into the unknown world that lay past the straits of Gibraltar. Using his rhetorical skills, he even seduces his men to join his folly. By the power of his reason, Ulysses sails so far that he actually catches sight of the mountain of Purgatory (the "South Pole"). The moment he does so, however, a storm rises, his boat founders, and, "as it pleased Another to order and command" (*Inferno* XXVI.129), he is washed into Hell. Ulysses stands for Dante as an object lesson of one who refused to curb his genius and was thereby destroyed. While those in upper Hell are guilty of wasting their gifts, those in lower Hell are guilty of using them in a perverse and ungodly manner.

As evil counselors use their rhetorical skills to lead others astray, so schismatics, the inhabitants of Bolgia Nine, use their gifts to promote civil strife between families, factions, religions, and nations. Dante clearly based their punishment on the mythological tale of Prometheus, he who stole the fire from Heaven and gave it to mortals. In retribution for his crime, Zeus chained Prometheus to a rock and sent an eagle to devour his liver: each night, the liver regenerated; each day, the eagle returned to feast again. In imitation of Prometheus's punishment, the damned souls of the schismatics march past a demon who, with his ever-sharp sword, hacks off their limbs or splits them in two. As they march around the ditch, their limbs regenerate or grow back together, only to be lopped off or severed again in an endless litany of blood and pain. Among these sowers of discord, Dante places the maimed soul of Mohammed, a decision that has caused Dante to be excoriated by Muslim countries for the past 700 years.

Interestingly, Dante does not put Mohammed where one would expect him to be; as Mohammed denied the Trinity and the incarnation, one would have expected the orthodox Dante to punish him in the burning coffins of the heretics. His decision to put him instead with the schismatics should remind modern Westerners who dismiss the Crusades as a wholly evil and avaricious enterprise that it was the followers of Mohammed who were in great part responsible for ripping apart the last remnants of the old Roman Empire. By seizing three of the original ecumenical sees (Alexandria, Jerusalem, and Antioch) and isolating the fourth (Constantinople), the followers of Mohammed not only robbed Christianity of her original churches—the seven cities mentioned in Revelation 2–3 fell to Islam within decades of Mohammed's death—but furthered the split between Western Catholicism (headquartered in Rome, the fifth see) and Eastern Orthodoxy (headquartered in Constantinople).

The falsifiers who inhabit Bolgia Ten do not live in fear of the demon with the sword, but that is because they do not need him. In keeping with the nature of their sin, they live in a state of eternal sickness, corruption, and decay. Imagine, writes Dante, if all the hospitals, leper colonies, and tubercular wards in the world were to be dumped into one stinking ditch; imagine that, and you will get merely a taste of the horror and wretchedness of Bolgia Ten.

The Traitors

In order to descend from level eight into the pit of level nine, the poets crawl into the hand of a fierce giant who lowers them down into the final abyss. The giants include not only Nimrod, builder of the Tower of Babel, but the rebellious Titans—those who dared assault Mount Olympus and were flung into Tartarus by Zeus. In these treacherous giants, Dante writes, we see embodied the danger that ensues when perverse reason is joined to immense strength.

Level nine is actually the fourth river of Hell (Cocytus), which Dante transforms into a frozen ice-cap. Within the icy grip of Cocytus, the traitors against family, country, guests, and lords are frozen in varying degrees. Many who read the *Inferno* are shocked to find that the worst sinners are punished not by fire but by ice, but Dante's choice to do so reveals again his powerful insight into human nature. To betray someone to whom one owes allegiance by blood, citizenship, hospitality, or covenant is to show oneself to be absolutely devoid of love. Only the eternal ice of Cocytus can serve as a fit home for the cold-hearted traitors. In a memorable detail, Dante informs us that the traitors against guests are so bad that they often descend to the ice before their bodies die, leaving a demon to inhabit their body for its remaining years of life.

The worst of the traitors, those who betrayed their lord, are submerged completely in Cocytus; they look, Dante writes, like pieces of straw trapped in glass. All that is but the three worst sinners of all time: Judas (who betrayed Christ, his spiritual lord) and Brutus and Cassius (who betrayed Julius Caesar, their political lord). For these most wretched of men, Dante devises a special torment. Frozen in the center of the ice stands the three-headed Satan, and, in each of his mouths, he chews forever on Brutus and Cassius (whose heads dangle out of his mouth) and Judas (who, being the worst of the three, lies head first in the hideous maw of the once-beautiful Lucifer).

Though most people today would likely consider a murderer to be a worse sinner than a traitor, Dante, along with most pre-modern people, saw things differently. And perhaps we are not all so different today. In 1953, two American civilians named Julius and Ethel Rosenberg were executed for passing military secrets to the Soviet Union. And I don't suppose there are many people in the world today who would name their son Judas or Ephialtes or Quisling.

13

Jesus, Paul, and John
New Testament Visions of the Afterlife

Whereas the Old Testament says relatively little about the afterlife, the New Testament has much to say on the subject. Jesus himself clearly believed in both Heaven and Hell and, when taken together, the "words in red" present us with a vivid and intimate picture of the afterlife. Many in elite Western circles have come, like the Jewish Sadducees and Greco-Roman Stoics of Jesus' day, to sneer at the whole notion of resurrected bodies, heavenly dwellings, and eternal rewards as a form of wish-fulfillment, of pie-in-the-sky-by-and-by. The fact remains, however, that a belief in the afterlife was clearly and repeatedly taught by Jesus and has always made up a central part of orthodox Christianity—so much so that apart from it, Christianity ceases to be Christianity. Indeed, when a group of resurrection-denying Sadducees try to "logically" disprove the resurrection (Matt 22:23–32), Jesus not only asserts his belief in it but insists that his belief is grounded in the Hebrew Scriptures. In Genesis and Exodus, Jesus reminds the Sadducees, God is often referred to as the God of Abraham, Isaac, and Jacob. Surely, he concludes, God is not a God of the dead but of the living.

The real problem, Jesus explains, is that the Sadducees neither understand the Bible nor the power of God; they think that if there is an afterlife, it must be just like our life on Earth. That they think this way is attested to by the hypothetical situation they construct to disprove the resurrection. In a sort of "anti-parable," they spin for Jesus the tale of an unlucky woman who is widowed no less than seven times. The Sadducees allow the pathos of the story to settle in and then hit Jesus with a seemingly unanswerable question: "Therefore in the resurrection whose wife shall she be of the seven? For they all had her" (verse 28). Rather than play their little game, Jesus cuts to the truth of the matter: "Ye do err, not knowing the scriptures, nor the power of God. For in the resurrection they neither marry, nor are given in marriage, but are as the angels of God in heaven" (verses 29–30). In Luke's account, we learn more fully what Jesus means by saying that we will be like the angels: "Neither can they die any more: for they are equal unto the angels; and are the children of God, being the children of the resurrection" (20:36). As we shall see later, this passage has often been misunderstood to say that we will *be* angels in Heaven, but that is not what Jesus says. His point is that we will experience a different *kind* of life that can't be understood simply by reference to our life in this world. One might as well try to understand the mysteries of the incarnation (the two-in-one) and the Trinity (the three-in-one) by studying college algebra.

Miracles and Parables

How then did Jesus mean us to understand the afterlife? Is it something wholly other or does it speak to our deepest yearnings? Perhaps the best place to start is with an episode from the Gospel of John from which comes a verse that has been heard at a billion Christian funerals around the world and across time. The setting is not far from Jerusalem in the town of Bethany, and the players include Jesus and two sisters whose brother has died and whose corpse has lain in a tomb for four days. When one of the sisters, Martha, sees Jesus coming in the distance, she runs to him and exclaims sadly:

> Lord, if thou hadst been here, my brother had not died. But I know, that even now, whatsoever thou wilt ask of God, God will give it thee. Jesus saith unto her, Thy brother shall rise again. Martha saith unto him, I know that he shall rise again in the resurrection at the last day. Jesus said unto her, I am the resurrection, and the life: he that believeth in me, though he were dead, yet shall he live: And whosoever liveth and believeth in me shall never die. Believest thou this? She saith unto him, Yea, Lord: I believe that thou art the Christ, the Son of God, which should come into the world. (John 11:21–27)

It is clear from the passage that Martha, like the Pharisees but not like the Sadducees, believes in the Old Testament promise of a future resurrection of the dead (Dan 12:2). While not denying this belief, Jesus makes a claim that would prove a stumbling block to the Jewish religious leaders and arrant nonsense to the Greek and Roman philosophers.

In contrast to the far-off resurrection dimly hinted at in the Old Testament and the shadowy, insubstantial Hades of Homer, Jesus proclaims that the power of resurrection, of a new life that transcends (rather than eviscerates) our present existence, is even now upon us . . . and that he himself *is* that Resurrection and Life. By claiming not only that he possesses within himself the power and reality of resurrection but that he can and will share that power with those who put their trust in him, Jesus suggests an intimacy between God and man that is lacking in the poetry and philosophy of the ancient world. Neither the Elysian Fields of Homer and Plato nor the Blessed Groves of Virgil promise mortals that they will share in the direct presence and the indestructible life of the eternal God. Indeed, the only place in the Old Testament where I find this kind of postmortem intimacy rises up out of the suffering of Job who, in the midst of his pain and agony, clings to a radical hope: "For I know that my redeemer liveth, and that he shall stand at the latter day upon the earth: And though after my skin worms destroy this body, yet in my flesh shall I see God: Whom I shall see for myself, and mine eyes shall behold, and not another; though my reins be consumed within me" (19:25–27).

Central to Job's hope is the twin belief that he shall still be fully and uniquely himself in the afterlife and that he shall dwell in the direct presence of God. Jesus promises his disciples a similar postmortem integrity and intimacy on the night before his crucifixion: "In my Father's house are many mansions. . . . I go to prepare a place for you. And if I go and prepare a place for you, I will come again, and receive you unto myself; that where I am, there ye may be also (John 14:2–4). The fact that modern scholarship has shown that the word "mansions" in the King James Version should more accurately by translated as "dwelling places" or "rooms" only increases the intimacy, for it depicts Heaven less as a row of discrete mansions than as a college dormitory thriving with fellowship. In either case, our future home in Heaven is one that God will not only fashion specifically *for* us but that he himself will dwell in *alongside* us.

What "proof" does Jesus offer to substantiate his extravagant promise? His own resurrection from the dead on the first Easter morning. Unlike Martha's brother, Lazarus, whom Jesus merely resuscitated, Jesus went through death and came out on the other side. And when he did, he appeared in a glorious resurrection body that could "walk through walls" and yet could eat and be touched, and that could be recognized as Jesus or not, seemingly in accordance with Jesus' wishes (John 20–21). The risen Christ stands both as a pledge of a future resurrection from the dead and its first fruits. His words of promise, that is to say, must be taken in conjunction with his own resurrection appearances—appearances that authorize his words even as they offer a glimpse of what resurrection *means*.

Later in this chapter, I shall develop further the New Testament understanding of the resurrection by looking closely at the Pauline epistles. For now, let us consider briefly what Jesus had to say about Hell.

Jesus on Hell

In what are surely the most frightening passages of the Gospels, Jesus describes Hell as a place of darkness, of weeping and gnashing of teeth (Matt 25:30), a place where the worm never dies and the fire is never quenched (Mark 9:48). It is so horrid that if an eye or hand were to cause us to go there, it would be better to gouge out that eye or cut off that hand (Mark 9:43–48). Unlike Heaven, that was prepared for us since the creation of the world (Matt 25:34), Hell was not originally made to house human beings; rather, it was made to house the rebellious angels who fell along with Satan (Matt 25:41). Whether or not we read the descriptions of fire and darkness as literal—the incompatibility of the two certainly suggests an allegorical element—Jesus clearly depicts Hell as a place of sadness, sorrow, and separation. It may be their own guilty conscience rather than worms that gnaw at the damned, but they *are* gnawed at in a way that is more actively painful than the mindless existence of the shades in Hades. Are the damned punished by means of the elaborate tortures described in Dante's inferno or in the Tartarus of Homer and Virgil? Jesus does not say for sure, but, again, he makes it clear that Hell *is* a place of suffering, even if that suffering is more mental and emotional than physical.

In Plato's Myth of Er and Virgil's *Aeneid* VI, the souls of the departed must face a forking path, with one fork leading down to Tartarus. In his Parable of the Sheep and the Goats (Matt 25:31–46), Jesus presents his own version of the forking path. At the end of the age, Jesus teaches, God will judge the nations and will separate the good from the evil, sending the good to a Heaven of eternal life and the evil to a Hell of eternal punishment. It is perhaps the inescapable eternality of Hell that disturbs readers of the Gospels the most; for, even if the punishments are more figurative and emotional than literal and physical, the thought that the damned must endure them forever is itself unendurable to most people. Indeed, though the traditional reading of Scripture posits Hell as a place of eternal torment, many recent theologians, seeking an alternative to this grim doctrine, have suggested that the damned will, at some point, be annihilated.

The theme of eternal separation, of the sifting of good and evil, appears often in Jesus' parables. It takes its most literal form in the Parable of the Wheat and the Tares and its subsequent explanation (Matt 13:24–30, 36–43), but it finds its most vivid and literary embodiment in the Parable of the Rich Man and Lazarus (Luke 16:19–31). The parable, which partakes of some of the qualities of a Platonic myth, concerns a heartless, ostentatious rich man (Dives in Latin) who gives nothing to the poor beggar (Lazarus) who lies by his gate. After a time, both men die and are carried to their final reward. Lazarus is carried by angels to Heaven ("the bosom of Abraham"), while Dives sinks to Hades where he lies in fiery torment. He begs Abraham to allow Lazarus to at least give him a drop of water to cool his tongue, but he is told that a great chasm lies between the two. Abraham also reminds Dives of his past life on Earth and the choices he made there: "Son, remember that thou in thy lifetime receivedst thy good things, and likewise Lazarus evil things: but now he is comforted, and thou are tormented" (verse 25). Though scholars still debate whether this parable should be taken literally or as a fictitious story meant to illustrate a point—nearly all of Jesus' other parables (e.g., the parable of the Prodigal Son) fit the latter category—it does illustrate powerfully, as do the myths of Plato and Virgil, that we live in an essentially moral universe of judgment and reward.

Still, unlike Plato and Virgil, Jesus holds out the hope of grace to all who believe and trust in him (John 3:16; 6:51; 11:25). This hope of a divine and overwhelming grace that is more powerful than sin, Satan, or death—of a mercy that can rescue us even on our deathbed—is not a part of the pagan view of the afterlife. True, the ancient world did boast a number of mystery religions that worshipped such gods as Demeter, Dionysus, Isis, Cybele, and Mithras, but these personal, passionate, often bloody folk cults existed apart from the great Greco-Roman poets and philosophers and are to the teachings of Jesus what a candle is to the sun. Ultimately, what is missing in paganism, even in its highest Platonic and Virgilean forms, is the concept of a single God who is both personal and holy. In Plato, the perfect, unchanging Forms provide a standard of truth but they are not personal; in Virgil, the Stoic gods who move history inspire duty (*pietas*) but not love or intimacy. The mystery cults sought union with a god or goddess who was anything but holy; the higher gods of Plato and Virgil partook of a kind of perfection but they did not reach out their arms to embrace the wayward children of the Earth. That is why it is only in the New Testament that Heaven and Hell are properly defined as the presence or absence of God.

The Resurrection Body

Though Jesus *is* the first fruits of the resurrection, it is the Apostle Paul who develops the full doctrine of the resurrection of the body. Indeed, it is Paul who makes it absolutely clear that a belief in the literal, bodily resurrection of Christ is the central, non-negotiable element of the Christian faith. If Christ did not rise, he boldly states, then our faith is useless and we are without hope in this world or the next (1 Cor 15:17). In the Christian understanding of the world, God created (at least) three beings to inhabit his universe: first he made the angels, who are purely spiritual; then he made the animals, who are purely physical; finally he made us, who are fully spiritual and fully physical. We are the great amphibians of the universe, not souls trapped in bodies—as Plato and the later Gnostics taught—but enfleshed souls. We, like Christ, are incarnate beings: not fully God and fully man like he was, but 100 percent physical and 100 percent spiritual. When God came to Earth as a man, he took upon himself our dual nature (though not really dual, since our body and soul are one); when he rose again from the dead, he did not return to the pure spiritual state of God the Father or God the Holy Spirit, but took upon himself a resurrection *body*. Though not all Christians are aware of it, the Bible and Christian doctrine not only teach that Jesus will forever be incarnate (fully God and fully human), but that we ourselves will someday be clothed in a resurrection body like that of the risen Christ.

Many Christians think that in Heaven we will be angels, but Christ taught not that we would *be* angels but that we would be *like* angels. It is not the Bible but Plato who imagined as his heavenly ideal disembodied souls flying free through the vast reaches of space. Still, though Christianity teaches that in Heaven we will continue to be physical/spiritual beings, it concedes a temporary period during which the dead will be disembodied. Only when Christ returns (the second coming) and the dead rise from their graves will we be awarded our resurrection bodies; until that time, we will remain, temporarily, in a state of nakedness. It is because of this gap between our deaths and the final resurrection that Dante has to provide airy bodies for his souls (see chapter 11). Various theories have existed within Christendom to account for the state of the soul between death and the resurrection: some argue that we will be held in a waiting place not unlike Hades and the Elysian Fields; others that we will be in Heaven in full communion with God; yet others that we will remain in a state of suspended animation until Christ's return, at which time both body and soul will rise again to be reunited in the air.

As for the resurrection body itself and the difference between it and our current, natural body, Paul has this to say: "It is sown in corruption; it is raised in incorruption: It is sown in dishonour; it is raised in glory: it is sown in weakness; it is raised in power: It is sown a natural body; it is raised a spiritual body (1 Cor 15:42–44). Our earthly body is like a seed that must die and be buried before it can be reborn into a new, more glorious body. "Except a corn of wheat fall into the ground and die," says Jesus in reference to his own coming death and resurrection, "it abideth alone: but if it die, it bringeth forth much fruit" (John 12:24). Think of the difference between the hard, dry acorn planted in the ground and the magnificent oak that springs out of it, and you will have some idea of the greater glory of the resurrection body.

But what shall the transition be like between the natural body and the glorified one: "Behold, I shew you a mystery; We shall not all sleep, but we shall all be changed, In a moment, in the twinkling of an eye, at the last trump: for the trumpet shall sound, and the dead shall be raised incorruptible, and we shall be changed" (1 Cor 15:51–52). In a parallel passage, Paul offers this sublime vision of Christ's return and our eternal union with him: "For the Lord himself shall descend from heaven with a shout, with the voice of the archangel, and with the trump of God: and the dead in Christ shall rise first: Then we which are alive and remain shall be caught up together with them in the clouds, to meet the Lord in the air: and so shall we ever be with the Lord" (1 Thess 4:16–17). Paul even asserts that we shall share in Christ's glory and be joint-heirs with him in Heaven, a teaching that Orthodox Christians call *theosis*.

Indeed, the whole creation—which, Paul tells us, was subject to futility after the fall—eagerly awaits the moment when the sons of God will be revealed in their full glory: "The whole creation groaneth and travaileth in pain together until now. And not only they, but ourselves also, which have the firstfruits of the Spirit, even we ourselves groan within ourselves, waiting for the adoption, to wit, the redemption of our body" (Rom 8:22–23). From the point of view of Christianity, Plato was partly right when he taught that our soul longs to be freed from the bondage of flesh. What he did not see was the final object of that longing. Lifted up by a greater Muse than Plato's, Paul's vision soars beyond Plato's wish for freedom from corruption to glimpse our true wish—not to be unclothed but to be re-clothed in a greater garment of glory: "For in this we groan, earnestly desiring to be clothed upon with our house which is from heaven: If so be that being clothed we shall not be found naked. For we that are in this tabernacle do groan, being burdened: not for that we would be unclothed, but clothed upon, that mortality might be swallowed up of life" (2 Cor 5:2–4). The

95

body is not to be condemned, as it was by Plato's philosophical heirs. It was created by God and declared good, and a time is coming when it will be redeemed, restored, and perfected.

How does Paul know these things? Christians, of course, have always believed Paul was inspired by the Holy Spirit, but Paul himself also hints at an experience from which he may have gained insight into the things of Heaven. In his second letter to the church in Corinth, Paul writes, somewhat elusively, of an experience in which he "was caught up into paradise, and heard unspeakable words, which it is not lawful for a man to utter" (2 Cor 12:4). Although the majority of biblical scholars interpret Paul's experience through the lens of apocalyptic literature with its heavenly journey motif, I would suggest that what Paul describes here is a life-after-life (or near-death) experience. I would further suggest that Paul had this experience several years earlier when he was stoned by an angry mob and left for dead (Acts 14:19). Regardless of the source of the vision, Paul says nothing more of what he saw and heard on his celestial journey. Still, his cryptic reference to a third Heaven provided biblical precedent for Dante's epic journey—one that would encompass not three but nine levels of Paradise.

The Throne Room of God and the New Jerusalem

Though Paul was not permitted to share what he saw, another New Testament writer boldly recounts his own experience of being raptured, while still in the body, into the heavenly regions. In Revelation, God rips away the veil that prevents mortal eyes from seeing spiritual things to afford John a vision both of Heaven and of God's greater plan for history (Revelation is a Latin translation of the original Greek title, *apocalypsis*, which means "uncovering"). In chapter 4, John is even vouchsafed a glimpse of the Throne Room of God, which he describes (in keeping with Isa 6 and Ezek 1) as a place of constant praise both by humanity (represented as twenty-four elders: twelve tribes of Israel and twelve apostles) and by six-winged, many-eyed angels with four faces that embody the fourfold nature of Christ (as he is presented in the four canonical Gospels). In an endless chorus, the elders and angels sing of God's holiness, power, and worth. Neither cute nor domesticated, John's angels (Isaiah identifies them as seraphim) are strange and terrifying creatures that are consumed with passion for God.

As the early chapters of Revelation offer a glimpse of the Throne Room, so the final three chapters bring together Heaven and Earth in a blaze of judgment and glory. Revelation 20 begins by offering a sublime image of the last judgment. Christ sits on a great white throne and from his face Earth and heavens flee in terror. He opens the book of life and from it judges all creation. Hell and sea together deliver up their dead that they may be judged. Those not found in the book of life are cast into a lake of fire, but for the blessed a glory awaits that even the imaginations of Plato and Virgil combined could not have conceived: "And I saw a new heaven and a new earth: for the first heaven and the first earth were passed away; and there was no more sea" (Rev 21:1). Just as many Christians think we will be angels in Heaven, so many think that our final destiny is to live in an ethereal Heaven. But that is not what the Scriptures teach. Just as our bodies will be redeemed, so shall the Earth share in the final resurrection. Rather than be taken up to Heaven, Heaven will come down to Earth and God shall dwell with his redeemed people: "And I heard a great voice out of heaven saying, Behold, the tabernacle of God is with men, and he will dwell with them, and they shall be his people, and God himself shall be with them, and be their God. And God shall wipe away all tears from their eyes; and there shall be no more death, neither sorrow, nor crying, neither shall there be any more pain: for the former things are passed away. And he that sat upon the throne said, Behold, I make all things new" (Rev 21:3–5).

And the place in which we shall dwell shall be a place like Eden but far more glorious: a place that is at once a restored garden and a restored city. Out of the sky shall descend the New Jerusalem, a perfect city with twelve pearly gates, streets of gold, and walls made of twelve precious stones. Through it shall run the river of life, clear as crystal, and along its banks shall grow the tree of life that shall bring healing to the nations. God will dwell with his people and be their light, and tears and crying shall be no more.

So shall be the new city, but that city shall also be a bride, and the new age, the true Golden Age Virgil yearns for in his Fourth Eclogue, shall be ushered in by a Great Marriage feast at which Christ (the Bridegroom) shall be wed to his Bride (the church). And as in earthly marriage, which, Paul tells us (Eph 5:31–32), foreshadows this crowning event, Bride and Bridegroom shall be two and yet one. The church shall unite with her God and Savior, but not in such a way that we shall be absorbed into an amorphous One Soul. Rather, we shall preserve our distinctness and individuality, even as we join in eternal union with he who is "Alpha and Omega, the beginning and the end, the first and the last" (Rev 22:13).

14

Dante's *Purgatorio* I

The Search for Freedom

Certainly the most misunderstood doctrine of the Roman Catholic Church is Purgatory. Most Protestants, and not a few Catholics, are convinced that Purgatory offers a second chance for salvation: a sort of probation for deciding whether the soul should descend to Hell or ascend to Heaven. But the church has never taught any such thing. All who make it to Purgatory will eventually ascend to Heaven. They do not go to Purgatory because their *salvation* is in doubt; they go because they lack the proper *sanctification* to enter the presence of God.

Indeed, Purgatory helps answer a perennial Protestant question: what happens to those who wait until their deathbed to accept Christ or to those who are saved and then fall back into sin? The Catholic answer is simple: they must first spend time in Purgatory where both their spiritual indolence and their desire for sin will be purged out of them through various punishments. Unlike the punishments of Hell, however, which are eternal and retributive, the ones in Purgatory are temporal and remedial: they have a purpose, and that purpose is to free the saved soul from all bondage to sin. In fact, far from resenting their punishments, the souls in Purgatory welcome them, for they know that when they have finished the process of purgation, they will be enabled to absorb as much of God's light and love as possible. All impediments washed away, they will be free to participate with their whole being in the glory of God.

The runner who trains for four years to participate in the Olympics will fare far better in the race than the one who has only trained for four months. His rigorous training will greatly increase his chances of winning, but it will do something else as well. It will allow him to take more joy and fulfillment in the actual running of the race. Were I to win an all-expense-paid trip to Rome on Thursday and immediately fly there on Friday, I would no doubt enjoy my vacation. But if I were given the chance to spend three months studying intensely the history and art of the Eternal City, think how much greater my enjoyment would be. I would not just see the glories of Rome in passing; I would be empowered to participate in them, to enter into the life of the city.

Purgatory is not about "earning our salvation," but, having already been saved by Christ's sacrifice on the cross, working with the Spirit to present ourselves as clean vessels. Out of pure grace and love, the Prince lifts Cinderella out of the cinders and takes her to his castle. But Cinderella would never think of entering her future home until she had the chance to wash, fix her hair, and put on her finest gown. The American Christian, in his somewhat adolescent way, asks if all of this is "fair." But Purgatory is not about fairness; it is about freedom.

Ante-Purgatory

Dante and Virgil's ascent up Purgatory begins at dawn on Easter Sunday when, dark and grimy from the pit of Hell, they emerge at the base of the mountain. They look less like poets on a grand adventure than sewage workers who have just popped out of a manhole! As they look above them at the southern sky, they see stars that no living man since Adam has seen. Dante has done more than escape from the clutches of Hell; he has been reborn from darkness into light. A whole new world lies open before him. Good Friday is past; the new life of Easter has begun.

When the gatekeeper of Purgatory spies the blackened visages of the two poets emerging from the "manhole," he is shocked and taken aback: no one has ever come to his island-mountain by *this* route before. He even wonders if the laws of the infernal pit have been broken without his knowledge. But Virgil quickly allays his fears and explains that Dante, who still breathes the air of the living, is on a divine mission.

This explanation calms the gatekeeper, but it does little to prepare the reader for the shock he receives when he learns the identity of the gatekeeper. He is none other than Cato the Younger, a Roman Senator of the first century B.C. who fought bravely to protect the Republic from strong men like Julius Caesar. Shortly after Caesar defeated Pompey, Cato, certain that Caesar would destroy the Republic and transform it into an Empire, fell upon his own sword. That Dante would chose a virtuous pagan, and a suicide at that, to guard Purgatory may at first seem to contradict his Christian scheme for the afterlife—until we recall that Cato killed himself not out of pride or despair, but for the sake of freedom. And the search for freedom is the very reason for which Purgatory exists.

After speaking with Cato, the poets are eager to begin their journey upward, but Cato, in true Dantean fashion, tells them that before they can *ascend* the mountain they must *descend* to the shore of the island. There, Dante must wash and tie a reed around his waist. When they reach the shore, they find a grassy spot protected by a cool breeze from the heat of the newly-risen sun. Virgil presses his palms into the grass, wetting them with the morning dew. In response, Dante lifts his "tear-stained cheeks to him, and there / he [makes him] clean, revealing [his] true color / under the residues of Hell's black air" (*Purgatorio* I.124–26). In this delicate and intimate scene, we see the power of Purgatory beginning to work: the power, that is, to so wash away the blemish of sin that our soul is restored to the pure state in which it was created.

Virgil then plucks a reed (whose pliant nature makes it an ideal symbol of humility) and ties it around Dante: "There, as it pleased another, he girded me. / Wonder of wonders! When he plucked a reed / another took its place there instantly" (I.130–32). Through a clever conflation of the Golden Bough (see chapter 6) and the miracle of Easter, Dante highlights the new life on which he is about to embark—and something else beside. When Ulysses tells Dante of his final voyage (see chapter 12), he explains that after he caught sight of Purgatory, a storm rose and, "as it pleased another" (God), he was drowned. By repeating this exact phrase in reference to Virgil's girding of him with the reed, Dante makes clear that he, unlike Ulysses, has been chosen by God to see Purgatory while still in the flesh. Both as pilgrim and as poet, Dante will visit supernatural realms closed not only to Odysseus and Homer but to Aeneas and Virgil as well.

As the poets stand by the shore, ready to begin their ascent, they catch sight of a swiftly-approaching boat laden with souls. These newly-blessed souls boarded the boat not at Acheron but by the shores of the Tiber in Rome. More wonderfully, they boast as their boatman not Charon or Phlegyas but a glorious angel who propels the divine craft by his wings alone—wings, Dante tells us, that never molt or lose their feathers. As the souls ride, they sing a psalm of the exodus: of Israel's release from Egyptian bondage. Among the souls, Dante recognizes Casella, a musician who had set some of Dante's poems to music. Casella and his fellow souls gather around the poets, and, as Casella plays one of the songs he wrote for Dante, they all pause in wonder at the beauty of the song. But Cato, seeing their loitering, scolds them and sends them scattering, like pigeons, up the side of the mountain.

In *Aeneid* VI, the Sibyl hurries Virgil on through most of his journey in the underworld. Dante imitates this haste in *Inferno* and then gives it a fuller, richer significance in *Purgatorio*. When it comes to seeking God, we must not delay, lest, like Dante, we fall off the path. On Mount Purgatory, this sense of urgency propels all of the souls to make full use of the time that is given them to prepare themselves for God. As long as the sun (symbol of God's grace) shines on the mountain, the souls continue their ascent and persist in their remedial punishments. When, however, the sun sets and darkness falls, they immediately lose their power and will to climb and fall into a deep sleep. Dante and Virgil spend three nights in Purgatory, and during each of those nights, Dante has a prophetic dream that helps keep him on his appointed path.

Ante-Purgatory, the first of the nine levels that circle the mountain, houses (temporarily) souls who, while on Earth, lost their sense of spiritual urgency and fell off the true path. Though some died in battle without extreme unction or were excommunicated from the sacramental life of the church, most simply delayed their salvation and dedication to Christ until the very last minute. As they, while in the flesh, made God wait on them, so now they must wait here on God's good pleasure before beginning their ascent, first to Eden, and then to Paradise. The wait is hard on them, but it also builds up within their hearts a burning desire for the Beatific Vision: to see God face-to-face.

Though the souls can do nothing themselves to reduce their stay in ante-Purgatory, the living *can* effect a reduction *on behalf* of the souls by performing one of two actions. The first is the saying of masses (prayers for the dead) in the name of the deceased; it is for this reason that many of the souls beg Dante to ask their relatives to pray for them. The second action is better known because of the pivotal role it played in the Reformation: the granting of a papal indulgence. Contrary to popular opinion, a papal indulgence cannot release a soul from Hell (even the pope has no power over Hell); all it can do is speed up a person's time in Purgatory. Of course, that does not mean that there weren't many charlatans—like Chaucer's Pardoner and Luther's nemesis, Tetzel—who led credulous crowds to believe that, for a price, their souls, and those of their relatives, could be freed from Hell. Dante's *Purgatorio* helps to explode this false understanding of indulgences, as it also helps to explode another misunderstood teaching of the church. Though a pope, through power of excommunication, can prevent someone from participating in the mass, he cannot thereby prevent him from asking for and receiving grace from Christ directly. True, the excommunicated person will be forced to spend more time in ante-Purgatory, but no pope has the power to cut us off from God's mercy. The church assists us in our road to salvation, but it does not own it: though community is vital to the Catholic Dante, the Platonic ideal of individual spiritual growth is just as strong an influence.

The Whip and the Rein

Once a soul leaves ante-Purgatory, it enters Purgatory-proper though a gate guarded by an angel. Before doing so himself, Dante dreams that he is being carried Heavenward by a golden eagle, an experience he compares to that of the mythical Ganymede: one of the few mortals to be taken bodily up to Olympus. As he dreams his Elijah-like dream (see 2 Kgs 2), Saint Lucia, patron saint of the blind, carries the sleeping Dante to the gate. Once there, he ascends three steps, whereupon a flaming sword engraves seven P's (for *peccatum*, "sin") upon his forehead. The seven P's represent the seven deadly sins (pride, envy, wrath, sloth, avarice, gluttony, and lust), each of which will be purged away on levels 2–8 of the mountain. As in Hell, these sins are graded in terms of severity; this time, however, levels 2–4 punish the greater sins while levels 5–8 punish the lesser. In both hierarchies, lust is accounted the least bad sin.

As Dante completes each of the seven levels, an angel appears and wipes the appropriate "P" off his forehead; with each cleansing, Dante becomes lighter and lighter until he is able to move swiftly up the remaining level. Each stage of Dante's purification process is reminiscent of the experiences of an initiate in one of the mysteries of ancient Greece: whether Eleusinian, Orphic, Pythagorean, or Neoplatonic. Indeed, through a clever use of verbal and visual repetition, Dante succeeds in making his progression through the seven deadly sins seem almost ritualistic and liturgical. Each level, for example, boasts its own special prayer and is linked to one of the Beatitudes (Matt 5). Thus the prideful are urged to remember how "blessed are the poor in spirit," while the wrathful and the gluttons are urged to recall the blessedness promised to the peacemakers and to those who hunger after righteousness.

In addition to each level having its own punishment, prayer, and beatitude, each provides an education in virtue and vice. The sinners in each level are both spurred on to virtue (the whip) and restrained from vice (the rein or bridle) by seeing or hearing visions, both of those who chose the path of virtue and were rewarded and those who indulged in vice and were punished. Of the paths of virtue (the whip), each is illustrated by an episode from the life of the Virgin Mary along with at least one figure from the Bible and from Greco-Roman history or myth. The paths of vice as well (the rein) are chosen equally from secular and sacred tales. By building these episodes into his epic, Dante delves the nature of vice and virtue in all humanity: Jew or Gentile, Christian or pagan. Dante knew that much of the greatness of Rome was sustained by the stories of virtue and vice that were told to the noble schoolboys of the Republic. In our own day, William J. Bennett, former US Secretary of Education, tried to revive this venerable Roman and medieval practice by publishing *The Book of Virtues*—a compilation of well-loved tales from sacred and secular sources that illustrate such virtues as courage, honesty, loyalty, and faith.

According to Christian theology, the worst sin of all is pride; it was through pride that the once beautiful angel of light, Lucifer, rebelled against God and was expelled from Heaven. In order to have not only the propensity for pride but the desire for it crushed out of them, the prideful circle the mountain on their hands and knees while huge boulders crush their backs. As in the inferno, the punishments are fitted exactly to the individual; in the case of level two, the boulders are larger or smaller depending on the severity of the sin. When the souls begin their weary crawl of humility (the virtue opposite to pride), they are invited to gaze upon carved stone figures of those who excelled in humility. As on all seven levels, the first exemplar of the virtue that defeats the vice is Mary. Here, we see Mary just after Gabriel has announced to her that she will bear the Son of God; in response to this news, Mary does not boast or resist but answers humbly: "Behold the handmaid of the Lord" (Luke 1:38). Beside the image of the Annunciation, we see an image of King David dancing humbly before the ark (2 Sam 6), while his prideful wife, Michal, scorns him for his lack of royal decorum. Beside David, a third image tells the story of how the virtuous pagan Emperor Trajan halted his march to help a poor widow who begged him for justice. Along with Mary, David, and Trajan, the souls of the prideful are urged to throw of their vainglory and step down from their pedestals of pride.

In contrast to these images, meant to whip the prideful on to the high virtue of humility, the rein of pride, which the souls see as they are about to depart from level two, provides them with a final warning of what pride does to those who give themselves over to it. Among the thirteen images of notorious sinners whose lives were consumed by pride, we encounter both Satan and Nimrod, the king responsible for building the Tower of Babel. As a pagan parallel to Nimrod, we see as well images of the Giants of Greek mythology who attempted, and failed, to overthrow Zeus and Olympus. Two characters from Ovid's *Metamorphoses* appear as well: Arachne, who challenged Athena to a sewing contest and was transformed into a spider for her arrogance; and Niobe, who boasted that her seven sons and seven daughters made her greater than the goddess Leto, who bore only Apollo and Artemis. As punishment for her boasting, Niobe's children and husband were killed, one by one, by arrows from the quivers of Leto's two children; Niobe herself was turned to a stone that even yet weeps water through its pores.

The envious who dwell on level three are punished not by crushing boulders but by having their eyes sewn shut. On Earth they sinned with their eyes, so here their eyes are closed that they might turn away from envy and desire only the glory of God. (Here and throughout I use the word "punishment" to describe the sufferings of those on the mountain, but it must always be remembered that the souls desire their punishments, for they exist to purify them both of the sin and their desire for it. In no sense is God exacting retribution upon the souls in Purgatory.) Since the envious cannot see, the whip and the rein come to them in the form of a voice that shouts out the names of those who put off envy and those who indulged it. The whip consists of Mary at Cana of Galilee (John 2), who showed her lack of envy (or, better, her presence of love) by requesting that Jesus provide wine for the wedding guests, Orestes, whose friendship with Pylades was legendary, and Jesus himself, who instructed his followers to love their enemies. The whip consists of Cain (Gen 4), whose jealousy led him to kill his own brother, and a mythical woman from Ovid (Aglauros) who betrayed her sister out of envious spite.

The wrathful of level three bounce their heads together as they move through stinging smoke, a fit illustration of the way wrath clouds our vision and our judgment. For these souls, mired as they are in a perpetual haze, the whip and rein come in visionary flashes that cut through the smoke. The virtuous who showed meekness instead of wrath include Mary scolding Jesus, but not overmuch, when he stayed behind at the temple (Luke 2:48) and Stephen forgiving the very people who stoned him to death (Acts 7:60). The wrathful include Haman, who tried to exterminate the Jews (Esth 3:6), and Amata, who resisted Aeneas' marriage to her daughter Lavinia and thus sparked the civil war that rages throughout the last half of the *Aeneid*.

Around and around level four, the slothful participate in an endless running race that builds up in them a passion for goodness and active virtue that they lacked in life. As they run, two in front shout out how Mary ran to see Elizabeth (Luke 1) and how Julius Caesar marched his troops all night to secure victory; meanwhile, two behind remind them of the Jews who died in the wilderness of Sinai and of the Trojans who abandoned Aeneas on his journey toward Rome (*Aeneid* V).

Before Dante can ascend to level five (avarice), night falls, and he has his second dream on the mountain. In his dream, Dante sees an ugly crone approaching him. Intrigued, Dante stares at her, and, as he does, she slowly transforms into a beautiful woman and begins to sing a seductive song. In her song, she identifies herself as one of the Sirens whose lovely voices almost led Odysseus off course (*Odyssey* XII). Dante proves impotent against the Siren's song, but is saved just in time by Virgil, who appears suddenly and rips open the witch, revealing her true inner ugliness. The dream is meant as a warning of how avarice (filthy lucre) lures us into thinking it is beautiful and desirable, and then drives us off course to our doom. The lesson is a familiar one, but Dante gives it new power and insight by showing how we are destroyed by something whose ugliness we were once aware of but forgot in our foolish reach for wealth.

To teach the avaricious the folly of following the Siren's lure—the folly, that is, of looking downward toward mundane things when they should be focused on things above—the avaricious are chained hand and foot, their faces pressed in the dirt. The punishment is a terrible one, for the souls cannot see the sun, but it is effective: when they are released from their chains, there is little danger of their ever looking down again. The tales of virtue and vice are spoken aloud: the former include Mary giving birth in a stable (Luke 1), Fabricius (a noble Roman) refusing bribes, and St. Nicholas giving his money to redeem virgins; the latter include King Midas, Ananias and Sapphira, who withheld money they promised to the early church (Acts 5), and Crassus, once the richest man in Rome and the equal of Caesar and Pompey.

15

Dante's *Purgatorio* II
Eden Restored

Just as there is a moment in *Inferno* when Virgil explains to Dante the major divisions of Hell, so is there a similar moment in *Purgatorio* when Virgil explains to Dante why the seven deadly sins are grouped the way they are on the mountain. Unexpectedly, Virgil links each of the deadly sins to love. In the case of the worst three sins (pride, envy, wrath), each represents a bad type of love that has been directed at one's neighbor. Normally, love should impel us to move out of ourselves toward others; this the prideful, envious, and wrathful do, but with malicious rather than charitable intent, wishing not the good but the ruin, shame, or injury of their neighbor. In contrast, the less bad sins (avarice, gluttony, lust) are not so much directed against others as they are misdirected toward improper objects. In Catholic theology, the enactment of a homosexual orientation is not sinful because it is fun or unseemly or forbidden, but because it represents a misdirection (or disordering) of erotic desire. Avarice, gluttony, and lust all turn healthy desire back against itself in a way that is essentially idolatrous and narcissistic. In between the three greater and lesser deadly sins lies sloth, which is best defined as a type of lax love—our desires are not misdirected; we are simply too lazy to pursue them.

Thus much about the nature of Purgatory Dante learns from Virgil. From Statius (see chapter 9), whom the poets meet on the level of avarice, Dante learns further details of which Virgil seems unaware. Statius, who has spent over a millennium on the mountain, explains to Dante that no one monitors the souls as they work their way through the various circles. Indeed, neither saint nor angel tells the soul when it has finished its penance and is ready to move on. The soul feels *in itself* that it has been released from bondage to sin and moves on of its own free will. When full penance has been done, and the soul is freed from all seven of the deadly sins, the mountain shakes with joy at the spiritual graduation. Though Dante certainly had Luke 15:10 in mind in constructing this memorable detail ("there is joy in the presence of the angels of God over one sinner that repenteth"), he likely was also influenced by Plato's Myth of Er, where Plato tells us that the Hell mouth shakes whenever a tyrant tries to escape. In a redemptive imitation of Plato (not directly, but filtered through such Roman writers as Cicero, Virgil, and Ovid), Dante transforms the angry Hell mouth into a joyous mountain.

From Statius' example, rather than his words, Dante learns one final detail about the soul's movement up Purgatory. Given that Statius spends no time on levels seven and eight but passes through them along with the poets, it seems clear that not all souls will spend time on every level of Purgatory; they need only spend time working out sins of which they are guilty. In a moment of humility, Dante admits to us, and to himself, that when he returns (postmortem) to the mountain, he will have to spend many years on the circle of pride.

Paradise Regained

Having left the level of avarice, Virgil, Dante, and Statius proceed onward to the levels of gluttony and lust. The punishment for the former, they discover, is to circle the mountain in a skeletal state of emaciation. Along the weary circuit of the gluttons stand two trees heavy with fruit. The fruit appeals to eye, nose, and tongue alike, but the gluttons are strictly forbidden from climbing the trees and plucking the fruit. From the first tree (the Tree of Life?), a voice celebrates Mary who thought of others' hunger at Cana of Galilee (John 2). It celebrates as well the moderation shown by Daniel, who refused to eat the royal food and wine of the Babylonian court (Dan 1), and by John the Baptist, who lived in the wilderness and fed on locusts and wild honey. Balancing sacred with secular, Judeo-Christian with Greco-Roman, the whip of gluttony also praises the matrons of the Roman Republic, who did not overindulge their flesh but preferred water to wine, and the inhabitants of the lost Golden Age celebrated by Hesiod and Ovid, who lived on a simple diet of acorns and mountain water. From the second tree (clearly identified as the Tree of the Knowledge of Good and Evil), a voice warns of the gluttony of Eve, whose eating of the forbidden fruit led to the fall, and of the centaurs, whose ravenous appetite for food and sex caused them to defile a wedding and led to a bloody war between the half-man/half-horse centaurs and a human tribe known as the Lapiths (this war is depicted in all its violent energy on the Elgin marbles which once graced the Parthenon).

The lustful of level eight sing praise songs as they walk through sheets of fire that purge away their misdirected desire. As they walk, they sing to each other not only of Mary's virginity but of the virginity of Apollo's sister, Diana, who, as patron goddess of the woods, took to herself young female votaries. And they sing as well of chaste couples who limited their sexuality to the bounds of faithful marriage. In contrast to the sexual purity of Mary, Diana, and the chaste couples, they shout out warnings against the sexual perversions of the inhabitants of Sodom and Gomorra and of Minos' queen, Pasiphae, whose unholy lust impelled her to lie with a bull and give birth to the monstrous Minotaur.

Although the lustful of level eight are the only ones who are punished by fire, Dante learns that in order to cross over into the Garden of Eden, all souls, no matter their sins, must pass through a wall of fire. There, in a white-hot sheet of flame, they receive their final purgation of all wrongful, lax, and misdirected love. Dante, terrified that he will be consumed by the fire, resists, but Virgil is able to coax him through by reminding him that Beatrice waits for him on the other side.

Shortly after Dante passes through the fire, the sun sets and he has his third and final dream on the mountain. This time, he dreams of Leah and Rachel, who, like Martha and Mary of Bethany (see Luke 10:38–42), represent the active and contemplative life. Once in Eden, he will meet a lovely woman named Matilda, who will herself take the role of the active life in contrast to the contemplative Beatrice. Even a cursory look at Dante's biography will reveal these two competing strains within the poet himself, who was powerfully drawn both to political and civic engagement and to deep philosophical and theological study. Indeed, whereas, up to this point, the *Divine Comedy* has placed more focus on action than contemplation, that proportion will be reversed as Dante journeys through Eden, the heavenly spheres, and the Empyrean of God.

Upon arriving in Eden, Dante is invited by Virgil to feast on those "golden apples men have sought / on many different boughs" (*Purgatorio* XXVII.116–17). The moment is a supremely Christian humanist one that merges biblical revelation about Eden with the almost universal pagan yearning for a lost Golden Age—one that Virgil himself celebrates in *Aeneid* VIII and the Fourth Eclogue. The Greek poets in particular spoke of a garden far in the west where enchanted golden apples grew that were guarded by a fierce dragon and by the lovely Hesperides, the daughters of Hesperus (the evening star and root of our word vespers). All men, Dante suggests, whatever their culture or religion, yearn for Eden and the Tree of Life. Indeed, as Dante listens to Virgil's words, he experiences something straight out of Plato's Myth of the Charioteer. Just as Plato says, in *Phaedrus* (see chapter 5), that when someone on Earth glimpses true beauty he feels the wings of his soul sprout feathers, so Dante, when he hears Virgil speak of the golden apples, is similarly transported: "Such waves of yearning to achieve the height / swept through my soul, that at each step I took / I felt my feathers growing for the flight" (XXVII.121–23).

Alas, it is a flight that Virgil will not be able to share. Having led Dante to the top of Purgatory and drawn for him the connection between Eden and the Golden Age, the greatest poet of antiquity and the supreme example of pagan wisdom and virtue confesses that he has now reached "the limit of [his] discernment" (XXVII.126). By the force of his classical reason and poetic art he has taken Dante back to man's original state, but he can go no further. Though Virgil will remain for several more cantos, it is here that he speaks his last words in the *Comedy*:

> Expect no more of me in word or deed:
>> here your will is upright, free, and whole,
>> and you would be in error not to heed
> whatever your own impulse prompts you to:
> lord of yourself I crown and mitre you. (XXVII.139–43)

Were a pastor or teacher to give such advice to a parishioner or student, he would be speaking foolishly and irresponsibly. No matter how moral and "good" a person may seem, his fallen nature, if left to indulge its desires without check, will lead him astray. In the restored Eden that will no longer be the case. Dante has been purged of all sin, and is therefore no longer capable of going astray. Purgatory, we must always remember, is about freedom. Now that Dante's desires have been freed from bondage to sin and his will freed from the perversions of lust and pride, he has become what he was created to be and is thus free to do what he ought to do. He is now a law unto himself, a full, free agent. It is for this reason that Virgil can declare Dante both king (political) and bishop (religious) over himself.

Dante has reached the state that Platonists and Stoics longed to reach—freedom from the ravages of desire, moral autonomy, spiritual self-sufficiency—but he has not sacrificed joy to do so. To the contrary, he now stands on the brink of a life, light, and joy that surpass even the dreams of Plato. True, Eden is *like* the Elysian Fields (and its Dantean counterpart, Limbo), but it is so much more passionate, so much more vital, so much more *real*. If I may use Plato in order to transcend him, we might say that

Eden is the true original of the Golden Age; it is the true Eternal Spring that the greatest pagan poets only glimpsed dimly in a bent and distorted mirror. And it is something else as well: the real Parnassus (the mountain of the Muses), the true source of all poetic inspiration.

Eden, Dante learns, is watered by two rivers (Lethe and Eunoë), whose source is not the tears of humanity. Unlike the four rivers of Hell, Lethe and Eunoë spring fresh and everlasting from the fountain of God. As in classical mythology, the souls must drink from Lethe, the river of forgetfulness; here, however, it is not their past lives that they must forget but the memory of sin—for God cannot have even the memory of sin in his presence. As for Eunoë (Greek for "good mind"), Dante invents this river as a counterpart to Lethe. Whereas Lethe washes away the memory of bad deeds, Eunoë strengthens in those who drink from it the memory of all their good deeds. Fire is used to purify metals, for it has the power both to eliminate dross and strengthen pure gold; Lethe and Eunoë, by their joint ministry, do the same for the human soul.

Boy Meets Girl

The medievals loved pageants—both on Earth and in the heavens—and one of the greatest sights that Dante sees in Eden reflects that love. As Dante, Virgil, and Statius look on with awe, a grand, liturgical procession wends its slow way through Eden. The procession—which calls up both the heavenly procession of Plato's *Phaedrus* and the procession of Roman history in *Aeneid* VI—is neither political nor military in nature. Rather, it presents, in a manner most strange to modern tastes, an allegorical celebration of the Bible and the church. Each book of the Old and New Testament is represented by a robed figure; between them marches the Griffin, a legendary beast with the body of a lion and the head and wings of an eagle.

Until the modern period, Christians saw in the Griffin a symbol of the dual natured, incarnate Christ, with the lion representing his humanity (the Lion of Judah) and the eagle representing his divinity (the eagle not only soars toward Heaven but has eyes so perfect that it can stare into the sun). The two-in-one nature of the Griffin embodies the original of a divine paradox whose perversion is seen in the monstrous duality of the Minotaur and the centaurs. The Griffin (Christ) pulls a chariot (the Church), which is attended on either side by the four classical virtues and the three theological virtues. Like Dante, the church is served by both reason and grace.

Generally speaking, as Dante approaches nearer and nearer to God, words fail him, and he is forced to turn to symbol and allegory. In the case of the procession through Eden, Dante uses it not only to convey the mystery of Christ and the church, but to mark the transition from Virgil to Beatrice. As the figure representing the Song of Solomon passes by Dante, it cries out in Latin, "Come my bride, from Lebanon." No sooner are these words spoken than Beatrice appears to the poets through a cloud of rosy flowers.

The moment he sees her, Dante feels the flame of his first love burn within him, and, as he has done so often before, he turns to share his feelings with Virgil. But Virgil is gone; in an instant, he has been transported back to Limbo. Dante is devastated by Virgil's disappearance, and he compares the loss of his master to the loss of Eden itself: a particularly powerful metaphor given the fact that Dante even now stands in the precincts of Eden. We the readers feel the loss as well, but Dante has subtly prepared us for it in two ways. First, when Dante says he feels the flame of love within him, he alludes to a line that Dido says in *Aeneid* IV when she falls in love with Aeneas. Second, when the angels cast flowers before Beatrice, they quote the lines Anchises uses to mourn Marcellus: "'Let me scatter lilies, / All I can hold'" (*Aeneid* VI). Taken together, the two allusions pay tribute to Virgil and the enduring legacy of his epic.

But Dante is given little time to grieve. A moment after he discovers that Virgil is gone, Beatrice calls him by name—the only time Dante's name is mentioned in the *Comedy*—and tells him, in a harsh tone, that she will give him far more to grieve for.

Though Dante idealizes Beatrice as the embodiment of divine grace, Beatrice Portinari was a real woman whom Dante first saw in Florence at the age of nine and again at the age of eighteen. Though he never courted or married her—she married someone else and died young—she remained in his mind an ideal of beauty. Indeed, just as the love of a single person marks the starting point for the ascent of the philosopher-lover in Plato's *Symposium* (see chapter 5), so Dante's love for Beatrice represents the poet-lover's first step on the road to spiritual enlightenment. It was the beauty of Beatrice that first awakened Dante's soul to higher things and that exerted an influence on him not unlike the influence of the heavenly spheres.

In the early 1290s, well over a decade before he began his *Comedy*, Dante had immortalized Beatrice in a sort-of epic dry-run, a loose collection of love sonnets and prose interludes that he titled *La Vita Nuova* (*The New Life*): a book as intricate (and obsessive!) in its use of numerology and astrology as the *Comedy*. While she lives, Beatrice's eyes and smile inspire the young poet to mystical heights, but, when she dies, he seeks consolation in a second, compassionate lady that he sees in a window. A final vision of Beatrice in Heaven, vouchsafed to the poet when he is twenty-seven (9 x 3), brings him back to his first devotion, and he experiences remorse over his "infidelity" to Beatrice. In the closing lines of *La Vita Nuova*, Dante swears that he will not write of her again until he is more worthy. When that time comes, he hopes to see her in all her heavenly glory and "to compose concerning her what has never been written in rhyme of any woman. And then may it please Him who is the Lord of courtesy that my soul may go to see the glory of my lady, that is of the blessed Beatrice, who now in glory beholds the face of Him *qui est per omnia secula benedictus* ['Who is blessed for ever']."[1]

In *Purgatorio* and *Paradiso* Dante does just that, but the reunion proves to be far less smooth than he perhaps had fantasized it would be. Beatrice has not forgotten that Dante strayed from her influence, and so she begins her long-awaited reunion with the poet by scolding him harshly. Immediately, the angels sing out in pity, begging the incensed Beatrice to be merciful to this nice Florentine man. Dante is moved to tears by their intercession, hoping that all now will be well, but Beatrice silences the angels, reminding them that they live their lives in Heaven and don't know the power of temptation on the fallen world from which Dante comes. Before Dante can drink from Lethe and enter Paradise, he must understand and confess fully his sins—and this Beatrice will make sure he does!

In the manner of a father confessor, Beatrice explains to Dante the exact nature of his sin: though graced with God-given gifts, Dante let them go to seed. Like the lazy servant in the parable of the Talents who buries his talent in the ground (see chapter 10), Dante has shown himself a bad steward of the poetic and philosophical gifts entrusted to him. For many years, Beatrice used her beauty to keep the inconstant poet on track, but when she died, he forgot her and turned his desires toward other worldly things, including other ladies, on whom he lavished his poetic praise. In short, Dante traded in the Beatific Vision for idols. Rather than follow Beatrice's soul to Heaven, Dante, like the adulterous lover of Francesca, followed her body down into the grave; like the avaricious on level six of Purgatory, he allowed his gaze to be drawn earthward toward mundane things.

During his years of spiritual and poetic idolatry, Beatrice prayed and sent Dante visions, but he, in his folly and sloth, ignored all her attempts to draw him back to the True Way. In the end, her only recourse was to descend to limbo and rouse Virgil to take Dante on his journey through Hell. In sharing this narrative, Beatrice not only exposes Dante's guilt (not for the sake of condemnation but so that it may be confessed and forgiven) but takes on, allegorically, the role both of Christ—who harrowed Hell for our salvation—and of God the Father. When read allegorically, Jesus'

---

1. Dante, *La Vita Nuova*, translated by Barbara Reynolds, 99.

parable of the Tenants (Matt 21:33–44) paints a picture of an active, passionate God who does all he can to call back his people from their idolatry and disobedience.

In the parable, a master plants a vineyard and hires tenants to work it; just so, God called Israel and established her in the Promised Land. Sadly, when harvest time comes, the tenants refuse to pay the master what they owe him; with great patience, the master sends servant after servant to collect the rent, but the evil tenants expel some and kill the others. Finally, the master sends his son. He hopes the tenants will respect his son, but instead, they drag him outside the vineyard and put him to death. Just so, when Israel turned her back on God, he tried every means to recall her: first he sent the law, then the prophets, and finally his Son. The love and dedication Beatrice has shown in trying to reclaim Dante from his sins is meant by the poet to point to God's covenant love for Israel.

The tenants, like the Pharisees against whom Jesus spoke the parable, reject all the attempts of the master to reconcile with them—even to the point of killing his one and only son—and, as a result, the vineyard is taken from them. Not so Dante. Beatrice's descent to limbo and the journey it initiates bring Dante to a full realization of his sins and a desire to return to the right path. With tears and sighs, Dante confesses that false pleasures led him astray the moment Beatrice left his sight. Had Dante tried to conceal his guilt, Beatrice explains, his guilt would still have been known to God, but here, "before our court, when souls upbraid / themselves for their own guilt in true remorse, / the grindstone is turned back against the blade" (XXXI.40–42). Before the eternal judge, the only way we can be declared innocent is to plead guilty and throw ourselves on the mercy of the court; only then will the edge of the sword of justice be dulled. Pleased by Dante's confession, Beatrice rehearses one last time his guilt that he may be stronger next time against the song of the Siren.

In rehearsing again his guilt and insisting after her death, the wings of Dante's soul should not "have been weighed down by any joy below— / love of a maid, or any other fleeting / and useless thing'" (XXXI.58–60), Beatrice reveals that in addition to being an allegory for the First and Second Person of the Trinity, she is also, quite literally, a jealous lover! As odd as it may sound, at the heart of his epic, Dante tells the oldest story in the world: boy meets girl; boy loses girl; boy gets girl back again. And yet, perhaps it is not so odd, for that is also the central story of the Bible. At its core, the Bible, too, is a love story: God takes a bride for himself (first Israel, then the church); she rejects him to commit spiritual idolatry; he forgives her and ransoms her back. God even allegorizes this love story by first instructing his prophet Hosea to marry a prostitute, and then, when she returns to her prostitution, to buy her back and restore her to her position as his beloved bride.

As we saw in chapter 13, the Bible ends not (like a Shakespearean tragedy) with war or judgment or death, but (like a Shakespearean comedy) with the Great Marriage of Christ and the church. The universe of Dante, like that of the Bible is, finally, a comic one. Our modern, cynical age tends to look down its nose at stories with happy endings, but the greatest stories of the human imagination—from the Bible to the *Odyssey*, the *Oresteia* to the *Divine Comedy*, *The Brother's Karamazov* to *The Lord of the Rings*—do not shy away from the joy and triumph of the happy ending.

16

Dante's *Paradiso* I

Journey into Light

Dante's progress through the nine levels of Paradise, which culminates in a vision of God, may best be described as a journey into light. Like a morning glory opening its petals to the sun, Dante's heart slowly swells and expands to take in the increased light that greets him as he approaches that divine light in which there is no shadow of turning. The process begins in *Purgatorio* XXXI, when Dante sees Beatrice stare at the Griffin. At this point in his journey, Dante's eyes are not prepared to look upon the glory of Christ, symbolized by the dual, incarnational nature of the Griffin. For now, he must settle for the reflected glory that shines in Beatrice's eyes. Even so on Earth, those who lack the spiritual discernment to see God's love and grace directly may catch glimpses of it in the faces and demeanors of those who are particularly close to God. In Eden, Dante must rest content to look at Beatrice looking at the Griffin, but a time will soon come when he too will be equipped to stare into the radiance not only of Christ's symbol but of Christ himself.

The naked eye of mortal man cannot stare into the sun without going blind, in the same way, a sinful, unprepared soul cannot look upon the glorious light of the All-Holy God without being burned. In Purgatory, the punishments exist not for the purpose of vengeance but as a vehicle for freeing the soul of all desire for sin. Here, in Paradise, we discover that they have another purpose: to train the eyes of the saints to yearn for the purer light which shines above. In Christian theology, we reach Heaven not by denying our desires but by purifying and expanding them. For the Buddhist, the Stoic, and the Neoplatonist, desire is the problem and so the solution involves the elimination of all desire. For the Christian, our desires were given us by God but were perverted and misdirected by sin. Salvation, then, does not mean removing our desires but restoring them to their original purpose and design. As such, we prepare for Heaven not by mortifying our emotions but by training them for a higher and better use. Imagine a man living in a dark room who is told that in twelve hours he will be placed in a room filled with dazzling light. Would he prepare himself for this experience by sitting in the dark for the next twelve hours? Would he not rather prepare himself by entering a brightly lit room, and then a brighter one, and then a brighter? This movement from bright to brighter is precisely the one that Dante follows, and it begins immediately in the opening canto of *Paradiso*.

As though she were an eagle, Beatrice turns her gaze skyward and stares directly and unwaveringly into the sun. At first, Dante only catches the reflection of the light in her eyes, but then, inspired by her devotion and yearning himself for the light, he raises his eyes to the sun. To have done so on Earth would have blinded him, but his senses have been strengthened by the air of Eden, man's proper place, and his drink from Eunoë. The sudden influx of so much celestial light transforms Dante the pilgrim, and Dante the poet is impelled to turn to a story from Ovid to describe the transformation. With poetic gusto, Dante compares himself to the mythical Glaucus, a humble fisherman who ate a herb he found by the shore and was instantly metamorphosed into a god of the sea. The metaphor is an apt one, and yet, ironically, it initiates an oft-repeated theme of *Paradiso* that highlights the limits, rather than the glory, of poetry. With each new influx of light and glory, Dante confesses more and more to his growing inability to find human words and images to express what he sees: "How speak trans-human change to human sense?" (*Paradiso* I.70). To assist him in his endeavors, Dante invokes both the muses and Apollo; nevertheless, he knows that what he has seen has struck so deeply into his being that it has surpassed the power of memory to dig it out.

But Dante's new-won ability to stare, eagle-like, into the sun is only the first of many surprises to greet the poet in his journey Heavenward. A greater surprise is about to be revealed.

Hierarchy Rightly Understood

To reach the depths of inferno and the heights of Purgatory, Dante was forced to walk, climb, and crawl, but to move from sphere to sphere in Paradise, he uses the far more thrilling method of locomotion. Only moments after looking into the blazing fire of the sun, Dante realizes, both to his joy and his terror, that his body is soaring upward through space. During the first two stages of his epic journey, Dante had questioned Virgil about each new wonder and mystery. During the final stage, Dante rarely asks Beatrice a direct question, not because he does not trust her but because she, possessing greater wisdom and insight than Virgil, is able to discern Dante's thoughts and pierce through his fears and confusions. Because of this ability, Beatrice generally answers his questions before he has fully articulated them.

In response to Dante's bewilderment as to how it is that he can fly, Beatrice explains that now that he has been purged of all sin, guilt, and heaviness, it is only natural that he should ascend upward: as natural as it is for a waterfall to flow downward. Within all of us, God has placed a natural, in-built desire to seek our proper place in relationship to him. And yet, though we are hard-wired with this yearning, we retain the power to go off course and, thus, frustrate our original purpose and design. As Virgil makes clear in *Inferno* III, when we lose the fear of God, our desires are perverted, and we end up yearning after the very things we dread. When this happens—when, that is, we misuse that reason and free will with which God gifted us at Creation—our base instincts take control and draw us downward. Or, to put it in the language of Plato's Myth of Er: though we were made to rise up and to the right, our lusts draw us down and to the left.

In a beautiful metaphor, Dante compares our souls to ships flying through space seeking our God-appointed port. Though many modern Americans and Europeans assume that the ideal state of man is egalitarian, with everyone possessing the same skills and the same "stuff," Dante and his fellow medievals understood that the very order of the cosmos depends on a hierarchical scheme in which everything has its place in God's divine architecture. Though geographically the medievals placed the Earth at the center of the cosmos, spiritually they placed God at the center. Everything in the universe, they believed—from angels to planets to men—had a set role and position vis-à-vis God. Yes, God created the universe out of love, but it is the universe's love for God that keeps it on course. It is not the impersonal laws of physics but their joyous love for God that causes the planets to spin.

In the heavenly realms Dante visits all is perfect and fixed; however, in the world that lies beneath the moon—the sub-lunar or terrestrial realm—all is in constant flux. As Dante moves past the first sphere (or heaven) of the moon, he makes a transition from what Plato calls the world of becoming (our own world of change, decay, and death) to the world of Being (the divine and unchanging realm of permanence and perfection). The souls who dwell above the moon in the paradisiacal world of Being desire only the will of God—a far cry from we who live on Earth under the influence of Dame Fortune (see *Inferno* VII), whose ever-changing Wheel ensures that nothing will remain constant or fixed.

In a recurring metaphor, Dante compares humanity to a ball of wax and God to a king who would impress his royal seal upon the wax that it might bear both his image and his will. Sometimes the impression of God's seal is clear and whole; more often than not, the wax resists the will of the Creator and mars the beautiful image that might have been. The metaphor is a common medieval one, and, though it appears in the Bible (see, for example, Hag 2:23 and 2 Cor 1:22), it likely goes back to Plato's *Timaeus*, the only dialogue of Plato available for much of the Middle Ages (that is why Dante and others got much of their Plato, as they did much of their Homer, second hand through Virgil, Ovid, Boethius, and others). At several points in *Paradiso*, Dante uses the image of the pure seal and the too-often intransigent wax to explain why the astrological influence of the stars takes varied forms in different people. Although Dante's heavenly bodies continually shed their essentially benign influence both on us and our planet, we retain our freedom and can make of these influences what we will. Thus, the same solar rays that turn clay hard and brittle make wax soft and pliable. As we follow Dante on his journey through the seven planetary spheres of the medieval cosmos, I shall pause to list the influences that they were believed to exert on both the natural and human realms.

The lowest heaven (or sphere) is the moon. By shedding its influence on the Earth, the moon produces silver, the only substance that, according to legend, can kill the moon-created werewolf. By means of that same influence it causes lunacy (from luna, "moon") in men, often impelling them to wander on the Earth. In Dante's heavenly scheme, the souls who reside in the sphere of the moon are those who, for whatever reason, were inconstant to a vow they had taken. It is here that Dante and Beatrice meet Piccarda, a nun who was forced to leave her convent by her brother so that she could make a political marriage.

After he hears her story, Dante wonders if Piccarda does not wish to rise to a higher station in Heaven. Can she be content to remain in the moon, when it lies the farthest from God? Would she not prefer to dwell, say, in the sphere of Jupiter or Saturn? Piccarda's reply offers solace to moderns who have a hard time accepting Dante's (and traditional Christian theology's) hierarchical view of this world and the next:

> Brother, the power of love, which is our bliss,
>
>   calms all our will. What we desire, we have.
>
>   There is in us no other thirst than this.

Were we to wish for any higher sphere,

> then our desires would not be in accord

> with the will of Him who wills us here. . . .

And so the posts we stand from sill to sill

> throughout this realm, please all the realm as much

> as they please Him who wills us to His will.

In His will is our peace. (*Paradiso* IIII.70–75, 82–85)

Piccarda's full desire is to be where God wills her to be; were she to move to a higher sphere, she would no longer be in God's will and would lose her peace and her joy. Though there are hierarchies in Heaven, every place in Heaven is equally paradise, for all the souls receive as much of God's love and light as they are able to hold.

Imagine two glasses: the first, a six-ounce glass, is filled with exactly six ounces of water; the second, an eight-ounce glass, is filled with exactly eight ounces of water. Which of the two glasses is more full? The answer, of course, it that both glasses are equally full, for each contains as much water as it can hold. In fact, were we to attempt to pour eight ounces into the six-ounce glass, the glass, if it could speak, would cry out to us to stop filling it with a liquid it cannot contain. The extra two ounces would cause it discomfort rather than pleasure. Dante himself explains it best in the opening stanza of *Paradiso*: "The glory of Him who moves all things rays forth / through all the universe, and is reflected / from each thing in proportion to its worth" (I.1–3). Dante's universe, like his epic, is one of perfect order, harmony, and balance. Discord can have no place in any quarter of the cosmos. Our position, vis-à-vis God, is neither arbitrary nor unjust; we dwell in that place from which we can absorb and reflect back the fullest amount of God's glory of which we are capable.

From Sphere to Sphere

But the wonder of Paradise is even greater than this. In the next canto, Beatrice explains to Dante that the souls he will encounter in each of the seven spheres are not really there. They have only manifested themselves there to aid Dante's limited understanding, in a manner analogous to the way Scripture accommodates our limited understanding by speaking of the invisible God in anthropomorphic terms. In reality, all the souls in Paradise exist in the Empyrean, in the tenth and true Heaven that lies outside of time and space. There, they dwell eternally in the direct presence of God. In that sense, Dante's progression up Paradise is a true progression, for, with each succeeding level, he comes closer and closer to glimpsing the ultimate truth through eyes increasingly able to bear God's light. In *La Vita Nuova*, the young Dante, daunted by the radiance of Beatrice, approaches her at first through a number of "screen ladies," lesser beauties he can gaze on without trembling. Most of what Dante sees in *Paradiso* are but lovely screens preparing him for his final vision.

Having soared on his heavenly flight past the sphere of the moon, Dante comes next to Mercury, the planet which produces quicksilver (or mercury) in the Earth and which makes men mercurial seekers of profit (the words for "Mercury" and "merchant" in Greek are related etymologically). Here, within the influence of Mercury, lie the souls of men of ambition, who sought honor, fame, and an active life. While there, Dante meets the Emperor Justinian, the greatest emperor of the Eastern (Byzantine) empire who codified Roman law, built the magnificent Hagia Sophia in Constantinople, and came very close to wresting back the fallen Western empire from the barbarians. In *Paradiso*, Dante presents him as a Virgilean figure and allows him nearly a full canto to survey, in epic terms, the history of Rome from Aeneas to the Guelph/Ghibbeline strife of Dante's Italy.

From Mercury, Dante rises upward to Venus, the planet of love, which makes men amorous and women beautiful and produces copper in the Earth. Venus (Aphrodite, in Greek) was born off the Greek isle of Cyprus, and it is from Cyprus that we get our word copper. Here dwell the lovers who did not give in to carnality (as did Paolo and Francesca) but who felt *caritas* (Greek, *agape*). Among them, Dante recognizes Rahab the harlot (Josh 2), whose *caritas* for the Jewish spies moved her to protect them from death.

Next in the heavenly hierarchy should come the Earth, but Dante's geocentric model places the sun there instead. The sun is the great eye and mind of the cosmos; it produces gold in the Earth and makes men wise and generous. Within the sphere of the sun, Dante sees the great theologians (or doctors) of the church. They appear to Dante and Beatrice in two circles (or garlands) of light, with twelve souls forming each garland. Some of the better-known theologians and philosophers that form this august company of twenty-four elders are Boethius, Solomon, the Venerable Bede, Aquinas, Bonaventure, Nathan (2 Sam 12), John Chrysostom, and Anselm. In a breathtaking display of light and color, the two circles of saints spin, intertwine, and glow like twin rainbows. As they spin, one soul from each garland (Aquinas and Bonaventure) comes forward and speaks with Dante and Beatrice.

In an act of supreme *caritas* that is indicative of all the souls in Paradise, Aquinas (a Dominican) celebrates the life of St. Francis, while Bonaventure (a Franciscan) praises St. Dominic. After praising the other's founder, they then proceed to attack the corruption of their own order. The fury of their vituperation generally shocks the modern reader, but their twin jeremiads against the Dominicans and Franciscans represent but the first in a long line of increasingly shrill attacks on the moral decay of both the papacy and the monastic orders. Even the lovely and gentle Beatrice indulges at several points in bitter invective. Though such strident and acrimonious censure might appear to have no place in Heaven, we must remember that Dante intends his *Comedy* for a living audience of Christians who have grown all too accustomed to clerical corruption. By viewing this corruption from the pure and removed perspective of Heaven, Dante exposes for his readers the wretched state of a Catholic Church whose papacy, at the time when *Paradiso* was composed, had been forcibly removed from Rome and compelled to reside in Avignon, France.

Mars, the fifth heavenly sphere, named for the Roman god of war, produces iron in the Earth and makes men Mars-like, or martial. Whereas bad men who receive the influence of Mars become killers and mercenaries, those whose hearts are pure are guided by the same influence to become warriors of God and martyrs for the faith. Among those whom Dante sees in the sphere of Mars are Joshua, Judas Maccabaeus, Charlemagne, Roland, and Cacciaguida, Dante's great-great-grandfather who died fighting in the Crusades. As Dante watches with awe, the souls of the warriors form themselves into the image of a giant crucifix. The image remains for a moment, and then one soul rays out from the cross like a shooting star. It is Cacciaguida, who appears to Dante with all the gravity and filial wisdom of Anchises appearing to Aeneas in the underworld or Paulus appearing to his son, Scipio, in a dream. Indeed, just as Anchises (in *Aeneid* VI) prepares Aeneas for what awaits him in Italy, so Cacciaguida instructs Dante in the exact nature of his coming exile. Likewise, just as Paulus (in Cicero's "Dream of Scipio") calls upon his son to live the life of an ethical Roman, so Cacciaguida inspires Dante to the same by conjuring up for him an image of the lost golden age of Florence and comparing it with the moral entropy of Dante's day.

Jupiter, the sixth sphere, is the best of all the planets to be born under. It produces tin in the Earth, makes men jovial, and brings the halcyon days. Here Dante meets the just rulers, and here he witnesses a third display of heavenly lights that surpasses even the most spectacular laser show of the twenty-first century. Across the expanse of the sky, the souls of the just flash out, letter by letter, a message in Latin that translates "Love righteousness, ye that are judges of the earth." Each letter fades away, but the last letter of the message ("M") remains hanging in the air. Then, in a flurry of light and motion, the souls arrange themselves around the M, forming the image of a giant flying eagle. Finally, the beak of the eagle moves, and all the souls speak in unison. All who dwell in the eagle are great rulers, but the six who make up the eye and brow of the eagle are celebrated as the six noblest souls. Two of them are Jewish kings (David and Hezekiah), two are Christian (Constantine and William II of Sicily), and two are pagan (Trajan and Ripheus). Dante is shocked (as are we) to find two pre-Christian rulers dwelling in Heaven rather than in Hell with the virtuous pagans.

The explanation he is given marks the consummation of Dante's Christian humanist vision of the afterlife.

17

Dante's *Paradiso* II

A View from the Stars

Trajan, emperor of Rome from 98–117, was not only a good emperor himself but was succeeded by three of Rome's finest emperors: Hadrian, Antoninus Pius, and Marcus Aurelius. He was highly respected throughout late antiquity and the Middle Ages for his just and intelligent rule of the Empire. Ripheus, on the other hand, is a legendary figure who makes a single appearance in Book II of the *Aeneid*. Virgil records his death during the fall of Troy and comments that he was the most just of all the Trojans. As Trajan died a pagan and Ripheus died over a millennium before Christ neither should appear in Heaven, much less in the exalted sphere of Jupiter —and yet here they are in the same company as David and Constantine.

Dante, who shares the puzzlement of the reader, asks how this can be and is answered by the unified voice of the Eagle. Trajan *did* go to his grave a follower of the false gods of Rome, but he was called back to life 500 years later by the prayers of Pope Gregory the Great, whose love for the just monarch compelled him to pray for this unprecedented miracle. Although his return to the flesh was brief, it was long enough to allow Trajan to accept the grace of Christ and thus ascend to the heavenly sphere of Jupiter. This lovely legend of Gregory's *caritas* was well known in Dante's day. In contrast, the legend of Ripheus that the Eagle tells was invented (uncharacteristically) by Dante for his epic. Because of his just and noble character, Ripheus received from the God of the Bible a prophetic vision of Christ and was thus enabled, like the Jewish David and Hezekiah, to put his faith in the messianic promise of Christ to come. From the day of his vision, the Eagle relates with joy, Ripheus turned aside from the pagan creed in which he was suckled and, like a Gentile John the Baptist, called upon his fellow Trojans to repent and change their ways.

Just as Christians today struggle over the fate of the hypothetical man in the middle of Africa who lives and dies without the opportunity of hearing the gospel, so Dante himself struggled with the perennial issue of what happens to those who are never given the chance to accept Christ's sacrifice on their behalf. By recounting the tale of Trajan's miraculous salvation and inventing a similar, but even more miraculous tale for Ripheus, Dante assures his reader, and himself, of God's justice, mercy, and sovereignty. No one can say for sure whether this man or that man is in Heaven or Hell, not because salvation is universal, but because God's grace is a mystery that we cannot fathom.

The conversion stories of Trajan and Ripheus testify to God's amazing grace, but they also perform a second, related function within the greater Christian humanist vision of the *Comedy*. That God's truth could pierce through to the lives of these two virtuous pagans stands as a reminder of (and an analogy to) God's presence in the highest poetry, history, and philosophy of the pre-Christian, Greco-Roman world. Indeed, one of the things that Dante learns from the Eagle is that it is often the case that virtuous pagans (like the Magi) come closer to God's truth than lapsed or legalistic believers (like the Pharisees). Jesus himself says as much when he warns the Jewish cities of Chorazin, Bethsaida, and Capernaum that it will be more tolerable for the pagan cities of Tyre, Sidon, and Sodom on the day of judgment than it will be for them, for had those ancient bastions of Gentile vice seen the miraculous signs performed in Capernaum they would have repented in sackcloth and ashes (Matt 11:20–24).

Celestial Perspective

Having learned all that God intended him to learn from the Eagle, Dante soars upward to the seventh sphere of Saturn. In sharp contrast to the jovial influence of Jupiter (Jove is an alternate name for Jupiter), the saturnine influence of Saturn produces lead in the Earth, causes disasters and plagues, and makes men heavy with melancholy. At least that is what it does to those who receive its influence in a negative way. The same celestial influence that makes bad men sullen and sarcastic transforms good men into the great mystics of the faith.

As Dante approaches Saturn, he sees a giant ladder stretching upward to the Empyrean. In constructing this ladder of divine contemplation, Dante clearly had in mind Jacob's dream (Gen 28:12), in which he saw a ladder extending from Earth to Heaven and the angels of God ascending and descending upon it. Here, however, it is not angels, but the bright souls of the contemplatives who, moved by *caritas*, leave the timeless, spaceless realm of the Empyrean and glide down the golden rungs of the ladder to meet with Dante. So rapt are they in their ceaseless contemplation of God that only one soul among them actually descends close enough to Dante to speak with him. He is a Benedictine monk named Peter Damian, but he has little good to say of his order. Rather, like Aquinas and Bonaventure, he attacks the corruption of his order with righteous anger and wrath. In response, the souls that stand poised on the rungs of the ladder roar out in a deafening group shout. The thunderous peal of their shout makes Dante's head reel, and he runs to Beatrice for protection as a child would to its mother.

Then in a moment that is so extreme it is almost comic, Saint Benedict himself appears and adds his own fierce condemnation of the order he founded. There was a time, he tells Dante, when his monks sought to ascend the rising path of Jacob's ladder, but now they have grown fat, lazy, greedy, and carnal. It is as if a Platonic philosopher who devoted his life to achieving a vision of the Forms were to abandon his search and embrace the shadows around him as the ultimate reality. Good beginnings, it seems, do not ensure good endings. What began as a commitment to draw near to God has given way to moral entropy and decay. They have traded in the Beatific Vision for gluttony, sloth, avarice, and lust.

Like the apocryphal books of Daniel and Revelation, Dante's *Comedy* is, in one sense, a cryptic and veiled—at times not so veiled—attack on the corruption of his day. Dante realized, as did Virgil and Cicero before him, that the eternal states of Heaven and Hell could allow him a removed perspective from which to view and critique the politics and religion of his age. In fact, in his meeting with Cacciaguida, Dante is instructed to spare no punches in his attack on corruption; only if he tells the unvarnished truth will his poem live forever. Dante's job as poet-prophet of the after-life demands that he tell the whole vision, that he not shy away from the evil men do, even when those men live in monasteries or conduct masses. In an interesting inversion of Revelation 10:9–10, Dante claims that if he completes his task properly, his epic poem will be bitter to the tongue but sweet to the stomach. Indeed, the exiled poet even dares to hope that he will someday return to Florence in triumph and be crowned with laurel for his accomplishments.

His meeting with the contemplatives at an end, Dante and Beatrice blaze across the sky like shooting stars. Their destination is the eighth sphere of the fixed stars (*stellatum* in Latin) where the constellations are hung in all their pristine and changeless beauty. With each succeeding level their ascent has been increasing in velocity; now, despite the millions of miles that separate Saturn from the fixed stars, Dante and Beatrice bridge the distance in a flash. On his way up, Dante, in a wonderful sci-fi fantasy moment, passes the constellation Gemini, under which he was born and to whose influence he partly owed his poetic genius. As he soars on toward his spiritual second birth, he hails Gemini and asks its aid for the epic task that awaits his return to Earth.

Though Dante has kept his eyes pointed Heavenward through most of his journey, Beatrice now calls on him to pause in the air and look back down on the universe below. Ever obedient to the wishes of Beatrice, Dante casts a backward glance on the vastness of space, on the seven spheres, and on the Earth, which now seems to him—as it did to Scipio in Cicero's "Dream"—a small, insignificant pebble lost in space. Forgetting for a moment his anger and invective, Dante dubs this dot in the cosmos "the dusty little threshing ground / that make us ravenous for our mad sins" (XXII.152–53). This dizzying vision of the smallness of Earth and her problems in the face of God's vast kingdom is one that will stay with Dante throughout his long, bitter exile, reminding him that his true citizenship is not below but above.

Celestial Hierarchies

During his sojourn among the fixed stars, Dante witnesses yet another celestial light and laser show. This time what he sees is a vision of the Triumph of Christ, of all those souls for whom he died and on whom his radiance shines as the sun shines on the Earth. Though the vision makes him swoon, it also so strengthens his eyes that he is finally able to look full on Beatrice's smile. The beauty of it is beyond the power of words to express, but Dante's baptized eyes can now throw off all screens and gaze directly on the most famous smile in the history of literature. Beatrice is overjoyed by Dante's progress, and she instructs him to look back at the Garden of Christ. But the stages of illumination are not so easily won. His eyes still lacking in the necessary purity, Dante, even now, cannot look on the Garden until Christ removes his direct radiance. He is, however, able to glimpse the new Eve of this greater Garden: the Virgin Mary, around whom spins in eternal love the messenger of the Annunciation, the Archangel Gabriel.

Strengthened further by this vision of the Mother of God, Dante is now ready to endure a very different kind of test. Like a young Catholic boy learning his catechism, Dante is "grilled" in quick succession on the exact nature and quality of the three theological virtues (faith, hope, and love).

As daunting as this test is for the nervous poet, it is rendered even more so by the fact that his catechizers are Peter (the apostle of faith), James (the apostle of hope), and John (the apostle of love). These three apostles, who made up the inner circle of Jesus' disciples (Mark 5:37; 9:2; 14:33), were considered by medievals to embody each of the virtues and, as such, they make excellent, if daunting teachers. The scholastic intricacies of the triple Socratic dialogue that ensues between Dante and Peter, James, and John do not here concern us, but it is worth noting that Dante bases his answers *both* on Scripture and on reason.

After passing the three tests, Dante is given the enviable opportunity to meet and question none other than Adam. From Adam he learns the humbling news that he and his wife only lasted six hours in Eden, that the true nature of their primal sin was disobedience, and that the original, God-given language that he spoke had degenerated long before the sin of Babel caused the tongues of men to be divided. Dante's interview with Adam at an end, Peter returns and, like Benedict attacking the order he founded, issues one final denunciation of the papacy that he himself fathered. From this point on, the invective cools, not because Dante's righteous anger disappears, but because the Earth becomes just too insignificant to worry about.

The ninth and final sphere to which Dante and Beatrice ascend before crossing over into the qualitatively different realm of the Empyrean is that of the *Primum Mobile*. Latin for "prime (or first) mover," the *Primum Mobile* should not be confused with God, who, in an Aristotelian formulation that was adopted by the church, is the Unmoved Mover. The *Primum Mobile* is the fastest of all the spheres and is the one that gives all the others their motion; by its movement of the stars and planets, it is also responsible for establishing time.

Here, in the highest sphere, Dante has a vision of the nine hierarchies of angels that spin, out of love, about their Creator. In descending order the angelic hierarchies, each of which corresponds to one of the nine spheres, are as follows: Seraphim, Cherubim, Thrones, Dominations, Virtues, Powers, Principalities, Archangels, and Angels. Though all the angelic orders praise God, only the lower three commune with man, carrying messages (like the one carried by Gabriel) between the heavenly and earthly realms. More than mere inhabitants of their appropriate sphere, each angel functions as the intelligence of its sphere, causing it to spin and to sing. (Together, the singing of the nine intelligences produces the music of the spheres.) Only the Earth neither sings nor spins, for only the Earth lacks an angelic intelligence—though, as alluded to earlier, Dante suggests (in *Inferno* VII) that Dame Fortune *is* the intelligence of Earth. Rather than cause the Earth to spin around God, the spinning of Fortune's wheel causes nations and individuals to rise and fall in a ceaseless parade of human folly.

In describing the nine angelic hierarchies, Dante looked not to passages from the Bible—which says little about the orders of angels, though it does make mention of the two lowest and two highest orders—but on a highly influential book (*Celestial Hierarchies*) thought to have been written by a first-century Athenian named Dionysius, whom Paul converted to the faith when he preached in Athens (Acts 17:34) and who served as the first Bishop of that renowned city. It was later discovered that the author was not actually Dionysius the Areopagite (known more commonly by the French version of his name, Denys) but a much later writer, often now referred to (understandably) as Pseudo-Dionysius. After mentioning Dionysius by name (XXVIII.130), Beatrice adds that Gregory the Great later modified Dionysius's hierarchies, but did so incorrectly. Gregory's innocent error, however, does not provoke a fresh invective. Rather, Beatrice tells Dante—with a winsome smile, I suspect—that the moment Gregory reached Heaven and realized his error, he broke into laughter. Heaven is a place of forgiveness and joy, and there are even numerous points in *Paradiso* where Dante himself is moved by what he sees to correct some of his own philosophical and theological errors from his earlier writings. There is no place for pride in Paradise, only goodness, truth, and beauty.

The Mystic Rose

Their journey through the nine spheres complete, Dante and Beatrice ascend at last to the Empyrean. To prepare his eyes for the even greater wonders and glories of the true Heaven, Dante stoops down and drinks from a river of light. His sight clarified by the light, he is finally ready to see the true eternal state of the blessed. The souls he has encountered thus far, we must remember, were only manifestations meant to assist his ignorance. In reality, all the souls dwell in the direct presence of God, grouped around him in an intricate pattern that resembles both a giant stadium with tiers on tiers of rows and a rose window in a cathedral that spirals outward in concentric circles. Within this mystic rose, whose petals never fade or fall, each soul has an assigned station, which it inhabits with complete joy and contentment. On one side of the rose rest all those who trusted in the prophecies of Christ to come (the righteous Jews); on the other side rest all those Christians who trusted in Christ incarnate. The former side is full, but the latter is still dotted with empty seats. When all of those seats are filled, Purgatory will be destroyed, and the end of the world will come. While God inhabits the center of the rose and the souls of the blessed fill the petals, the angels, like a swarm of bees, fly back and forth in a ceaseless exchange of love and grace.

Dante is so moved by the vision of the mystic rose that he turns to share it with Beatrice, but Beatrice, like Virgil before her, has departed. In a flash, she has returned to her station in the mystic rose. This time, however, Dante feels no sorrow, for, though she is now millions of miles away, Dante sees her with perfect clarity. In the purity of the air of Heaven, the tyranny of space is shattered. Dante, aglow with *caritas*, hails her for braving Hell to release him from his bondage to sin. In response, Beatrice smiles at him one last time, then turns her face to stare into the face of God. Her mission completed, she has returned to eternal contemplation of the Beatific Vision.

As Virgil was replaced by Beatrice, so Beatrice is herself replaced by one final guide: Saint Bernard, a famous scholar and defender of orthodoxy whose contemplative side included a passionate devotion to Mary. In a prayer that is as simple as it is profound, Bernard first praises the Virgin for being the turning point of God's salvation history, then petitions her to strengthen Dante's eyes that he may gaze in full upon the Triune God, and then beseeches her to protect Dante lest the vision drive him mad or puff him up with pride. Mary, like Beatrice before her, smiles upon Bernard with eyes of love and then turns her gaze back to God.

Meanwhile, as Dante prepares to receive, and also to describe, his vision of God, he turns suddenly, and shockingly, toward a type of metaphoric language that is more erotic than philosophical: "And I, who neared the goal of all my nature, / felt my soul, at the climax of its yearning, / suddenly, as it ought, grow calm with rapture" (XXXIII.46–48). Dante's use here of sexual imagery may at first seem odd, but nearly all the great Christian mystics—from St. John of the Cross to Theresa of Avila to Julian of Norwich—have resorted to such language and imagery to describe their intimate encounters with God. In Christian theology, it must be remembered, the church is referred to collectively as the bride of Christ, and the destiny of the bride is to be married eternally to Christ the bridegroom. In fact, St. Paul himself speaks of the two-into-one nature of marriage and sexuality as a foreshadowing of the Great Marriage of Christ and the church (Eph 5:31–32).

Dante tries to find the right words to explain his intimate union with the Godhead, but his memory is ravished by the sight and swoons away. He feels like a man who has had a powerful dream, but then wakes to find that the details have slipped away, leaving behind only the emotions associated with them; or again, like footsteps in the snow that fade in the light of the sun; or yet again, alluding one last time to Virgil's *Aeneid*, like the prophetic leaves of the Sibyl, which blow away on the wind when the door to her cave is thrown open. Well, not exactly the last time, for several lines later, Dante returns to Virgil's image of the Sibylline leaves to describe the complete unity that rests within God alone. As he grows worthier to see, Dante understands how God "conceives / all things in a single volume bound by Love / of which the universe is the scattered leaves" (XXXIII.85–87).

In the inferno, the circle is used to represent futility; in Heaven, it represents eternal perfection. Not surprisingly, therefore, the Triune God manifests himself to Dante as three circles that differ in color but share the same circumference: the second circle (Christ) comes out of the first (God the Father), while the third (the Holy Spirit) is a pure fire breathed equally by the other two. Within the second circle, Dante perceives both the image of God and of man. He yearns to understand this mystery (the incarnation), and how he fits into it, but he cannot; then, suddenly, in a flash of light that cleaves his mind, the answer to the mystery is revealed to him.

But Dante does not share with us this surpassing, and highly personal, revelation; to know that, we must go on our own journey to the stars.

18

Milton's *Paradise Lost* I

Better to Reign in Hell

Homer, Virgil, Dante . . . and then comes Milton. But with a twist. Virgil's *Aeneid* is inconceivable without Homer's *Iliad* and *Odyssey*. Likewise, Dante's *Divine Comedy* is inconceivable without the previous epics of Homer and Virgil. But with Milton's *Paradise Lost*, an odd, and to my mind disturbing, shift occurs in the epic sequence. True, *Paradise Lost* is inconceivable apart from the *Iliad*, *Odyssey*, and *Aeneid*, but the same cannot be said for the *Divine Comedy*. Indeed, though I am more than willing to be challenged on this point, I would argue there is not a single *clear, unambiguous* tribute or reference to the *Commedia* in the twelve books of Milton's epic. Now, since Milton borrows from the same Greco-Roman and biblical sources as Dante, numerous *links* exist between Dante and Milton's depictions of Heaven and Hell: links that I will take pains to enumerate and interpret over the course of the next two chapters. But links and poetic influence are very different things.

J. R. R. Tolkien often insisted, sometimes irascibly, that his *Lord of the Rings* owed nothing to Wagner's Ring Cycle. Many fans of Tolkien who are also fans of Wagner, and who thus see the many obvious parallels between the two works, will sometimes dismiss Tolkien's protestations—*unless* they are also familiar with the *Nibelungenlied*, the *Volsunga Saga*, and the *Eddas* (works that provided source material for *both* the Ring Cycle and the *Lord of the Rings*). Just as Tolkien did not need to listen to Wagner to access the Scandinavian legends that underlie portions of his epic fantasy, so Milton did not need to read Dante to access the Greco-Roman, Judeo-Christian heritage that gives structure and density to both of their epics.

The analogy is, I think, an accurate one, but it has one flaw. Though Tolkien *may* have been telling the truth when he disclaimed knowledge of the Ring Cycle, Milton—who devoted five years of his life to reading through the vast legacy of European literature—was well acquainted with Dante's journey through Hell, Purgatory, and Heaven. Why then did Milton go to such pains to dissociate his epic from that of Dante? I would suggest three reasons: 1) as a self-consciously ambitious poet, Milton wanted to present himself (and England) as the true heir to Virgil (and the Augustan Age of Rome); 2) as a Protestant of Puritan convictions, Milton wanted to distance himself from the Catholic vision and theology of Dante; 3) as a would-be molder of late Renaissance mores whose worldview was far closer to that of the High Middle Ages than he might have liked to admit, Milton sought to wrest from Dante (and thus Aquinas as well) the right to define and shape the dialogue between humanism and Christianity, Athens and Jerusalem, Platonism and the creeds of the church.

Whichever of these reasons was uppermost in Milton's mind—and I do believe that all three played at least some role in the construction of *Paradise Lost*—the fact remains that Milton's epic was as theologically, philosophically, and aesthetically galvanizing in the seventeenth century, not to mention the three centuries that would follow it, as Dante's was in the fourteenth. Even today, many devout Protestants who know their Bibles well would be shocked to discover how much their views of Heaven and Hell, devils and angels rest not on Scripture but on *Paradise Lost*—which I sometimes like to refer to, only half facetiously, as the sixty-seventh book of the Bible.

Myself Am Hell

By combining scattered biblical references with his own fertile imagination and his exhaustive knowledge of all previous sacred and secular portrayals of Heaven and Hell, Milton (1608–74) succeeded in doing what no poet before him had even attempted. He fashioned a detailed, highly dramatic, theologically profound account of a cosmic event that the Bible only hints at in an obscure, allusive manner: Satan's rebellion against God and his fall from Heaven.

In Milton's telling, Satan begins as a magnificent archangel (Lucifer, the angel of light) who dwells in the presence of God. But evil is soon found in him. When God the Father appoints the Son (Christ) as Lord over all and orders all knees to bow to him, Satan refuses. Rather than take second place to God and Christ, Satan rebels and succeeds in seducing one third of the angels to his cause. For a while, Satan holds the good angels at bay—partly by using what may best be described as celestial cannons—but his victory is short lived. Christ himself enters the battle and, using less than half his power, drives the rebels back to the gates of Heaven. In fear they cast *themselves* out of Heaven and fall for nine days.

Hell is terrified by the spectacle of the falling angels and seeks to flee, but her foundations are sunk too deep into the Earth for her to move. In the end, she is forced to receive Satan and his unfaithful crew: "Hell at last / Yawning received them whole, and on them closed, / Hell their fit habitation fraught with fire / Unquenchable, the house of woe and pain" (VI.874–77).[1] In Plato's Myth of Er (see chapter 5), when a tyrant tries to leave the underworld, the cavernous mouth of Hell shakes and the sinner is tortured and cast into Tartarus. So here, the fallen angels (now devils) are swallowed whole by the abyss and descend to the lowest pit of Hell: which Milton, in keeping with both the classical tradition and 2 Peter 2:4 (see chapter 2), identifies as Tartarus. Though Milton makes no direct reference to the sign that stands over the entrance to Dante's inferno ("Abandon all hope, ye who enter here"), he makes it clear that the sorrow, pain, and despair of Hell are as eternal and unquenchable as the fire.

In the opening scene of *Paradise Lost*, Milton gives a fuller description of Tartarus that effortlessly weaves details from Homer, Plato, Virgil, and the parables of Jesus. It is a place devoid of peace, rest, and hope:

> A dungeon horrible, on all sides round
>
> As one great furnace flamed, yet from those flames
>
> No light, but rather darkness visible
>
> Served only to discover sights of woe,
>
> Regions of sorrow, doleful shades, where peace
>
> And rest can never dwell, hope never comes
>
> That comes to all; but torture without end
>
> Still urges, and a fiery deluge, fed
>
> With ever-burning sulphur unconsumed. (I.61–69)

In chapter 13, I argued that the fact that the Gospels present us with two mutually exclusive images of Hell (darkness and fire) suggests that such descriptions cannot be taken in a purely literal fashion. Milton, with great poetic flair, "solves" this paradox through one of his most memorable oxymorons: "darkness visible." In Milton's vision of Hell, the "ever-burning

---

1. Milton, *Paradise Lost*, edited by Scott Elledge, 161; further references will be given in the text by book and line numbers.

sulphur" rages like a "great furnace," but those flames give off "no light." Sharing Dante's Augustinian understanding of sin as negation, Milton presents the fires of Hell as a perversion of the burning bush (Exod 3): both burn without burning out; however, whereas the latter brings the light of revelation to Moses and the light of freedom to the children of Israel, the former gives neither illumination nor release from bondage.

Once the full nature of their defeat and imprisonment becomes plain to Satan, he calls for a counsel of demons over which he presides like an Eastern potentate. Scorning the horrors of his prison, Satan announces that he does not repent his actions and that he will never yield to God's authority. Like Dante's sinners, Satan feels neither remorse nor shame, only a sense of injured merit. Indeed, in what is surely the best known line from the epic, the defeated Satan boldly proclaims his tragic choice: "Better to reign in Hell, than serve in heav'n" (I.263). If the only alternative to Hell is submission to God, Satan will embrace the sufferings of Hell, where at least he can exert unfettered his infernal will to power. As prideful as he is unyielding, Milton's Satan is supremely defined by his utter refusal to serve.

Unwilling to repent and heal his broken relationship with his Creator, Satan chooses the course of further torment and degradation, taking a perverse joy in the fact that their prison lies far removed from the presence of God. Indeed, rather than pine for Heaven, the devils choose to create their own realm and kingdom in Hell: an "infernal world" where they can "reign secure" (I.251, 261). Though this may sound like a counsel of despair, Satan takes refuge in his belief that "The mind is its own place, and in itself / Can make a heav'n of Hell, a Hell of heav'n" (I.254–5). That is to say, Satan dismisses the disjunction between the bliss of Heaven and the misery of Hell by reducing it to a difference in point-of-view. Hell, he attempts to convince himself is not intrinsically horrible; it is only his perceptions of Hell and Heaven that make the former seem horrible and the latter seem glorious. He is wrong. Later, as Satan, newly escaped from Hell, approaches Eden, Milton comments that the fallen archangel has not truly freed himself from the grip of Tartarus: "For within him Hell / He brings, and round about him, nor from Hell / One step no more than from himself can fly / By change of place" (IV.20–23). No matter how far he may fly, Satan cannot escape the Hell that is within him. Though Milton's Hell is a real place of torment, the greater Hell is the one that dwells in the twisted and perverse soul of Satan and his minions. In fact, only moments later, Satan himself realizes the terrible truth of his existential imprisonment and exclaims: "Which way I fly is Hell; myself am Hell" (IV.75). Like Dante before him, Milton was a poet who understood not only the philosophy and theology of Hell, but the psychology of sin that undergirds it.

Pandemonium

As for his depiction of Satan's fellow demons, Milton, whether consciously or not, also parallels Dante's powerfully Christian humanist vision of Hell and its inhabitants. In an epic simile that also functions as an allegory, Milton compares the devils to the Titans who rebelled against Jove (Zeus). By making this connection, neither Milton nor Dante mean to suggest that there was "really" a group of Titans who attempted to overthrow the Olympians; rather, their intent is to present the pagan myth as a shadow of—and a pointer to—the Christian truth. Milton, however, develops and expands the connection by linking his devils not only to the Titans of Greek mythology but to the pagan deities of the Canaanites, Philistines, Babylonians, and Egyptians. Eventually, Milton makes clear, Satan's cohorts will invade the Earth and take on the names of Belial, Moloch, Beelzebub, Ashtaroth, Osiris, and Mammon. In fact, to drive the connection home, Milton, in an epic anachronism, refers to his demons by those very names.

Seizing the theological and aesthetic middle ground between the iconoclastic, pagan-aversive zeal of his fellow Puritans and the more epicurean, Greco-Roman orientation of Renaissance Catholic and Anglo-Catholic poets and artists, Milton presents the Greek deities as the *least* vicious of the lot. That is to say, whereas Milton exposes the pagan gods of the Middle East as evil to the core, he depicts his Olympian gods as dwelling in the cold middle air in a moral state that is more passively stoic than actively evil. On the one hand, the classical, *Aeneid*-loving Milton cannot resist linking his epic tale to those of Homer and Virgil; on the other, Milton the Puritan revolutionary must ensure that all false gods be revealed as demons. Indeed, to accommodate both sides of his religious and poetic psyche, Milton often provides his readers with a "true" Christian reading of an erring Greek fable.

This desire to find a middle ground also manifests itself in Milton's controversial choice to allow his devils some degree of tragic grandeur. At the beginning of the epic, Satan is described as being huge in form and as possessing, though in eclipse, some of his original glory. His demons also show great, Aeneas-like initiative in founding and constructing their capitol city of Pandemonium (Milton's own coinage; it means "all devils"). However, Milton does not, contrary to popular opinion (see chapter 21), allow his devils to retain their initial grandeur. At the very moment that the devils, in false glory, enter Pandemonium, they are transformed from Titans to dwarves. Satan himself, though given some qualities of the epic hero, is increasingly shown to be wrathful, envious, and proud; morally speaking, the Titanic rebel is a pygmy.

Having gathered in court, the devils debate their next course of action. Their speeches are masterpieces of sophistry and self-delusion that reveal how sin corrupts both our passions and our reason. In the end they decide that if they cannot overthrow God, they can at least pervert his goodness and his future plans. They have heard rumors of God's new creation (man) and decide to sabotage it as a way of striking back at God. To accomplish their petty, spiteful plan, they send Satan on an epic journey: not *into* Hell (like Odysseus, Aeneas, and Dante), but *out* of Hell to God's newly created Earth.

As he leaves, Satan instructs his devils to make a thorough search of Hell: a command that allows Milton to provide readers with a condensed tour of the underworld that echoes Homer and Plato, Virgil and Dante. True to the tradition, Milton catalogs the

> four infernal rivers that disgorge
> Into the burning lake their baleful streams:
> Abhorred Styx the flood of deadly hate,
> Sad Acheron of sorrow, black and deep;
> Cocytus, named of lamentation loud
> Heard on the rueful stream; fierce Phlegethon
> Whose waves of torrent fire inflame with rage. (II.575–81)

To the four standard rivers of Hell, Milton adds Lethe, the river of forgetfulness, but gives it, as did Dante before him, a fresh, Christian inflection. In Plato and Virgil, souls drink from Lethe before being reborn in new bodies. Reincarnation being incompatible with Christian theology, poets like Dante and Milton are forced to find a new use for the river. In Dante's restored Eden, the blessed souls drink from Lethe so that they may forget even the memory of sin; in Milton's Hell, the torment of the damned is increased by *not* allowing them to drink from Lethe—even one drop of which would cause them "to lose / In sweet forgetfulness all pain and woe" (II.607–8).

On either side of Lethe lie two fields where sinners are punished: the one is a "frozen continent" of snow and ice; the other burns with fire. While avoiding a direct reference to Dante's *Inferno*, Milton makes it clear that God uses both fire and ice to punish—and embody the true nature of— malice and treachery. The Furies ferry the damned over the river where they

> feel by turns the bitter change
> Of fierce extremes, extremes by chance more fierce,
> From beds of raging fire to starve in ice
> Their soft ethereal warmth, and there to pine

Immovable, infixed, and frozen round,
Periods of time, thence hurried back to fire. (II.598–603).

Each time they cross the river, they long to drink from Lethe but are prevented by Medusa. Like the great archetypal sinner, Tantalus, they can never reach the water they yearn for. The fallen angels, like the fallen humans, seek desperately to find a pleasant region of Hell, but they too are unsuccessful. For Hell, explains Milton in somber words of warning, is

A universe of death, which God by curse
Created evil, for evil only good,
Where all life dies, death lives, and nature breeds,
Perverse, all monstrous, all prodigious things,
Abominable, inutterable, and worse
Than fables yet have feigned, or fear conceived. (II.622–27)

The true and full nature of Hell—grotesque, twisted, unspeakable—is worse than any mortal has ever conceived in a nightmare or any poet has ever imagined in verse: even, so Milton seems to imply, the great Dante Alighieri!

Satan, Sin, and Death

Meanwhile, Satan proceeds to the massive gates of Hell, which are perpetually guarded by two fearsome porters: Sin and Death. In what is surely the most eerily original episode in *Paradise Lost* (one worthy of Dante at his best), Milton gives an account of the birth of Sin and Death that is so tangible and vivid that it seems more real than allegorical. In a perversion of the birth of Athena (goddess of wisdom) out of the head of Zeus, Sin bursts full-grown out of Satan's head as he plans his conspiracy against God. But the horror does not cease there. Satan, filled with lust for the beauty of Sin, rapes his own daughter, who conceives in her incestuous womb the abhorred offspring of Satan and Sin: Death. She will, however, take no joy from the birth; when her time arrives, Death literally tears itself out of her, permanently misshaping her lower body in the process. No sooner is he out of the womb than Death turns against its mother and rapes her as well. This time she gives birth to a legion of vicious dogs that continually dive inside of her to gnaw on her bowels and then burst out of her womb anew.

Out of lustful loyalty to her father, and a shared hatred of God, Sin and Death open the gates and allow Satan to escape from his infernal prison. The action is a momentous one, for, once opened, the gates can never be shut again. Though Milton does not say it directly, the incident may be interpreted as a perversion of the harrowing of Hell, the very incident that allowed Dante to enter Hell while still in his mortal body.

Set free from Tartarus, Satan journeys through regions of Chaos on the long way to Earth. For Milton, as for Plato and Dante, God is a God of order and harmony; he is, however, absent in the nether regions of the Earth, and, in his absence, all form and pattern collapse into discord and chaos. In this misty region of anarchy, the four elements (earth, air, fire, and water) and their opposing qualities (hot and cold, moist and dry) war with each other in perpetual confusion. As the Lord of Chaos hates God as much as Satan, the two villains make a pact, thus allowing Satan to proceed to Earth, where he successfully tempts Eve to eat of the apple.

When the evil deed is done, Sin, who still guards the gates of Hell, feels her power swelling. She calls on Death and the two build a causeway from Hell to Earth. Milton, borrowing an image from Herodotus's epic history of the Persian War, compares the causeway to the bridge over the Hellespont that the tyrant Xerxes built to facilitate his invasion of Greece. As before, Satan is consistently linked to Oriental despots whose lust for power and contempt for human dignity stand as a perpetual threat to Western freedom and democracy.

Milton makes it clear that this causeway is the wide road that leads to destruction that Jesus warns against in the Sermon on the Mount (Matt 7:13–14); because of it, Hell and our world become "one realm, one continent / Of easy thoroughfare" (X.392–93). Satan commands Sin and Death to cross the causeway and stake out their territory on Earth. He then returns to Pandemonium, assembles the devils, and makes a rousing speech of his successful seduction of Eve. He expects a thunderous applause but is greeted only by a hiss, for all the devils have been transformed into snakes; in true Dantean fashion, the devils become on the outside what they already are within. Satan too is transformed first into a monstrous serpent and then into a dragon.

To increase the anguish of the demons, God causes a tree to grow in Hell that is ripe with fruit. The serpents, who have now been divested of all their former glory, swarm around the tree and partake of its fruit. But their gluttonous behavior does nothing to assuage their hunger and thirst: for the fruit, like that which tempted Eve, looks beautiful on the outside but tastes like dust and ashes. And yet, though the fruit is bitter, the serpents, in their delusion, continue to eat it. In a final act of divine justice, God decrees that once a year the devils must reenact this humiliating ritual; Sin and Death, in contrast, are allowed free reign on Earth to "lick up the draff and filth" (X.630) of the now-corrupted Earth.

19

Milton's *Paradise Lost* II

Better to Serve in Heaven

While on his journey from Hell to Earth, Satan passes through the shadowy region of limbo. But Milton's limbo—which, at this point in time, is empty—bares only the slightest resemblance to that of Dante. Dante's Catholic limbo holds the virtuous pagans, who, though they lack hope, are afforded some dignity; Milton's Protestant limbo is a Limbo of Vanity, a "Paradise of Fools" (III.496). Here on this insubstantial "windy sea of land" (III.440) are blown "Both all things vain, and all who in vain things / Built their fond hopes of glory or lasting fame, / Or happiness in this or th' other life" (III.448–50). Those who sought only an earthly reward and the praise of men, who devoted themselves only to superstitions and empty zeal, end up here in this Dantean land of wasted gifts, broken dreams, and missed opportunities.

During his journey through Hades, Aeneas sees an ancient elm under whose leaves cling numberless false dreams. Milton's limbo is similarly a place of great sadness and quiet despair. A sort-of fusion of Dante's limbo and vestibule (where dwell the damned souls of the opportunists), Milton's limbo is populated by those whose works proved futile, who refused to engage with life or God in any real or profitable way. It is in limbo—and not, Milton makes clear, in the circle of the fickle moon—that the makers of all the "abortive" and "monstrous" works of man find their final resting place: the proud giants of Genesis 6, sprung from the unnatural mingling of mortals and angels; the arrogant builders of the Tower of Babel, whose unholy aspirations brought only ruin and division; pompous, passionless philosophers like Empedocles who foolishly took their own lives as a road to godhood.

Here also are those of the Catholic Church whom the Protestant Milton considered to have devoted their lives to folly: not only pilgrims whose visits to the Holy Land brought them closer to the dead (but not the risen) Christ, but friars of the Carmelite, Franciscan, and Dominican orders whose isolation and asceticism drew them away from, rather than closer to, the true God of the Bible. In a disturbing passage, Milton imagines members of these three orders proceeding to the very gate of St. Peter, only to be blown out of Heaven along with their cowls, relics, indulgences, and papal bulls. Unlike Dante, who soundly criticizes the corruption of the medieval monastic orders as a way of encouraging renewal, Milton rejects them out of hand as worthless and vain.

Though I myself share Milton's low Protestant orientation and theology, I must confess that his anti-Catholicism (partly understandable given the religious controversies of his day) has the effect of lessening the scope of his epic. Despite the overwhelming power of its poetic imagery and its ringing affirmation of human free will, *Paradise Lost* somehow lacks the rich humanism and *joie de vivre* of the *Commedia*. Ironically, though Milton is more cautious than Dante about allowing pagan elements into his Christian worldview, it is Milton, and not Dante, who ultimately falls prey to the cold, fatalistic stoicism of Virgil. Critics continue to debate whether Shakespeare was raised Protestant or Catholic, but the fact remains that his comedies and romances are strongly Catholic in spirit—a spirit they share with the *Commedia* and *Canterbury Tales* but not with *Paradise Lost*. By "Catholic spirit," I refer to a strongly incarnational, sacramental vision that holds in creative tension man's glorification and degradation, that embraces fully both word and image, and that finds traces of God's grandeur, holiness, and grace in the meanest of earthly objects. Inasmuch as it falls short of that vision, *Paradise Lost*, to my mind at least, is less satisfying than the *Commedia*.

Still, there are compensations, particularly in the depth and breadth of Milton's cosmology.

This Pendant World

As he leaves limbo, Satan sees again the universe through which he fell: a universe that combines the best of classical, medieval, and renaissance thought. At the age of thirty, Milton traveled through Florence, where he met the great Galileo—old, blind, and under (house) arrest, as Milton himself would one day be. The poet of *Paradise Lost* was well versed in the Florentine's controversial astronomical theories and could have done for Galileo's heliocentric model what Dante had done for Ptolemy's geocentric one. He chose instead to create an ordered, sympathetic universe that could stand, and that *continues* to stand, as a scientific, theological, philosophical, and aesthetic nexus between the ancient and modern world.

In fact, when the still unfallen Adam asks the angel Raphael a number of searching questions about the nature and construction of the universe, he receives this reply:

> To ask or search I blame thee not, for heav'n
> Is as the book of God before thee set,
> Wherein to read his wondrous works, and learn
> His seasons, hours, or days, or months, or years:
> This to attain, whether heav'n move or earth,
> Imports not, if thou reckon right; the rest
> From man or angel the great Architect
> Did wisely to conceal, and not divulge
> His secrets to be scanned by them who ought
> Rather admire. (VIII.66–75)

Christian theology—*both* Catholic and Protestant, medieval and renaissance—has always understood that God speaks to us through two books: the book of his Word (the Bible and Christ himself), through which comes God's direct or special revelation, and the book of nature, through which comes his indirect or general revelation. (Galileo famously remarked that the former tells us how to go to Heaven, while the latter tells us how the heavens go.) God has so equipped us that we naturally yearn to read the chapters and verses of his wondrous creation; however, as Raphael warns Adam, we must not let our inquisitiveness get the best of us. The Bible tells us all that we need to know for salvation, but it is does not invite us to unpack God's majesty or to unweave the paradoxes of the Trinity and the incarnation. Even so, though God gave us eyes and minds to study the stars, he did not mean for us to so codify and systematize the heavens as to rob them of their mystery. Just as the Bible should impel us to worship, rather than "figure out" God, so the heavens, properly understood, should provoke in us something greater than mere intellectual curiosity: namely, admiration, thanksgiving, and awe.

In the passage quoted above, Raphael diplomatically refuses to reveal to Adam whether the Earth remains still while the heavens move, or whether (as Galileo taught) it is the Earth that moves through the heavens.

A few lines later, Raphael scolds Adam and his astronomical heirs for taking for claiming that because the Earth is smaller and less bright than the sun, it must therefore be of less value. Our often vain arguments about the shape and motion of the stars, Raphael boldly suggests, provoke laughter in the Creator who is amused by our squabbles over heavenly bodies that dance millions of miles above our heads. That is not to say that Raphael discourages Adam and his human descendants from studying the stars. Rather, he reminds him (and us) that our attempts to fashion a systematic cosmology are but so many attempts to "save appearances" (VIII.82)—to make sense of the information we receive through our eyes. Over the next three centuries, the heirs of Galileo would move away from the classical, medieval, and (mostly) renaissance attempt to save appearances and would posit that nature and the universe are what they are apart from our observations of them. Ironically, over the last three decades, quantum physicists have returned, in part, to the medieval view: arguing that our perceptions of nature actually alter nature. Dante and Milton would both have been pleased!

Although Raphael holds back from Adam full knowledge of how the heavens go, he does provide him with a detailed narrative of God's creation of the universe. According to Milton, Heaven and Earth came into being when God turned round his "golden compasses" (VII.225) through the primal chaos, setting a boundary within which divine harmony would rule. By first purging out the "black tartareous cold infernal dregs / Adverse to life" (VII.238–39), and then ordering what remains through a process of separation and discernment (light from dark, land from water, and so forth), God slowly gives shape to the cosmos. On the one hand, Milton's description of the stages of Creation mimics closely the six days of Genesis 1, which begins with the Spirit of God hovering over the primal waters and ends with a universe in which everything is in its proper place and sphere. On the other, Milton, tapping the overwhelming energy (I almost wrote "irresponsible energy") of Protestantism, boldly breaks from the orthodox Christian doctrine that God created the world *ex nihilo* ("out of nothing"). Milton rejects this teaching, favoring instead the Platonic (and generally pagan) view that posits God as an artist who creates by giving shape and form to undifferentiated matter—rather as people today make gingerbread men by pressing cookie cutters into raw, unformed dough.

Still, though Milton's rejection of *ex nihilo* creation threatens to move him out of the bounds of Christian orthodoxy, his position does little to disrupt the biblical purity of his epic. The problem, I would argue, is not that Milton favors the pagan view over the Christian, but that he simply does not understand the doctrine he rejects. Creation *ex nihilo* does not mean that

God created every object in our universe out of nothing. Quite the contrary! With the exception of verse 1, the first chapter of Genesis presents precisely the picture Milton incarnates in his poem: God as artist who shapes chaos into order. The doctrine of creation *ex nihilo* (which is suggested in Gen 1:1 and stated more clearly in Heb 11:3) merely affirms that in the beginning only the Triune God existed. Matter and God are not equally eternal. God *created* the matter, which he later *shaped* into the universe. This radical notion, that does not appear in any ancient book outside the Bible, was rejected by most scientists for the last two centuries . . . until the discovery of the Big Bang proved—as much as such things *can* be proved—that the Bible was right to posit a moment of creation at which matter and space came into being *out of nothing*.

As for the specific details of his universe, Milton, while careful not to come down firmly on either the geocentric or heliocentric side, does lay out his cosmological model in a fashion that cleaves quite closely to Dante's Ptolemaic universe. Milton retains the same nine spheres (the seven planets + the fixed stars + the *Primum Mobile*), but adds a tenth, crystalline sphere between the fixed stars and the *Primum Mobile* (III.482). He also adds a memorable detail that he borrows from Homer (*Iliad* VIII.18–29) and then Christianizes: attached to the floor of Heaven runs a golden chain, upon which hangs "this pendant world" (II.1052). In chapter 8, I noted that the root meaning of the word *kosmos* is "ornament," and that the ancients and medievals used that word, for they believed not only that the universe was the ornament of God but that it was therefore something we could love as we do all beautiful things. By referring to our universe as a "pendant world," Milton affirms his continuity with the poets and stargazers of the past.

Stairway to Heaven

As Satan continues his journey to Eden, he casts his gaze skyward, revealing yet another facet of Milton's aesthetic cosmology. In Genesis 28, Jacob is vouchsafed a vision of a ladder (or stairway) that stretches from Earth to Heaven and upon which the angels of God ascend and descend. During his airy flight, Satan sees this very stairway stretching down from Heaven. According to Dante's *Paradiso*, Jacob's ladder extends from Saturn to the Empyrean and is mounted by the great contemplatives of the faith; Milton characteristically omits any reference to Dante's ladder, fashioning instead his own unique reading of Jacob's vision. For Milton, the stairway Satan sees is the same stairway Lazarus will one day be carried up by angels (Luke 16:22) and alongside which Elijah will one day fly in his golden chariot (2

Kgs 2:11). Before the fall, we learn, the stairway was wide and stretched down to Paradise (Milton's name for the garden part of Eden); after the fall, it grew thinner and moved to the Promised Land. And all the while it grew thinner, Sin's causeway grew wider.

Although the stairway, which enables angels to pass back and forth between Heaven and Earth, is normally closed to devilish traffic, when Satan arrives, the stairway allows him entrance—less to facilitate his journey than to taunt him for his final impotence. Granted safe passage, Satan ascends the stairway to the sun; as he nears his goal, he casts a backward glance and gets a Dantean view of the stars. Though the vision provokes neither praise nor thanksgiving in his cold, proud heart, Satan is granted the privilege of watching the stars as they dance in harmony, producing days, months, and years. He is also allowed to glimpse the life-giving virtue of the sun that penetrates and vitalizes all things. Just as Milton was well-versed in the theories of Galileo, so was he a student of alchemy—one of the goals of which was to discover the philosopher's stone that would turn base metals into gold and endow its possessor with eternal life. For Milton, the sun itself is the long sought after philosopher's stone that sheds down its influence upon the Earth and its inhabitants.

Alas, life-hating Satan receives no benefit from the virtuous influence of the sun. No sooner does he reach the sun then he disguises himself as a good angel (as an angel of light—see 2 Cor 11:14) and fools the angel Uriel into revealing the location of the Earth. In allowing Uriel to be hoodwinked by Satan, Milton does not mean his readers to dismiss the angels as credulous fools. Uriel is taken in by Satan, not out of naïveté, but out of guileless innocence and a blessed inability to engage in or detect hypocrisy.

Though they lack the power and majesty of Dante's angels, Milton's angels are developed more fully as characters who converse with humans but are unique from them. For example, Milton's angels possess a wisdom that not only surpasses our own but is of a different kind and quality; whereas we think discursively (by consecutive reasoning), the angels apprehend directly through intuition (V.485–90). As for the angelic nature itself, Milton explains that though they are pure spirit and lack bodies, they are capable of all the sensual pleasures available to man. Like us, they partake of food, but instead of turning to waste, the food they consume transubstantiates into spirit (V.404–50). Most shockingly (and originally), Milton asserts that angels engage in sexual relations, for, he reasons, sex is a part of love and without love there is no happiness (VIII.620–21). When angels make love, however, they have neither bones nor joints to act as obstacles:

> Easier than air with air, if Spirits embrace,

Total they mix, union of pure with pure

Desiring; nor restrained conveyance need

As flesh to mix with flesh, or soul with soul. (VIII.626–29)

Readers familiar with the writings of the Christian mystics are not overly shocked by the sexual language that Dante uses in the final canto of *Paradiso* to express his union with God. But no knowledge of ancient, medieval, or renaissance writing can adequately prepare the reader for this outrageous and yet strangely compelling description of angel sex. To call Milton a proto-hippie is to do him a gross injustice. The poet of *Paradise Lost* is simply in a category of his own!

The Unmoved Mover

But let us now leave devils, planets, and angels behind to ascend to the very throne of God. Having spent Books I and II in Hell, Milton begins Book III with a celebration of light that rivals Dante's *Paradiso*. In direct contrast to the perpetual darkness of Hell, God dwells forever in unapproachable light and is himself light: a light that is not only a force and a stream but that possesses creative properties. It is that light that shines in the darkness, and the darkness can neither overthrow nor comprehend (John 1:5). It is the light that God spoke into being on the first day of creation (Gen 1:3) and that "lighteth every man that cometh into the world" (John 1:9).

The journey from Hell (Books I and II) to Heaven (III) is a poetic one, yet Milton, like Dante, makes it a personal journey as well by calling on light itself to allow him, as a poet, to make the climb. In keeping with epic convention, Milton seeks divine inspiration to assist him in his poetic task; however, the Greek muses invoked by Homer and Virgil will not suffice to inspire the kind of epic Milton desires to write. Thus, though he invokes the "heavenly muse" at the outset of Book I, he makes it clear that he is speaking of a higher divine force by identifying this muse as the inspirer of Moses (I.6–10). Likewise, the muse he invokes in Book III embodies a greater, biblical force that the highest pagan poets only glimpsed in shadow. To this muse Milton speaks with confidence and humility:

Thee I revisit now with bolder wing,

Escaped the Stygian pool, though long detained

In that obscure sojourn, while in my flight

Through utter and through middle darkness borne

With other notes than to th' Orphean lyre

> I sung of Chaos and eternal Night,
>
> Taught by the Heav'nly Muse to venture down
>
> The dark descent, and up to reascend. (III.13–20).

Like Dante himself, Milton has descended in order to ascend, has braved chaos and the land of Styx that he may now rise up to Heaven. He has encountered things unseen and unimagined by Hell's first visitor (Orpheus) and has traversed more levels of God's universe than Plato or Virgil was able to conceive.

But Milton has a special problem not faced by Dante. By the time he began composition on *Paradise Lost*, Milton was blind, his eyes no longer able to receive the light of the heavens. Still, like all great artists, Milton uses his weakness as a strength. First, his blindness links him with the greatest poet and prophet of Greece (Homer and Tiresias), promising him access both to beauty and to truth. Second, his blindness forces him to turn from an external, physical light to an internal, spiritual light—one better suited for apprehending the invisible God. Like a Platonic philosopher, Milton has learned to forsake earthly shadows that deceive and weigh down and rise to the eternal, unchanging Forms that clarify and uplift.

Guided by his inward eye, Milton leads us up to God who dwells in the pure Empyrean. From his throne, God bends down and surveys, in a single glance, all the spheres, the chaos leading to Hell, and Satan's ascent. His glance reaches every corner of the universe and takes in past, present, and future simultaneously. Many today view Milton's God negatively as a cold immobile force who lacks the energy of Satan, but that is only because we moderns privilege reckless action over regal composure. In keeping with theologians and philosophers from Aristotle to Aquinas, Milton celebrates God as the Unmoved Mover; his sovereignty is so total that he need not move to effect his will. As Milton says of God in one of his sonnets: "His state / Is kingly: thousands at his bidding speed / And post o'er land and ocean without rest" (Sonnet 19.11–13). If our age cannot appreciate the absolute sovereignty of Milton's God, it is only because we have lost the ability to see glory and grandeur in earthly hierarchy and kingship.

Milton did not suffer from this lack of vision. Like Homer's Zeus or Virgil's Jupiter, Milton's God rules the court of Heaven and sets forth all that will happen in the epic—but with one key distinction. While Zeus and Jupiter are finally overruled by a shadowy fate that they cannot fully fathom, Milton's God lies above even the control of fate and destiny. Together with Christ, he foresees the fall and plans even now for the atonement. He even, in a flash of eschatological vision that surpasses both Virgil and Dante, looks ahead to the Final Judgment and the resurrection of the dead:

Hell, her numbers full,
Thenceforth shall be forever shut. Meanwhile
The world shall burn, and from her ashes spring
New heav'n and earth, wherein the just shall dwell,
And after all their tribulations long
See golden days, fruitful of golden deeds. (III.332–37)

Like Dante, Milton cannot help but end with a partly classical image that calls up Virgil's eschatological Fourth Eclogue. Indeed, in a supreme Dantean, Christian-humanist moment, Milton hails the stars as the true home of the pagan happy isles (III.565–70).

In response to God's prophecy of the future, the angels shout together their hosannas and cast down their golden crowns before the thrones of God and of Christ (Rev 4). Then they take their golden harps in hand and play. As they praise God "omnipotent / Immutable, immortal, infinite . . . Author of all being, / Fountain of light" (III.372–75), they must shield their eyes from God's glory with their wings.

Compared to the power and light of God, Satan is nothing but a peevish pipsqueak.

20

Bunyan and Donne
Death and Beyond

In chapter 18, I placed Milton on a continuum between zealous Puritans on the one hand, and "hedonistic" Catholics and Anglo-Catholics on the other. Perhaps the best way to define that middle ground is to contrast Milton's vision of the afterlife with those of two roughly contemporary Johns who were born twenty years after and thirty-six years before the poet of *Paradise Lost*: John Bunyan (1628–88) and John Donne (1572–1631). The former was a fiery and intractable Puritan who spent twelve years in prison for preaching his nonconformist views; the latter a Catholic-raised convert to Anglo-Catholicism who began his life as a rake and a man about town but ended it as a celebrated preacher and Dean of Saint Paul's Cathedral.

In his masterpiece, *Pilgrim's Progress*, Bunyan fashions his own limbo of vanity; however, whereas Milton places his in the heavens, Bunyan locates his in an earthly, temporal place called Vanity Fair (a name he coined). Though today the word "fair" conjures up rides and entertainment, Bunyan's fair is an outdoor market where all commodities—from food to religion—are sold: "houses, lands, trades, places, honors, preferments, titles, countries, kingdoms, lusts, pleasures; and delights of all sorts, as harlots, wives, husbands, children, masters, servants, lives, blood, bodies, souls, silver, gold, pearls, precious stones, and what not" (521).[1] Like Milton's limbo, Bunyan's Fair has a distinctly anti-Catholic slant: "the ware of Rome and her merchandise is greatly promoted in this fair; only our English nation,

1. For ease of reference, all quotes from Bunyan and Donne will be taken from *Seventeenth Century Prose and Poetry*, 2nd ed., edited by Alexander Witherspoon and Frank Warnke. Prose selections will be referenced in the text by page number; poetry selections will be referenced by line number.

with some others, have taken a dislike thereat" (521). Any involvement with the world threatens to sully the soul and impede the spiritual progress of the pilgrim.

Donne, in contrast, fashions in his sermons, devotionals, Holy Sonnets, and sacred poems, a vision that, though aware of the dangers of worldliness, is reluctant to eschew all the beauties that God's world has to offer—even if they are adorned with ribbons, paint, and perfume. In his poem, "Satire III," Donne, while critiquing the Catholic argument that Rome's great age demands obedience, warns against the near-asceticism of Geneva (headquarters of the more extreme forms of Protestantism). The Puritan, he writes,

> loves her only, who at Geneva is called
> Religion, plain, simple, sullen, young,
> Contemptuous, yet unhandsome; as among
> Lecherous humors, there is one that judges
> No wenches wholesome but coarse country drudges. (50–54)

Ugliness, Donne is quick to remind us, is not a virtue in and of itself; neither is beauty to be summarily dismissed as an impediment to the Christian walk. When Jesus taught, in the Sermon on the Mount, that the man who looks at a woman with lust in his eye has committed adultery in his heart, he shifted the burden of lust from the body that is looked at to the eye that does the looking. The austere, flesh-denying Puritan Donne parodies is so lecherous-minded that he equates virtue in women with external coarseness rather than internal purity. He rejects the beauty of the world, not because it is inherently sinful, but because he can see in it only sin.

When placed alongside *Paradise Lost*, Bunyan and Donne's opposing visions of Earth, Heaven, and Hell form a triptych along which can be scanned the marvelous array of Christian ideas and imagery on display in England's restless and fertile seventeenth century.

From the City of Destruction to the Celestial City

Since its first publication in 1678, *Pilgrim's Progress* has remained one of the most widely read books in the English language. It has never gone out of print, and it was, for many decades, the second most popular book after the Bible. Written in a simple but poetic prose that combines everyday speech with the cadences of the authorized (King James) Bible, *Pilgrim's Progress* tells the story of Christian, a simple man who is warned by Evangelist to flee from the wrath to come. Though his family and neighbors laugh at his resolve to leave his country (the City of Destruction), Christian puts his fingers in his ears, cries out "Life! life! eternal life!," and runs off in search of the Celestial City (Heaven/New Jerusalem).

Pilgrim's Progress, like Dante's *Comedy* (another work that purified and ennobled vernacular speech), successfully fuses the literary device of allegory with that most perennial of archetypes: the quest narrative. Nevertheless, despite the similarity in form, the two works are quite different. As a Puritan, rather than a Catholic allegory, *Pilgrim's Progress* avoids all pagan references and uses the Bible as its sole authority. This difference makes Bunyan's epic pilgrimage both more limited and more expansive than Dante's: limited because it severs itself from the creative well-springs of Homer, Virgil, and Plato; expansive because it is thereby forced to forge a radically new landscape, imagery, and psychology. And that landscape, for all its universal appeal, is finally an individual, internal one.

Unlike Dante, who, despite his yearning for Heaven, was intimately involved with the political and cultural institutions of his day, Bunyan's Christian is a sojourner in the land. For him, nearly everything in our world represents a snare, a diversion, or a false path. (Though moderns take for granted that it was the Christians of the so-called Dark Ages who considered our world a vale of tears, that notion is often more strongly felt in Puritan writings than in medieval Catholic ones!) Bunyan's Puritans, like those who left to found the American colony at Plymouth Rock, identified strongly with the Jews of the exodus. As such, they tended to follow the Old Testament dictum to remove oneself from the unbeliever.

It is for this reason, I would argue, that the dichotomy Bunyan establishes between Heaven and Hell is almost identical to the one he establishes between Heaven and Earth! The quest-journey for Heaven is not so much a matter of following the rising path—as it is for Plato and Dante—as it is a matter of continually choosing between light and dark, the kingdom of God and the kingdom of Satan. Unfortunately, Satan's kingdom extends from Hell to Earth and manifests itself in every earthly sphere: from church to state to family, from school to marketplace to gentry. Though Bunyan does not reference *Paradise Lost*, he would likely have agreed with Milton's allegory of sin and death building a causeway between Hell and Earth. The things of this Earth are simply too compromised to merit our attention and devotion. The high Christian-humanist calling that cries out from the pages of the *Comedy* and that speaks in slightly muted tones in *Paradise Lost* falls into near silence in the somber pages of *Pilgrim's Progress*.

One place where Bunyan's firm dichotomy between Heaven and Earth, light and dark comes most sharply into focus is during Christian's epic battle with the demonic Apollyon (Greek for "destruction"). During the battle,

Christian is tempted to forsake his pilgrimage to the Celestial City and return to the service of Satan, he who is the Lord of the City of Destruction and of Vanity Fair. Unabashed, he rebukes Apollyon and boldly replies: "O thou destroying Apollyon! to speak truth, I like His service, His wages, His servants, His government, His company, and country better than thine; and therefore leave off to persuade me further; I am His servant, and I will follow Him" (514). Bunyan allows for little overlap or converse between what Augustine dubbed the City of God and the City of Man. Whereas Dante, and less so Milton, tries to build a bridge or stairway from classical pagan virtues to the fuller Christian virtues, Bunyan erects a wall of separation.

Escaping from the world, rather than redeeming it, is the focus of *Pilgrim's Progress*, an epic struggle that can only be sustained by a powerful vision of Heaven. In the form of a catechistic dialogue between Christian and a fair-weather fellow pilgrim named Pliable, Bunyan states clearly the nature of that heavenly kingdom that is the goal of every true Christian pilgrim. Pliable asks Christian to share with him what the book he carries (the Bible) has to say about the kingdom he seeks:

> CHRISTIAN: There is an endless kingdom to be inhabited, and everlasting life to be given us, that we may inhabit that kingdom for ever.
>
> PLIABLE: Well said; and what else?
>
> CHRISTIAN: There are crowns of glory to be given us, and garments that will make us shine like the sun in the firmament of Heaven.
>
> PLIABLE: This is very pleasant; and what else?
>
> CHRISTIAN: There shall be no more crying, nor sorrow; for He that is owner of the place will wipe all tears from our eyes.
>
> PLIABLE: And what company shall we have there?
>
> CHRISTIAN: There we shall be with seraphims and cherubims, creatures that will dazzle your eyes to look on them. There also you shall meet with thousands and ten thousands that have gone before us to that place; none of them are hurtful, but loving and holy; every one walking in the sight of God, and standing in his presence with acceptance for ever. In a word, there we shall see the elders with their golden crowns; there we shall see the holy virgins with their golden harps; there we shall see men that by the world were cut in pieces, burnt in flames, eaten of beasts, drowned in the seas, for the love they bare to the Lord of the

place, all well, and clothed with immortality as with a garment.
(505)

To the Puritan Bunyan, Heaven represents not only a higher form of life (one of worship and joy) but a higher congregation (what Calvin referred to as the hidden elect). In place of the hierarchical and monarchical Heaven of the Catholic Dante, Bunyan, in keeping with Hebrews 11 and Revelation 4–7, presents Heaven as a place of reward and fellowship for those who have suffered oppression together. Oddly, Bunyan's biblical vision, purged of all reference to classical sources, is strikingly similar to the image of Heaven conjured by Socrates at the end of his *Apology* (see chapter 4): a place where fellow sufferers of injustice can commiserate in peace and joy.

As he nears the end of his earthly sojourn and sees in the distance the pearly gates and golden streets of the Celestial City, Christian learns that before he can enter it, he must pass through a river (the River Jordan) that Bunyan identifies as death. Only Enoch and Elijah, Christian is told, ever reached the city without going under the waters. Though Bunyan's description of the Celestial City is taken directly from John's description of the New Jerusalem (Rev 21–22; see chapter 13), his mention of the river that must first be crossed is an addition of his own—though it is based on allegorical readings of Scripture that date back to St. Paul. Earlier in the chapter, I noted the Puritan tendency to compare their own experiences of persecution to the exodus. This tendency would later be imitated by American slaves who interpreted their own struggles and longings for freedom in terms of the Jewish movement from Egyptian bondage to possession of the Promised Land. In the Negro spirituals that rose up out of those longings, the act of crossing the River Jordan signifies both death and heavenly rest. The fact that it was Joshua (Yeshua in Hebrew; Jesus in Greek) who led the Israelites across the Jordan into the Land of Milk and Honey adds particular resonance both to the Negro spirituals and to the closing section of *Pilgrim's Progress*.

Once he has crossed to the other side of the shore and reached what American evangelicals like to call the "great by-and-by," Christian is reunited with all the saints in eternal fellowship. There he looks forward to attending the wedding feast of the Lamb and praising God for eternity.

And there we expect Bunyan will end his narrative . . . but he does not. *Pilgrim's Progress*, though it climaxes in Heaven, actually ends on a sobering note. As Christian looks back across the river, he sees one of his companions, Ignorance, board a boat. Rather than walk through the waters, Ignorance chooses to be ferried by a figure ominously named Vain-hope. Thus arrived, Ignorance enters the City—but no one greets him; instead two angels seize him, bind him, and carry him above the mountain where they cast him through a door in the side of the hill. "Then I saw," concludes Bunyan, "that there was a way to Hell, even from the gates of Heaven, as well as from the City of Destruction!"

The razor edge of Heaven and Hell is sharp indeed!

The Resurrection of the Dead

Bunyan's legacy is a strong one, but his was not the only Protestant voice in seventeenth-century England to exert a lasting influence on the Western world's conception of the afterlife. If John Bunyan denied the world and John Milton accepted it grudgingly, John Donne sought to engage and redeem it through a rich and sensual imagination that was less suspicious of the flesh and that embraced higher pagan wisdom as a vehicle for seeking after eternal truths. One of the markers of Donne's wider vision is his willingness to allude to, and *learn from*, Dante.

For example, in two of his many sermons, Donne offers images of damnation and of salvation that shimmer with the visual and philosophical imagery of the *Divine Comedy*. The worst part of damnation, writes Donne in Sermon LXXVII (1640 folio), is not to fall into the hands of God, but to fall out of them, to be cast off and forgotten. How terrible, he muses, that

> God should frustrate all his own purposes and practices upon me and leave me and cast me away as though I had cost him nothing; that this God at last should let this soul go away as a smoke, as a vapor, as a bubble; and that then this soul cannot be a smoke, a vapor, nor a bubble but must lie in darkness as long as the Lord of light is light itself, and never a spark of that light reach to my soul. (105)

Though the light/dark dichotomy of this passage may also be found in *Pilgrim's Progress* and *Paradise Lost*, Donne adds to it a psychological horror and dread that is more indicative of the *Inferno*. By withdrawing his direct presence from Hell, God leaves the damned to their own devices, an existential torment that can only lead to the kind of sick and pointless games that the sinners play endlessly in Dante's inferno.

For the redeemed, however, the eternal nature of their postmortem state takes on a very different quality. The death of the saints, writes Donne in Sermon XXVII, births them "into another life, into the glory of God" (104); it is a process that ends one circle (our mortal life on this Earth) and begins another (our immortal life in the presence of God):

for immortality and eternity is a circle too; not a circle where two points meet but a circle made at once; this life is a circle made with a compass that passes from point to point; that life is a circle stamped with a print, an endless and perfect circle as soon as it begins. (104)

In *Inferno*, the circle represents futility, but in *Paradiso*, the same symbol is used to represent the timeless, uncreated nature of the Triune God. In contrasting our life on Earth with our life in Heaven, Donne makes a similar distinction, but does Dante one better. To help incarnate the subtle difference between the two, Donne visualizes the imperfect, time-enslaved progression of our creaturely life as a circle drawn by a swinging compass and the perfect, eternal essence of our heavenly life as a circle stamped all at once—like a signet ring pressed into wax. Or, as Plato might have put it, the first circle exists in the world of becoming, the second in the world of Being.

More than Bunyan or Milton, perhaps even more that Dante, Donne discerned that our passage from Earth to Heaven, time to eternity was not a movement but a metamorphosis, not a transmigration but a transfiguration. The change from our old body to our resurrection body is not just quantitative but qualitative, a difference not in degree but in kind. Christians of Donne's day believed in a very literal final resurrection wherein all the atoms of our body—whether burned, frozen, or decomposed, whether covered with Earth or plunged in the sea—would rise up in the clouds and be reassembled in an instant. Over the course of his dual career as poet and preacher, Donne made several attempts to capture the power of that apocalyptic moment when the trumpet would sound and the dead would rise from their graves. To my mind, he succeeded most fully in the opening lines of Holy Sonnet VII:

> At the round earth's imagined corners blow
> Your trumpets, angels, and arise, arise
> From death you numberless infinities
> Of souls, and to your scattered bodies go. (1–4)

In a mere four lines, Donne delves the many facets of the resurrection of the dead: its paradoxical nature (expressed by the oxymoronic image of a round earth with corners); its border-shattering urgency ("blow / Your trumpets," "arise / From death," and "infinities / Of souls" all push themselves over the natural boundary of the end of the line); its vastness of scope (the seemingly redundant but powerfully apt phrase "numberless infinities"); and its kinetic energy (the rising souls go in search of "scattered bodies").

And yet even these lines do not capture the fullness of the mystery. What truly fascinated Donne and his contemporaries about the resurrection of the body was the promise it carried that corruption would some day blossom into new life. In one of his sermons (XXVI) he reassures his parishioners that though our dust be scattered to the four corners of the Earth, God remembers each particle and will gather them all at judgment day:

> It is not with God as it is with man; we do, but God does not forget the dead; and as long as God is with them they are with him. "As he puts all thy tears into his bottles," so he puts all the grains of thy dust into his cabinet, and the winds that scatter, the waters that wash them away carry them not out of his sight. (105)

The image is a sublime one that reminds us that the same God who controls the motions of planets and suns controls as well the most insignificant of atoms. Jesus assures us in the Sermon on the Mount that God has counted every hair on our head; Donne expands that assurance to include every speck of dust of which we are so fearfully and wonderfully made.

Donne's propensity for sublime imagery is everywhere evident in his poetry and prose, but it is balanced, and paradoxically strengthened, by an equally strong propensity for the grotesque. Indeed, one of the most characteristic aspects of Donne's work is its tendency to mingle exaltation of the human form with a disgust for our animal nature. Shakespeare's *Hamlet* expresses this same duality, this same gravitation toward and away from physicality, when in his famous "What a piece of work is a man" speech (Act II, Scene ii), he first praises man for being like an angel in action and a god in apprehension, and then ends by dismissing him as nothing more than a "quintessence of dust." In Sermon XIV (1649 folio), Donne captures this same duality by first comforting his parishioners' fears of the resurrection, and then ruminating, with an almost perverse glee, on the diverse places where our atoms may be found:

> In what wrinkle, in what furrow, in what bowel of the earth lie all the grains of the ashes of a body burnt a thousand years since? In what corner, in what ventricle of the sea lies all the jelly of a body drowned in the general Flood? (106)

Even more grotesque—and yet somehow strangely beautiful—Donne shares with us, in a poem entitled "The Relic," his plan for ensuring that he will see his lover one last time before the end. He has tied a bracelet of her hair around his wrist so that, on Judgment Day, when she goes from place to place in search of her scattered body, she will have to visit his tomb to retrieve her hair.

More than any other English poet, Donne infuses his speculations of the afterlife with a wit, a tension, and a vibrancy that is still unmatched today. No other poet could so boldly ridicule death for his puffed-up sense of self-importance as Donne does in the opening lines of Holy Sonnet X: "Death, be not proud, though some have called thee / Mighty and dreadful, for thou art not so" (1–2). And no other poet would dare to continue on in the same vein: first mocking death for affording us release and rest while remaining himself a slave to fate and kings; then lampooning him for keeping company with vile poisons and diseases; then insolently asserting that poppies make us sleep as well as him; and finally reminding him of how different his fate shall be than ours: "One short sleep past, we wake eternally, / And Death shall be no more; Death, thou shalt die" (13–14).

21

Satan as Hero

Romanticism and the Inward Turn

Although I ended chapter 19 by labeling Milton's Satan a "peevish pipsqueak," and although I believe Milton himself wished us to view Satan as such, the fact remains that Milton's Satan, at least in the first half of *Paradise Lost*, possesses qualities that link him to the epic and tragic heroes of the ancient world: like Homer's Achilles, he demands respect befitting his nature and status; like Homer's Odysseus and Virgil's Aeneas, he goes on an epic journey through dangerous and chaotic realms; like Aeschylus' Prometheus, he resists what he sees as the tyrannical authority of the chief deity; like Sophocles' Oedipus, he will not cease to fulfill his mission despite warnings of doom; like Euripides' Medea, he feels wronged and slighted and exacts a revenge that is so horrible it takes on sublime dimensions. Most of these links, of course, were forced upon Milton by his decision to write a dramatic epic in imitation of the great pagan masterpieces of Greece and Rome—but that all important "of course" was lost upon the British Romantic poets who spearheaded a radical change in the way the Western poetic tradition would henceforth perceive and depict angels and devils, Heaven and Hell.

Born out of the French Revolution and its goal to topple old hierarchies, purge "dead" traditions, and remake society, the British Romantic movement was eager to read afresh the classic literature of the past and find in it a message befitting their new, revolutionary age. The zeitgeist of Romanticism called for energy, imagination, and innovation over reason, logic, and order, and they found those qualities not in Milton's God but in his Satan.

Satan as Hero

In his essay, "A Defense of Poetry," Percy Bysshe Shelley (1792–1822) offers a revisionist interpretation of *Paradiso* and *Paradise Lost* that claims to uncover a hidden agenda in Dante and Milton that critics of their day were unwilling, and perhaps unable, to see. In chapter 16, I highlighted Dante's decision to place the soul of Ripheus (a Trojan soldier who appears briefly in *Aeneid* II) with the souls of the just leaders who dwell in the sphere of Jupiter. Dante's decision to include a pagan in Paradise, I argued, was predicated on his Christian-humanist faith that the lesser vision of pagan writers like Plato and Virgil could lead upward to, and find their fulfillment in, the greater revelation of Christ and the Bible. Shelley, who argues that Dante observes "a most heretical caprice in his distribution of rewards and punishments" (1106),[1] reads the Ripheus episode as an aesthetic cover for Dante's cryptic heterodoxy. Indeed, in a passage that is itself quite cryptic, Shelley has the following to say about the true beliefs of Dante and Milton, poets whom he claims—quite accurately, I think—are rivals:

> The poetry of Dante may be considered as the bridge thrown over the stream of time, which unites the modern and ancient World. The distorted notions of invisible things which Dante and his rival Milton have idealized, are merely the mask and the mantle in which these great poets walk through eternity enveloped and disguised. It is a difficult question to determine how far they were conscious of the distinction which must have subsisted in their minds between their own creeds and that of the people. (1106)

In this rather shameless specimen of special pleading, Shelley, whether he intended to or not, speaks for countless numbers of modern, highly educated secular humanists who reject the supernatural (and thus Heaven and Hell, angels and devils) but who nevertheless harbor a passionate love for the *Divine Comedy* and *Paradise Lost*. Shelley and his fellow Romantics made Dante and Milton "safe" for those wishing to sever their poetic power from their philosophical and theological beliefs.

If I seem here to be putting words in Shelley's mouth, consider what he has to say, just one sentence later, about the true message, protagonist, and genius of *Paradise Lost*:

---

1. For ease of reference, all quotes from the Romantic poets in this chapter and the next will be taken from *English Romantic Poetry and Prose*, edited by Russell Noyes. Prose selections will be referenced in the text by page number; poetry selections will be referenced by line number.

Milton's poem contains within itself a philosophical refutation of that system, of which, by a strange and natural antithesis, it has been a chief popular support. Nothing can exceed the energy and magnificence of the character of Satan as expressed in "Paradise Lost." It is a mistake to suppose that he could ever have been intended for the popular personification of evil. Implacable hate, patient cunning, and a sleepless refinement of device to inflict the extremist anguish on an enemy, these things are evil; and, although venial in a slave, are not to be forgiven in a tyrant; although redeemed by much that ennobles his defeat in one subdued, are marked by all that dishonors his conquest in the victor. And Milton's Devil as a moral being is as far superior to his God, as One who perseveres in some purpose which he has conceived to be excellent in spite of adversity and torture, is to One who in the cold security of undoubted triumph inflicts the most horrible revenge upon his enemy, not from any mistaken notion of inducing him to repent of a perseverance in enmity, but with the alleged design of exasperating him to deserve new torments. Milton has so far violated the popular creed (if this shall be judged to be a violation) as to have alleged no superiority of moral virtue to his God over his Devil. And this bold neglect of a direct moral purpose is the most decisive proof of the supremacy of Milton's genius. (1106–7)

The popular reading of *Paradise Lost*, Shelley asserts, is refuted by Milton's *true* intent: to hail Satan as the hero and God as the tyrant of the universe. As a child of the French Revolution, Shelley discerned in Milton's Satan an energy and a magnificence lacking in his God. In fact, reading *Paradise Lost* through revolutionary eyes convinced Shelley that Milton's God was one who not only lacked the energy of Satan but stood in opposition to it—an opposition that sparked in Satan a noble desire to rebel against Jehovah's crushing authority and unnatural hierarchy.

Despite their differences, both Dante and Milton, following in the wake of Aristotle and Aquinas, hailed God as the Unmoved Mover. In sharp contrast, Shelley, who privileged risk over security, passion over stoic harmony, was disgusted by what he saw as the smug self-satisfaction and stony aloofness of Milton's Jehovah. Though Shelley, like so many of his academic heirs, all but worshipped the genius of Dante and Milton, he would not have been comfortable in either of their Heavens: to him, their God would have seemed as cold and remote as Olympian Zeus. If Shelley ascribed to any religion, it was the religion of Plato; and yet, though much of his mature work is undergirded by Platonism, Shelley would have found Plato's pristine world of Being rigid, static, and incompatible with life.

Percy Shelley was truly a devil's advocate, as intent on critiquing what he saw as God's repressive nature as in giving the devil his due. Still, to be fair to Shelley, it is clear the poet was aware of Satan's shortcomings. That is why, I would argue, he sought out another hero who possessed the same restive and indomitable energy, but whose motives were purer and whose heart inclined to the misery of man. He found that hero in Prometheus, the Greek Titan who stole fire from Olympian Zeus and gave it to man, and who further concealed from Zeus the secret information that alone could prevent Zeus's overthrow (Prometheus in Greek means "forethought"). For these two crimes, Prometheus was chained to a high rock in the Caucuses: each day a vulture devoured his liver; each night the liver regenerated, only to be devoured again at the return of day. In his masterful "closet tragedy" (a tragedy meant to be read rather than performed), *Prometheus Unbound*, Shelley presents Prometheus as a character who combines the purity and self-sacrifice of the crucified Christ with the revolutionary fervor and tyrant-hating defiance of Satan. In his preface to the play—a play that is modeled closely on Milton's closet tragedy, *Samson Agonistes*—Shelley makes clear that his Titan represents a more perfect version of Milton's Satan:

> The only imaginary being, resembling in any degree Prometheus, is Satan; and Prometheus is, in my judgment, a more poetical character than Satan, because, in addition to courage, and majesty, and firm and patient opposition to omnipotent force, he is susceptible of being described as exempt from the taints of ambition, envy, revenge, and a desire for personal aggrandizement, which, in the hero of *Paradise Lost*, interfere with the interest. The character of Satan engenders in the mind a pernicious casuistry which leads us to weigh his faults with his wrongs, and to excuse the former because the latter exceed all measure. In the minds of those who consider that magnificent fiction with a religious feeling it engenders something worse. But Prometheus is, as it were, the type of the highest perfection of moral and intellectual nature impelled by the purest and the truest motives to the best and noblest ends. (982)

Those familiar with the *Prometheus Bound* of Aeschylus will recognize that Shelley has reconfigured the myth so as to increase both the selfless purity of Prometheus and the cruel tyranny of Zeus. In Aeschylus, both characters are given an equal number of vices and virtues; furthermore, though pity is expressed for Prometheus, the standard Greek reading of the myth—one echoed not only by Aeschylus but by Dante and Milton as well—is that the Titans were the rebels and that Zeus's confining of them to Tartarus was finally a just and good thing.

Shelley will have nothing of it. His Zeus (Jupiter) is a lawless usurper and irredeemable bully whom Prometheus is right to resist. Indeed, whereas Greek myth insisted that Prometheus ultimately revealed the secret and prevented Zeus's overthrow, Shelley ends his play with the dethronement of Zeus, the release of Prometheus, and the restoration of an Edenic world of absolute equality and unrestricted freedom. Significantly, Shelley's contemporary, John Keats (1795–1821), also wrote an (unfinished) epic work in the mode of Milton (*Hyperion*) in which he effected the same Romantic reversal of Titans and Olympians—a theme he expanded on further in his (also unfinished) Dantean revision of the epic (*The Fall of Hyperion*). In exalting the rebellious but good-natured Titans over the proud and tyrannical Olympians, Shelley and Keats were likely influenced by a passage in *Aeneid* VIII, where Virgil relates an Italian tradition that links the Titans (led by Saturn) to the Golden Age of Italy. Still, Virgil, like his Greek predecessors and medieval and renaissance heirs, agreed in their presentation of Zeus as a just and lawful, if erratic, ruler. This was something that neither Keats nor Shelley was willing to do.

The Byronic Hero

Nor William Blake either! A generation younger than Keats and Shelley, Blake (1757–1827) paved the way for Shelley's reading of *Paradise Lost* by insisting that Milton's Satan is superior in all ways to his God. In his *Marriage of Heaven and Hell* (see next chapter), Blake argues that Milton's God is less interesting, forceful, and sympathetic than his Satan. Here is his explanation for this anomaly: "The reason Milton wrote in fetters when he wrote of Angels & God, and at liberty when of Devils & Hell is because he was a true Poet and of the Devil's party without knowing it" (211). What Blake suggests here is that Milton the poet was stifled by the restrictions of the Platonic-Christian God he celebrates in his epic, but was set free by the energy of Satan and Hell. However, just as Dante's proto-Christian Virgil was used by God to announce Christ's birth in the Fourth Eclogue, so Milton was used unconsciously by Satan to champion liberty and energy. Convinced of the truth of this satanic eschatology, Blake later wrote an esoteric epic poem titled *Milton* in which he chronicles, in apocalyptic language, Milton's decision to leave Paradise and remake himself through Blake!

Blake's radical readings of Milton and his "hero" not only influenced Keats and Shelley, but the other great poet of their generation, Lord Byron

(1788–1824). Byron was so enamored of Milton's Satan that he modeled a new type of hero after him: a hero who is still with us today. This distinctively Romantic protagonist, quickly dubbed the Byronic hero, is a man who has committed a taboo sin or acquired forbidden knowledge and, as a result, has been cut off from humanity. He is a man of grandeur and power, at times almost super-human, but he is forced, mostly by his own sense of guilt and alienation, to live on the margins of society. He is, like Byron himself, moody, impulsive, and overly self-conscious; though generally young in years, he is always old in experience. He exists as a tribe of one who has made a cult out of his own pain; indeed, he takes great pride in his suffering, for he alone can bear it.

Byron developed his new archetype in a series of (mostly forgotten) oriental tales in verse, and then perfected him in two works of great poetic and psychological power: *Childe Harold's Pilgrimage* and a closet tragedy (*Manfred*) about a Faust-like character who has committed incest and, by so doing, destroyed his sister. Byron, accused of incest himself, and Shelley, an early proponent of free love, were themselves real-life Byronic heroes. Forerunners of the Byronic hero include not only Satan and Prometheus, but Cain, Orestes, Oedipus, Faust, the Wandering Jew, Mephistopheles, Hamlet, Macbeth, Don Juan, and the Fisher King. Post-Byron examples of this fertile archetype include Heathcliff, Dr. Frankenstein, Ahab, Dracula, Dr. Jekyll, Captain Nemo, Dorian Gray, Raskolnikov, the Phantom of the Opera, Darth Vader, Gollum, Batman, and most of the characters who appear in the stories of Edgar Allen Poe, the operas of Wagner, and the films of Orson Welles.

No matter the age or the country in which he appears, the hell the Byronic hero must suffer is always an internal one: he is always his own worst enemy, his own executioner. Like Milton's Satan, he will not submit or yield, no matter the pain, the torment, or the exile. Ultimately, the Byronic hero lives within his own tortured mind, his motto that of Milton's Satan: "The mind is its own place, and in itself / Can make a heav'n of Hell, a Hell of heav'n."

The Journey Within

As the Romantics reinterpreted Satan, so did they reinterpret the epic journey to Heaven and Hell that Milton himself reinterpreted in *Paradise Lost*. Though far less radical than Blake, Byron, or Shelley, William Wordsworth (1770–1850) played perhaps the central role in re-imagining for post-French Revolution Europe what such a journey might look like in a world whose focus had shifted from the supernatural to the natural, the external to the internal.

The young Wordsworth was determined to write an epic for his age as great as those of Homer, Virgil, Dante, and Milton. In the prospectus for his proposed (but unfinished) epic, *The Recluse*, he asserts that to accomplish his task he must "tread on shadowy ground, must sink / Deep—and, aloft ascending, breathe in worlds / To which the Heaven of Heavens is but a veil" (28–30). As a would-be epic poet, Wordsworth knows he must be prepared to brave the same supernatural journeys undertaken by Dante and Milton, but Wordsworth claims his pilgrimage will carry him both higher and deeper. In bold, Miltonic language that shocked even the heterodox Blake, Wordsworth goes on to boast just *how* high and deep he is prepared to go:

> All strength—all terror, single or in bands,
> That ever was put forth in personal form—
> Jehovah—with his thunder, and the choir
> Of shouting Angels, and the empyreal thrones—
> I pass them unalarmed. Not Chaos, not
> The darkest pit of lowest Erebus,
> Nor aught of blinder vacancy, scooped out
> By help of dreams—can breed such fear and awe
> As fall upon us often when we look
> Into our Minds, into the Mind of Man—
> My haunt, and the main region of my song. (31–41)

Wordsworth's journey, it appears, will not (like those of Dante and Milton) take him down into the Earth or up into the sky, but into his own mind.

In true Romantic fashion, Wordsworth interiorizes the epic journey: the path he treads will take him through an internalized landscape of the soul, a psychic journey within. Though Wordsworth the man possessed a Christian faith that grew more orthodox as he aged, Wordsworth the poet indulged a more pantheistic view that perceived the supernatural as being spread throughout nature and that found spiritual enlightenment by encountering the divine within. In fact, he goes on in the next section of his prospectus to argue Eden can be restored, but only when nature and the mind of man are joined in an incarnational marriage pattered on the great marriage of Christ and the church. But before that day arrives, poets like Wordsworth will have to have the courage to delve deeply into the hidden recesses of the mind. Indeed, I would argue Wordsworth and his fellow Romantics are the true discoverers of the unconscious; Freud only added a scientific nomenclature. It was the Romantic poets who first mapped the vast oceans and continents that dwell within the mind of man. Within that mind, Wordsworth believed, there lay a universe of joy and awe, wonder and terror that surpassed even the epic pilgrimage of Dante and the epic, if diabolical, flight of Satan.

Wordsworth's dear friend and fellow poet Samuel Taylor Coleridge (1772–1834) also constructed many of his own poems along the lines of an internal journey into the seemingly inaccessible regions of the psyche. In his finest example of such a poem, *The Rime of the Ancient Mariner*, he even succeeded in inventing one of the great prototypes of the Byronic hero. Written in medieval ballad rhythm, the poem takes us on a fantastic sea voyage around the world, a voyage whose navigational chart offers an aesthetic map of a tormented soul. In the poem, the Ancient Mariner commits a foolish and immoral act (he shoots an innocent albatross) that alienates him from both the world of nature and of man. To atone for his senseless crime, the Mariner is made to suffer a physically and emotionally intense penance of guilt and remorse—although, as his journey leads finally to a type of salvation, it would be more accurate to call it purgatorial rather than infernal.

Actually, to be even more precise, the final state of the Mariner mirrors the limbo existence of Dante's Virgil. A life-long penance is laid upon Coleridge's Byronic hero whereby he must roam the world warning others to avoid his own terrible fate. Like Virgil leading Statius to Christ, the Mariner has the power to heal and restore those who heed his words, but is unable himself to find rest and peace. As is true of all epic poets, the Romantic seeks inspiration; he even desires, as did Dante and Milton, to be a poet-prophet speaking wisdom and warning to his corrupt age. Unfortunately for the Romantic, that inspiration comes with a price: no sooner does he receive it than he finds that the sought-after knowledge is, in reality, a forbidden fruit that further isolates him from society. Or to quote three heavy lines from the opening scene of Byron's *Manfred*:

> Sorrow is knowledge: they who know the most
> Must mourn the deepest o'er the fatal truth,
> The Tree of Knowledge is not that of Life. (10–12)

Byron borrows his lines from Ecclesiastes (1:18) and Genesis 3, but alas, he is unable himself to complete the journey from fall to redemption.

Internalizing the Nekuia

Though the work is somewhat less known than the other Romantic poems discussed above, Blake's lovely and delicate *Book of Thel* provides us with one last example of the Romantic reworking of classic, medieval, and renaissance notions of Heaven and Hell. A sort of mini-epic (it is less than 150 lines long), *The Book of Thel* transports its readers to a fairy world where a young, untested princess yearns to come of age. In the first three sections of the poem, the young Thel speaks to a lily, a cloud, a worm, and a clod of clay in hopes of finding some meaning and purpose for her existence. She learns from these allegorized figures that she is of use and that even the humblest clod of clay is precious in the sight of God.

We expect that the poem will end when Thel learns these simple truths, but it does not. In the fourth and final section, Thel braves the underworld in the form of an epic *nekuia* that recalls both the Hades of Homer and Virgil and the Sheol of the Old Testament:

> The eternal gates' terrific porter [sin and death for Milton] lifted
>   the northern bar:
> Thel entered in & saw the secrets of the land unknown.
> She saw the couches of the dead, & where the fibrous roots
> Of every heart on earth infixes deep its restless twists:
> A land of sorrows & of tears where never smile was seen. (104–8)

Thel wanders through this dark valley—which signifies not only the abode of the dead and the roots of the natural world but her own unformed psyche—and listens to its "dolours and lamentations" (110). In the end, she arrives, as we all must, at her own grave.

It is here that the thrill and adventure of her epic rite of passage loses its aura of romance. From out the grave the innocent Thel hears a voice that speaks to her of the horrors and hypocrisies that enter our soul through our five senses, speaks too of the loss of innocence that comes with sexuality. But the virgin Thel is not yet ready to enter into a fallen world of physicality, to be penetrated either by sexual contact or by worms (after she is dead). Seized by a fit of terror, she screams and flees from the underworld.

Blake's Hades is not a place for theology or theodicy; it is an arena for facing our fears. A full century before Freud, Blake's *nekuia* provides us with an interiorized psychic journey of the id (Thel in Greek means "I want") in search of self-awareness.

22

Heaven is a State of Mind

Blake's *Marriage of Heaven and Hell*

It is impossible to exaggerate the impact the French Revolution had on late eighteenth- and early nineteenth-century Europe. When the people of Paris rose up on July 14, 1789, and stormed the Bastille—a state prison which held, not criminals in the modern sense of the word, but political offenders who had fallen foul of the aristocracy—it seemed to promise a new dawn of liberty, equality, and fraternity. Everything seemed possible: if a nation wanted freedom, it needed only to stand up, shake off its fetters, and pronounce itself free. And the same held, or so it seemed, for each individual. Authority, hierarchy, tradition, privilege: all were to be swept away by an irresistible flood of revolutionary energy.

If we view the events of 1789 from the optimistic perspective of our modern Western democracies, we will likely picture happy, well-dressed citizens exercising their right to vote. If we take a darker view of the same events—especially if we take into account that the French Revolution later morphed into the Reign of Terror, during which thousands of aristocrats and other undesirables lost their heads to Madame le Guillotine—we will see a nation of mini-Satans raising their fists in defiance and arrogantly proclaiming: "we will not serve." To us, the two visions seem contradictory, but they were not so for Shelley and Byron. The authors of *Prometheus Unbound* and *Manfred* hailed satanic energy as heroic and saw the toppling of Milton's authoritarian and repressive Unmoved Mover as a good thing, no matter the cost. And they were not the only poets who felt that way.

If Shelley and Byron hailed satanic energy as heroic, then Blake all but worshipped it. Written in the first flush of the French Revolution, Blake's

Marriage of Heaven and Hell is a veritable hymn to the revolutionary, apocalyptic force of Milton's Satan, a force that not only shatters physical chains but what Blake, in a poem called "London," referred to as "mind-forged manacles." Fragmented, esoteric, heavily symbolic, composed in a strange mixture of prose and verse, the *Marriage* nevertheless possesses a quasi-mystical energy that cannot be easily dismissed. With the urgency and abandon of an Old Testament prophet, Blake rips away the veil and allows us to peer into the forces that propel history forward and that underlie our little human systems of philosophy and religion. Ironically, the twin targets of his half polemical/half ironic work are worldviews that for the last three hundred years have stood in opposition to one another: secular humanism (which privileges reason over imagination) and orthodox Christianity (which privileges Heaven over Hell).

During the eighteenth-century Enlightenment, scientists like Newton, men of letters like Voltaire, and poets like Alexander Pope celebrated a cosmos that was just as ordered as that of Dante and Milton, but which was far less personal. In their essentially deistic works—especially Pope's verse epistle-cum-mini-epic-cum-theodicy, *An Essay on Man*—they present us with a clockwork universe set in motion by an absentee watchmaker God who started the watch going but left it to run on its own without divine intervention. Though all three of these men believed in God, their vision paved the way for a more secular-humanist (as opposed to Christian-humanist) view of the world, one in which miracle is replaced by law and wonder gives way to calculation. It was a world Blake refused to live in.

And yet he refused just as strongly to live in a world where right and wrong, virtue and vice were defined by commandments written in stone, and where a fearless rebel like Satan was thoroughly condemned while a divine autocrat was allowed to set absolute standards for good and evil. Though Blake seems to have been fairly orthodox in his younger years, he slowly gravitated away from any form of creedal Christianity to construct his own intensely personal vision of God and man, the natural and the supernatural, salvation and damnation. ("I must create my own system," he once quipped, "or be enslaved by another man's.") The formulas around which Christians and secular humanists structure their beliefs and their lives were felt by Blake to be equally constrictive and unnatural.

Urizen v. Orc

Indeed, at the very outset of *The Marriage of Heaven and Hell*, Blake establishes—and then deconstructs—a dichotomy that underlies Christian *and* Enlightenment thought:

> Without Contraries is no progression. Attraction and Repulsion, Reason and Energy, Love and Hate, are necessary to Human existence.

> From these contraries spring what the religious call Good & Evil. Good is the passive that obeys Reason. Evil is the active springing from Energy.

> Good is Heaven. Evil is Hell. (210)

Both reason and energy, Blake argues, are necessary for the perpetuation of the human race, but religion—and science, as the rest of the *Marriage* makes clear—refuses to hold the two in tension or accept the dichotomy as a life-giving one. Instead, reason and energy, when perceived through the eyes of pure (Newtonian) reason or doctrinal (Dantean/Miltonic) faith, become synonymous with love and hate, good and evil, Heaven and Hell. Blake, as Romantic poet-prophet, plays devil's advocate and tries to restore the integrity of the two sides of the contrary—or, better, the two poles of the binary. In his zeal, however, he comes close to switching (rather than reconciling) the binary, exalting energy to the detriment, and even overthrow, of reason.

In his later, increasingly esoteric works, Blake would embody and wrestle with these and other contraries through the medium of a complex mythology that he devoted several decades to constructing. The system would come to include two rival deities (Urizen and Orc) who would embody the two sides of the reason/energy binary in a powerful, even visceral way. In fact, whereas most of Blake's mythological characters are hard to grasp and rarely merit the effort needed to unpack them, Urizen and Orc remain potent allegorical (Blake would have said symbolic) figures for the Romantic struggle between tradition and revolution.

Blake's Urizen (probably meant to sound like "you reason") is an old, jealous, restrictive, vengeful deity who crushes all freedom and creativity. Blake linked him to Jehovah, the Old Testament God who speaks to man only in the form of Thou Shalt Nots and who feels threatened by all rivals, whether human, natural, or divine. He is supremely the Unmoved Mover of Milton, though he also bears a resemblance to the Olympian Zeus/Jupiter who chains Prometheus to the rock and imprisons the Titans in Tartarus.

Urizen is the power behind the British and French throne that was torn down by the American and French Revolutions (born thirteen years before Wordsworth, Blake was eighteen when Independence was declared in the colonies of the New World).

In direct contrast to Urizen, Orc (probably named after Orcus, one of the many Roman names for Hades) is a young, fiery, fetter-shattering god who challenges the restrictive rules and systems of Urizen. He embodies both the revolutionary energy released by the Storming of the Bastille and the intuitive, non-rational wisdom disseminated by Romantic poet-prophets driven mad by inspiration. He embodies as well the forbidden knowledge of the fire filched by Prometheus, the taboo fratricide of Cain, and the spiritual-political defiance of Milton's Satan. Orc itself is neither good nor evil; it is simply energy: unleashed, unstoppable, inexorable. Like Nietzsche's superman (*übermensch*), Orc is *beyond* good and evil; he exerts his will to power without reference to any bourgeois, schoolboy notions of right and wrong. Interestingly, the best and most precise metaphor for understanding Orc is found in one of the icons of pop culture: the strongly archetypal Star Wars films. In the world of Yoda, Obi Wan Kenobi, and Luke Skywalker, the Force is conceived as an energy field that is itself neutral, but which can be channeled either for good or evil. Like the Force, Orc can be used to create, revive, and renew; but it also has a dark side: one that tears down, destroys, and obliterates.

For too long, Blake felt, Western theology, philosophy, and poetry had tried to bind the energy of Orc (Titans/Satan) and confine it to the underworld (Tartarus/Hell). Until the revolutions in America and France, they had succeeded in demonizing energy as an evil, Hell-born force that threatened the stability, harmony, and rationality of a stoic Heaven watched over by a cold-deterministic (or arbitrary-absentee) God. Worse yet, they first erected a false dichotomy between body and soul, then made the body the exclusive dwelling place of evil energy, and ended by fashioning a God who would punish that evil energy in Hell. In contrast to this view, Blake asserts, in his *Marriage*, that "the following Contraries to these are true":

> 1. Man has no Body distinct from his Soul; for that call'd Body is a portion of Soul discern'd by the five Senses, the chief inlets of Soul in this age.

> 2. Energy is the only life, and is from the body; and Reason is the bound or outward circumference of Energy.

> 3. Energy is Eternal Delight. (210)

Energy, Blake makes clear, animates *both* body and soul; reason, far from being the proper (God-given *or* scientific) guide to the soul is itself but the outward boundary of energy. Furthermore, true life and joy flow out of energy, which is the fire and the genius that effects growth in body and soul.

In contrast to Dante and the Platonists, whose rising path to Heaven and the world of Being calls for balance and restraint, Blake prophetically declares, in a section of the *Marriage* entitled "The Proverbs of Hell" that "the road of excess leads to the palace of wisdom" (211). This same satanic theme of excess over restraint is echoed in several other proverbs:

> He who desires but acts not, breeds pestilence.
>
> The lust of the goat is the bounty of God.
>
> The wrath of the lion is the wisdom of God.
>
> The cistern contains: the fountain overflows.
>
> The tygers of wrath are wiser than the horses of instruction.
>
> You never know what is enough unless you know what is more than enough.
>
> Sooner murder an infant in its cradle than nurse unacted desires. (211–12)

The Proverbs of Solomon counsel a life of prudence and self-control that avoids extremes and resists sinful temptations to over-indulgence; Blake's "Proverbs of Hell" teach that prudence and self-control lead only to repression and stagnation. Blake's Proverbs, that is to say, are really *anti-proverbs* that subvert the very intent of religious instruction; they train their initiates not to become servants of God but Byronic heroes.

In a particularly shocking passage, one that predates by a century Nietzsche's critique of religion as a slave ethic, Blake censures those who enforce restraint on themselves and others: "Those who restrain desire, do so because theirs is weak enough to be restrained; and the restrainer or reason usurps its place & governs the unwilling" (210). The weak and self-enslaved fear energy and therefore use the dual power of religion and reason to legislate against those who would indulge and channel that energy. And the same dynamic holds true on the spiritual level. The angels—whom Blake scorns as passive lackeys of Milton's Urizen-God—share the same slave ethic as their timorous human counterparts and slander the devils who would assert their will to power. Why then do the angels not join the devils and share in their energy? Because, Blake explains, to the weak, repressed angelic mind, the "enjoyments of Genius . . . look like torment and insanity" (211).

In a later passage of great mythic force, Blake elaborates further on the perpetual war between those who would restrain energy and desire and those who would set it free: "The Giants who formed this world into its sensual existence, and now seem to live in its chains are in truth the causes of its life & the sources of all activity; but the chains are the cunning of weak and tame minds which have power to resist energy" (213). These Giants are, of course, the Titans, who, in Blake's Romantic re-working of classical and Christian mythology, are transformed from proud rebels into the primal sources of Orcic energy. They are chthonic ("of the earth") powers, volcanoes of energy that once animated the world but are now chained by slavish-minded men and gods who use religion and philosophy as weapons. Such men Blake labels devourers; they seek to stem the prolific energy of the Giants. Ironically, just as the Zeus who puts Prometheus in chains is the same god whom Prometheus helped put in power, so the slavish-minded betray the very source of their life and power. They enslave and are themselves enslaved by Blake's "mind-forged manacles." Their slavery is an internal one, and only the power of Orc can set them free. In Blake's economy, Dante's heavenly search for freedom takes a downward turn!

The passage and the assumptions that underlie it are radical indeed, but Blake dares go one step further to make the Bible and *Paradise Lost* complicit in a spiritual subterfuge of the highest order. Whereas the name "Satan" in Hebrew means "accuser" or "slanderer" (the role he plays in the book of Job) in *Paradise Lost*, Blake claims, it is the Messiah (or Christ) who is the true Satan: for in the epic, it is Christ (not Lucifer) who accuses and condemns.

Cleansing the Doors of Perception

In the previous chapter, I surveyed the Romantic tendency to internalize traditional notions of Heaven and Hell, a tendency that both illustrates and embodies Satan's egocentric claim (in *Paradise Lost*) that "The mind is its own place, and in itself / Can make a heav'n of hell, a hell of heav'n." The claim is one that resonates through nearly all of Blake's work, but it reaches its fullest and most audacious form in a section of the *Marriage* entitled "A Memorable Fancy." If, in his "Proverbs of Hell," Blake takes on the guise of a satanic Solomon, in his "Memorable Fancy," he puts on the mantel of Jesus himself to construct an unforgettable parable that enshrines Satan's claim as a theological and metaphysical (anti-)truth. In the parable, an angel comes to Blake and warns,

> "O pitiable foolish young man! O horrible! O dreadful state! consider the hot burning dungeon thou art preparing for thyself to all eternity, to which thou art going in such a career."

I said, "Perhaps you will be willing to shew me my eternal lot, & we will contemplate together upon it, and see whether your lot or mine is most desirable."

So he took me thro' a stable & thro' a church & down into the church vault, at the end of which was a mill: thro' the mill we went, and came to a cave: down the winding cavern we groped our tedious way, till a void boundless as a nether sky appear'd beneath us.

By degrees we beheld the infinite Abyss, fiery as the smoke of a burning city; beneath us, at an immense distance, was the sun, black but shining; round it were fiery tracks on which revolv'd vast spiders, crawling after their prey, which flew, or rather swum, in the infinite deep, in the most terrific shapes of animals sprung from corruption; & the air was full of them, & seem'd composed of them: these are Devils, and are called Powers of the air. I now asked my companion which was my eternal lot? he said, "between the black & white spiders . . ." (213–14)

Blake's imagery is both Dantean and Miltonic in its horror and corruption, but here the parallel stops; for as soon as the angel leaves Blake alone in his Tartarean dungeon, a change occurs:

My friend the Angel climb'd up from his station into the mill. I remain'd alone; & then this appearance was no more, but I found myself sitting on a pleasant bank beside a river by moonlight, hearing a harper, who sung to the harp; & his theme was: "The man who never alters his opinion is like standing water, & breeds reptiles of the mind."

But I arose, and sought for the mill, & there I found my Angel, who, surprised, asked me, how I escaped?

I answered, "All that we saw was owing to your metaphysics: for when you ran away, I found myself on a bank by moonlight hearing a harper . . ." (214)

The message of Blake's parable is clear: Hell is not an intrinsically terrible place; it is only because our perceptions have been shaped by a religious (pro-reason, anti-energy) metaphysic that we see it that way. If we could only free ourselves from the restrictive visions of Plato, Dante, and Milton, we would see that Hell is not a pit of eternal torment and darkness but a place of peace and beauty. Heaven and Hell, Blake would have us believe, are not to be defined as the presence or absence of God; instead, they are to be interpreted as states of mind, as two contrary ways of perceiving reality that can either free or enslave the soul. As the harper's song suggests, the best kind of perception, the kind that frees the mind and creates a "heav'n of hell," is dynamic, volatile, ever shifting and shaping anew.

Earlier in the *Marriage*, Blake sums up the full import of his internalization of Heaven and Hell in a powerful aphorism that reads like a saying from the Gnostic Gospel of Thomas: "If the doors of perception were cleansed every thing would appear to man as it is, infinite. For man has closed himself up, till he sees all things thro' narrow chinks of his cavern" (213). There is a touch here of Plato's Allegory of the Cave, of the need for the true philosopher to recognize and forsake the illusions of our world as mere shadows of shadows. There is even a touch of Dante's purgatorial journey into light, with its need to shift one's vision away from the mundane and the physical and to prepare one's eyes for the glory of God. But Blake's finally solipsistic vision is far more radical: things are not as they are, but as they are perceived; it is our perceptions that create the world around us and not vice versa.

Blake, who was an artist as well as a poet, etched his poems into engraving plates that included drawings and border designs; he even invented a new engraving method that made use of an acid wash. In the *Marriage*, Blake, the supreme Romantic poet-prophet, explains that his "infernal method" of printing is itself part of his radical program. In Heaven, corrosives destroy; in Hell, they are "salutary and medicinal, melting apparent surfaces away, and displaying the infinite which was hid" (213).

23

Heaven is Reality

C. S. Lewis's *The Great Divorce*

Blake hailed the marriage of Heaven and Hell in 1790. A century-and-a-half later, while a would-be Nietzschean *übermensch* with a truly satanic will to power led his Nazi party toward world domination, an Oxford don named C. S. Lewis (1898–1963) wrote a response and a challenge to Blake's wedding announcement. Written in the form of a brief, modern updating of Dante's *Divine Comedy*, Lewis's deceptively simple *The Great Divorce* (1946) boldly puts asunder that which Blake (not God) had too hastily joined together.

Best known for *The Chronicles of Narnia*, Lewis brought with him to the task of refuting Blake—not only theologically and philosophically, but psychologically and aesthetically as well—two essential qualifications. First, Lewis was arguably the finest and most effective Christian apologist of the twentieth century. In such books as *Mere Christianity*, *Miracles*, and *The Problem of Pain*, Lewis defended church doctrine and the greater Christian worldview. He showed that a modern man trained in reason, logic, and science could, without putting aside his brain or experiencing cognitive dissonance, embrace such paradoxical metaphysical realities as the Trinity, the incarnation, the atonement, and the resurrection. What that means in relation to the thesis of this book is that an educated lover of Dante and Milton need not make an artificial and unnecessary breach between the power of their poetry and the truth of their subject matter. Though both of their epics are allegorical-mythic in form, the narratives are undergirded by eternal truths about the nature of God, man, and the universe.

Closely allied to his role as defender of the faith, Lewis the English professor was also a committed apologist for the literature and culture of the classical, medieval, and renaissance periods. In such highly acclaimed academic works as *The Allegory of Love*, *A Preface to Paradise Lost*, and *The Discarded Image*, he went so far as to defend the cosmological model that nurtured the epic visions of Homer, Plato, Virgil, Dante, and Milton. Without advocating a return to the geocentric model of Dante, Lewis helped twentieth-century readers gain a wider perspective *on* models: when it comes to competing paradigms of the universe, the proper distinction is not between absolute truth and absolute falsehood but between a modern age that privileges laws and mechanism and a medieval age that privileged hierarchy and pageantry. Despite Galileo's claim that the universe *is* as he saw it through his telescope, Lewis argued, convincingly I think, that we more often than not see in the universe what we project on to it.

Partly to help moderns experience an ordered and personal universe from the inside—in the way that Dante and his fellow medievals did—Lewis wrote *The Chronicles of Narnia* and a trilogy of science fiction novels (*Out of the Silent Planet*, *Perelandra*, *That Hideous Strength*). In all ten of these fantastical works, Lewis brings to shimmering life a meaningful cosmos in sympathy with both God and man. Still, and here is the genius of Lewis that empowered him to write *The Great Divorce*, he was able to create fairy-tale lands of child-like wonder and numinous awe that nevertheless work in tandem with a firm Judeo-Christian understanding of good and evil, right and wrong, virtue and vice. Mystery and doctrine are as firmly compatible as science and religion or reason and faith. The secular humanist *can* have the beauty of Dante and Milton's poetry without sacrificing his or her beliefs, just as the Christian can have his or her assertion of universal moral values without sacrificing the myth or the magic.

Living in the Shadowlands

The premise behind Lewis's brilliantly imaginative tour-de-force is that, by God's grace, the damned souls in Hell are allowed, if they so choose, to take holidays to Heaven. They make the trip by boarding a celestial omnibus driven by a dazzling angel that is clearly patterned on the one who (in Dante's *Purgatorio*) pilots the boat from Rome to Purgatory. When the damned souls disembark from the bus, they are met by the blessed soul of a former friend or family member who converses with them and attempts to convince them, even now, to repent and embrace God's love. Sadly, for all but one of the sinners, the attempt fails: for the sinner categorically refuses to give up whatever idol he has erected in the place of God. Despite the fact they have experienced the despair and wretchedness of Hell and can see spread out before them the joys of Heaven, Lewis's sinners *knowingly* and *willfully* choose misery over grace.

The sinner's choice, Lewis argues, can best be expressed by the words of Milton's Satan, "Better to reign in hell, than serve in heav'n." In the end, "there is always something [the damned] prefer to joy."[1] Like Satan, they would rather nurse pride and injured merit than ask forgiveness of God. For Lewis, there can be no marriage of Heaven and Hell, for the saint who dwells in the former has taken a very different vow from the sinner who dwells in the latter. Heaven is reserved for those who say to God what Jesus said in the Garden of Gethsemane: "Thy will be done"; Hell, in contrast, houses those to whom God says, "*Thy* will be done." The good/evil dichotomy *is* a real one, but the basis of the dichotomy is neither energy nor genius. All that matters is the end toward which we direct our energy and genius. If we direct it toward God, Heaven will open before us; if we turn it backward onto ourselves, we will be engulfed by Hell and will lose our desire and ability to yearn for Heaven.

Building not only on the traditional Christian theology of Dante and Milton but on the metaphysics of Plato, Lewis asserts in *The Great Divorce* that Heaven and Hell are real, distinct, diametrically opposed places. And yet, at the same time, he accepts half of Blake's solipsistic, idealistic philosophy. Hell *is*, in the final analysis, a state of mind, an inward, egocentric narcissism that shrivels our human potential. But Heaven is the very opposite. Heaven is reality itself, a reality that our mind does not create but must submit to. In *Miracles*, Lewis deplores the modern habit of speaking about Heaven and God in negative terms: we are corporeal, God is non-corporeal; Earth is physical, Heaven is non-physical. The truth is actually the reverse. God and Heaven are not less than man and Earth, but *more*: they are *trans*-corporeal and *meta*-physical.

Though orthodox Christianity rejects the Platonic belief that our world is only an illusion and our body a prison house for the soul, it does accept the deeper truth *behind* Platonism—that *compared to* the ultimate reality and "thingness" of Heaven for which we were made, our existence on this present Earth is tantamount to living in what Lewis (in *The Last Battle*) calls the shadowlands. Just as the resurrection body Paul describes in 1 Corinthians 15 (see chapter 13) is like our current body but far more substantial and real, so does the New Jerusalem in which we will someday dwell

---

1. C. S. Lewis, *The Great Divorce*, 69; further references will be given in the text by page number.

have a substance and a reality against which our current cities will pale into nothingness. Plato's distinction between the world of Being and the world of becoming—reflected in the medieval cosmological model's positing of the moon as the transition point between the unchanging perfection above and the ceaseless change below—provides Lewis with the key to deconstructing Blake's own deconstruction of Heaven and Hell.

That deconstruction begins in the opening chapters of *The Great Divorce*, with Lewis's reimagining of Hell. Like both the *Comedy* and *Pilgrim's Progress*, *The Great Divorce* presents itself as a dream-vision in which the protagonist perceives the truth about our mortal and immortal lives. In Lewis's dream-vision, he wakes to find himself, not in Dante's Dark Wood, but in the run-down streets of a dimly-lit town he eventually identifies as Hell. As anyone familiar with Lewis would expect, his vision of Hell borrows heavily from the theology and philosophy of Plato, Dante, and Milton. But that does not prevent Lewis from shocking us with a number of surprises. Fans of Plato, Dante, and Milton will search in vain for shuddering Hell-mouths or graphic punishments or fire and ice. Instead, Lewis presents us with a cheerless, endlessly-drizzling town plunged in perpetual twilight. It is a colorless, lightless, lifeless place: dismal, drab, and isolated. Like the soul-crushing, anti-humanistic worlds of T. S. Eliot's *Waste Land* and Orwell's *1984*, Lewis's Hell is devoid of laughter, joy, or fellowship. Had Lewis been American, he might have compared it to Las Vegas during the day, when the essential dinginess of the place lies exposed to the glare of the sun, with no neon signs to shroud it in false gaiety.

Aside from the bus stop where people await their ride to Heaven, the town is empty. The reason for this, Lewis later learns, is that as soon as people arrive in the town, they quarrel with their neighbors and move elsewhere: a move facilitated by the fact that the inhabitants of the town need only imagine a house, and it immediately appears. Shortly after the move, however, they quarrel again with their new set of neighbors, and move even further out. Because of these frequent moves, the majority of the inhabitants now live so far from the town (and from each other) that it would take them a thousand years to travel back to the bus stop.

At first, Lewis—the protagonist in the story, rather than the author—naively wonders if any of the people in Hell get to visit famous tyrants who left their mark on history. One of his fellow passengers on the bus replies that two enterprising residents once decided to travel out to see Napoleon, a journey that took them 15,000 Hell years to complete. At the end of the journey, they did manage to find his house and peer in through the window, but they did not speak with him. In place of the charismatic child of the French Revolution they went out to find, they saw only a tired-looking, fat little man pacing his house, endlessly blaming each of his generals in turn for his defeat at Waterloo. Even if they wanted to speak with him, it would have done them no good. Like most of the sinners, Napoleon is so self-absorbed that he doesn't even know he is in Hell. He just continues on doing what he did on the Earth, with the vital exception that nobody now cares for him or listens to him.

Like Dante, Lewis firmly believed that Hell is ultimately a place that *we* chose, that it is, in fact, a place where the damned *want* to go, for it promises to give them their sin for eternity without the threat of intervention by God. What makes Lewis's treatment of this spiritual and psychological truth unique from that of Dante—if not unique from all other speculations on the nature of the afterlife—is its suggestion there are no active torments in Hell. Hell's absolute and total separation from the love and presence of God—and with it, all goals and yearnings, all that is meaningful and purposeful—is punishment enough. Like the Byronic hero, the inhabitants of Hell are their own worst enemies, their own executioners.

The notion is a radical one, but it rests on an even more radical premise that Dante only hints at in his *Inferno*: Hell is a process rather than a destination. For Lewis, Hell is not so much a pit that we are thrown into on account of a single, heinous sin (like those of Tantalus or Sisyphus), as it is a marsh that we slide into one peccadillo at a time. Each time we choose ourselves or our sins over God, each time we reject God's offer of grace, we surrender another spark of our humanity. And with each such loss we become less and less the kind of being who desires to spend eternity in the presence of God, and more and more the type of being who desires only to be left alone to cling to himself and his sin forever. In the end, the infernal process of sin and self-absorption causes us to (quite literally) de-humanize ourselves.

It is for that reason that, in Lewis's splendid *Screwtape Letters*, a senior devil named Screwtape advises his nephew Wormwood (a junior devil in the lowerarchy of Hell) not to be deceived by his youthful desire to catch up the human he is tempting in a magnificent sin of biblical proportions. True, the big sins are fun, and it certainly is entertaining to watch humans squirm, but the biggest sinners are often the ones who become the most committed saints. No, Screwtape advises, it is much safer to tempt mortals with a long series of dull little sins. That way the human won't even know what is happening to him. He will think he is doing just fine, when in fact every little decision he has made has drawn him inexorable away from God and toward the darkness outside—a darkness that will eventually fill and devour his soul. "The safest road to Hell," Screwtape concludes, "is the gradual one—the gentle slope, soft underfoot, without sudden turnings, without milestones, without signposts."[2]

Infernal Case Studies

This insidious process of dehumanization by which a mortal man made in the image of God fashions himself anew into a creature made for Hell is rendered disturbingly palpable in *The Great Divorce* through a series of what may best be described as case studies. As Lewis wanders through the breathtaking landscapes of Heaven, he overhears a number of conversations between recalcitrant damned souls and the blessed saints sent to minister to them. Just as a book written by a Freudian psychologist might illustrate each major phobia through a single representative patient, so Lewis explores the sins that keep us from grace, not by assigning them various levels (as Dante does), but by providing us with a dozen or so case-study conversations.

One of the simplest but most profound of these case studies involves a woman whose besetting sin appears at first to be so minor, so inconsequential that it seems hardly worthy of damnation. The sinner in question, far from being a mass murderer or tyrant, is merely a garrulous, grumbling old woman who won't cease her "pity-party" long enough to listen to the saint sent to help her. To Lewis she seems far from evil—only a grumbler, really—but Lewis's Virgilean guide (George MacDonald) explains to him that he is brushing over the essential questions: "whether she is a grumbler, or only a grumble" (74). If there's even an ember of humanity left inside of her, the angels can nurse the flame till it blazes again, but if all that is left is ashes, nothing can be done. The garrulous woman eventually returns to Hell, not because she is (theologically speaking) beyond salvation, but because there is nothing left in her to save.

Like all of Lewis's sinners, the woman is an insubstantial, person-less ghost, rather like the bloodless shades Odysseus encounters during his *nekuia*. In contrast to the supple, virile, glowing forms of the saints (whom Lewis calls the "real people"), the sinners appear to be greasy stains on a window. They are so weak, so small and shriveled that they cannot even bend the grass of Heaven. In a powerful image that sets the reader's mind reeling, MacDonald explains that Hell is so small and Heaven so vast that if the smallest bird in Heaven were to swallow all of Hell, it would not even notice it. MacDonald then goes on to set Lewis's mind reeling as well by telling the astonished traveler that the bus ride he took from Hell to Heaven was not one of transportation but of magnification. The bus did not fly to

2. C. S. Lewis, *The Screwtape Letters*, 56.

Heaven as a plane might fly from London to New York; it expanded out of a nearly microscopic hole in the grassy turf of Heaven.

Plato and Dante, I believe, would have agreed with Lewis's contention that Hell's inhabitants are self-deceived about the insignificance of their infernal prison. And they would have concurred as well with his portrait of a landscape painter who was first drawn to art because he desired to capture the numinous, ineffable light that lay just behind the landscape he was painting. As he progressed in his craft, however, he lost his initial longing for the light and became obsessed with the medium of art *as* a medium. That is to say, though he began as a good Platonic philosopher/ lover, one whose first step toward the Forms is the love of a specific object or person (chapter 5), he ended by abandoning the search. What should have been a means to a higher end (the Good, the Beatific Vision) became an end in itself. His initial desire, one that should have drawn him upward to Heaven, was twisted earthward and led him instead to Hell.

Lewis's Hell bears a strong resemblance to Plato's Cave—both are places of stagnation and illusion—but with one vital distinction. Lewis's cave-dwellers get to see the real, outside world, yet *still* reject it. The psychological depth of Lewis's work rivals Dante's in its exploration of addictive, self-destructive behavior. Both knew (as Plato did not) that we *can* knowingly choose what hurts us: a theological and psychological truth that Lewis embodies in a third case study about a mother who has taken the bus to Heaven to see the blessed soul of her son, who died when he was young. Immediately upon arrival, she insists on seeing her son, but is told that before she can do so, she must learn to desire God. She replies indignantly that God *is* Love, and that any God that would not let her see her son must be a false one. What, after all, the incensed mother exclaims, can be holier than her mother-love?

The woman claims, rightly, that God is Love (1 John 4:16), but what she really means is that Love is God. Her son, or, to be more precise, her smothering, manipulative love for her son is her God. If God won't step aside, she's ready to drag her son down with her to Hell where she can really care for him. (In a parallel case study, Lewis introduces us to a controlling wife who would do the same for her unambitious husband!) Probably by design, Lewis's "mother from Hell" shares many similarities with Dante's Francesca (chapter 11). Like Dante's adulteress, she has taken an aspect of God (love) and fashioned it into an idol which draws her away from God toward her own narcissism. But Lewis goes beyond Dante to explore the deeper, theological-psychological truth that underlies the mother's problem: namely, that it is more often the *nobler* emotions (art, mother love, patriotism) that keep us from God because they can more effectively masquerade as the real thing. Satan, after all, is not a murderer or fornicator who made it big; he is a fallen angel who once stood high in the celestial hierarchy.

Indeed, the only sinner who accepts the offer to remain in Heaven is a man enslaved by the far less socially acceptable sin of lust. His lewd, pornographic desires are embodied in a lizard that sits on his shoulder and whispers carnal thoughts in his ear. The saint who dialogues with him offers to kill the serpent, but the sinner is afraid it will be painful and tries to put off his decision. Finally, in desperation, he calls out to God, and the angel crushes the serpent. What follows is a wondrous metamorphosis in the mode of Ovid, Dante, and Milton—but this time, it is a transfiguration that leads not to horror but to glory. As the saved sinner grows and becomes substantial, the serpent morphs into a powerful and noble stallion (a symbol of pure virility). With great joy, the man mounts the horse and rides on his back into the mountains of Heaven. As he rides, the Earth rejoices to be trodden upon and thus consummated by the horse.

For Lewis, the reason that lust (and other base passions) cannot enter Heaven is not because it is too strong, but because it is too weak for the thundering, passionate desire of Heaven. Lewis's Heaven is one of pure joy, a joy, he insists, that is unsullied by any pity for the damned. Like Dante, Lewis must learn to harden his heart against the sinners, not merely because it is wrong to pity those whom God has justly condemned—which is the reason Dante gives—but because God will not allow Heaven to be spoiled by that spiteful, binding, manipulative pity that seeks to spread its misery. Heaven is above such things.

24

Science and the Afterlife

From Utopia to Dystopia

It remains to consider what the two earnest generations who domi-
nated England between the death of Blake and the birth of Lewis had
to say about Heaven and Hell. I refer, of course, to the Victorians, those
most enterprising of Brits who—with a little help from American manifest
destiny—spread the blessings of democracy, technology, and the free
market across the globe. While the Romantics internalized Heaven, casting
their eye backward to a restored Eden, the Victorians externalized it with a
vengeance, casting their eye forward toward a secular version of the New
Jerusalem.

For the Victorians, Heaven was neither a state of mind to be gained
through cleansed perception, nor a divine home to be inherited after death,
but an earthly goal to be built by hard work and social planning. That is not
to say that the Victorians abandoned the Christian faith of their fathers.
Though many in literary and academic circles slowly gravitated toward
theological liberalism (a school of thought that takes a non-supernatural
approach to Scripture and emphasizes Jesus the teacher and social reformer
over Jesus the incarnate Son of God), most Victorians still believed and took
seriously the Bible's call on their lives. Rather than simply capitulate to secular
humanism—as most of Europe would do over the course of the twentieth
century—the Victorians preserved their traditional faith, but nurtured
alongside it a new one: positivism. Put simply, positivism is the belief that,
through science, technology, and enlightened government, man can propel
himself into an ideal, perfect world of peace, equality, and plenty. In seeking
to fulfill the call of positivism, the Victorians would not only reshape and

bring to Earth mankind's desire for Heaven but leave a rich humanitarian legacy that is still with us today.

The Victorian Dream

The most common word used to describe this perfect world of peace and equality is utopia, a word coined by Sir Thomas More (he who lost his head to Henry VIII) and which, ironically, means "no place" in Greek. It was an irony that did not dissuade the Victorians, who felt quite sure that they could build this "no place" in the real world. In fact, the nineteenth century spawned a diverse group of idealists known as utopian socialists who fashioned actual working communities in which all labor and goods were shared. Some of these planned communities even found their way to America, with one of them (Brook Farm) being famously parodied by Nathaniel Hawthorne in his novel, *The Blithedale Romance.*

The Victorian faith in the possibility of utopia rested on two separate foundations. The first involved a radical change in anthropology that exerted a strong influence on the leaders of the French Revolution. Whereas the Bible taught that the problem with man, the thing holding him back from perfecting himself and his society, was sin, rebellion, and disobedience, many Enlightenment thinkers (most notably, Jean-Jacques Rousseau) argued that the real problem with man was not sin but ignorance and poverty. The shift can perhaps best by viewed in the most beloved work of Victorian England's most beloved novelist, Charles Dickens.

Midway through *A Christmas Carol*, Scrooge meets with the Ghost of Christmas Present and is allowed to witness what Christmas means to the poor and dispossessed of England. Near the end of his interview with the Ghost, Scrooge notices something rustling under Father Christmas's cloak. The Ghost, happy to satisfy Scrooge's curiosity, lifts his cloak, revealing two filthy, wretched children. Scrooge asks if the urchins belong to the Ghost and is told in reply that they are not his children but man's. The boy, he explains, is ignorance, and the girl is want (that is, poverty). He sternly warns Scrooge of the danger the children pose to society, adding that, of the two, ignorance presents the greater threat.

According to the traditional, Judeo-Christian view, a view held by Dante and Milton alike, evil lies within each individual heart and cannot be eradicated by human effort. The best church and state can do is rein in pride, lust, and greed through moral and ethical legislation, religious training, and, if necessary, military force. Instilling in people yearning for heavenly rewards and fear of eternal punishments in Hell constituted one of the prime methods for controlling the deceit and wickedness of the human heart. In contrast, the Victorians believed proper social planning and universal public education could eradicate poverty and ignorance, and, by so doing, usher in a brave new world of prosperity and brotherhood.

Stories of Heaven and Hell need not be eliminated, just given a new, more this-worldly inflection. Hell came more and more to be seen, not in terms of the afterlife, but as a description of the socio-economic ills that ravaged modern urban centers. The hellish plight of London's poor is captured not only in such Dickens' novels as *Oliver Twist* and *David Copperfield*, but in the etchings of Gustave Doré, who, in addition to illustrating *The Divine Comedy*, *Paradise Lost*, and *The Rime of the Ancient Mariner*, produced a series of beautiful but disturbing sketches that express both pity and outrage for living conditions in England's supposedly glorious and civilized capital.

As for Heaven, rather than abandon this world for the next, the Victorians sought to bring Heaven to Earth: a utopian vision that was supported by the second foundation of Victorian positivism: the growth of science and technology. Rapid advances in commerce, health care, communication, and transportation seemed to hold out the promise that we would one day learn to control nature and force her to serve the will of man. Such is the world envisioned in the optimistic, utopian works of H. G. Wells, a world of sanitized, shimmering glass buildings ruled by enlightened leaders for the good of all. Needless to say, this utopian dream was dashed by the horrors of the First World War and completely put to death by the dreadful unleashing of the Atom Bomb at the end of the Second.

We moderns can no longer naively trust in the benefits of science and technology, but for those who lived in the bright dawn of the Industrial Age, all things seemed possible. Lord Alfred Tennyson (1809–92), he who most embodied the positivism of his age, often celebrated in verse the glories of utopia to come. In his poem, "Locksley Hall," he tells the story of an overly-Romantic, embittered young man whose heart is broken when his beloved marries another and who, in the manner of a Byronic hero, isolates himself from society. Near the end of the poem, however, he abandons his Romantic, Hamlet-like over-self-consciousness and identifies himself with the Victorian zeitgeist of positivism. Yes, he muses, for a little while longer there will be war and rumors of war, but, in the end, utopia *will* come:

> Till the war drum throbbed no longer, and the battle flags were furled
> In the Parliament of man, the Federation of the world.
> There the common sense of most shall hold a fretful realm in awe,
> And the kindly earth shall slumber, lapped in universal law. (127–30)[1]

1. All quotes from Tennyson will be taken from *Tennyson's Poetry*, second edition, edited by Robert W. Hill, Jr.; line numbers will be given in the text.

Not since the glory days of the Roman Empire—particularly as celebrated in Virgil's *Aeneid*, the language of which Tennyson closely imitates—had Europe indulged such a vision: not just world conquest, but the victory of law, order, and civilization over nature, division, and barbarism. The great Roman roads would be rebuilt, and commerce would flourish again, but this time scientific social planning would ensure that all would share in the benefits of trade, not just the wealthy few. The messianic prophecies of Isaiah 11:1–9 and Virgil's Fourth Eclogue were to be made a reality in Victorian England. A fusion of the lost Pax Romana of Caesar Augustus and the coming New Jerusalem would meet in the real time and place of London.

If "Locksley Hall" tells of a would-be Byronic hero who allies himself to the Victorian dream of a new Rome, Tennyson's epic, *In Memoriam A. H. H.* (which, like those of Dante and Milton, is also a theodicy), traces his own personal growth from grieving Romantic to committed Victorian. At first plunged into despair and isolation by the death of his young friend, Arthur Henry Hallam, Tennyson slowly comes to identify with his age's spirit of progress. In *In Memoriam* #106, written on the occasion of the third New Year's Eve after the death of Hallam, Tennyson issues a prophetic utopian call that has lost none of its visionary potency. Read in full, the poem embodies all the facets that made up the Victorian dream of Heaven on Earth:

> Ring out, wild bells, to the wild sky,
>   The flying cloud, the frosty light:
>   The year is dying in the night;
> Ring out, wild bells, and let him die.
>
> Ring out the old, ring in the new,
>   Ring happy bells, across the snow:
>   The year is going, let him go;
> Ring out the false, ring in the true.
>
> Ring out the grief that saps the mind,
>   For those that here we see no more;
>   Ring out the feud of rich and poor,
> Ring in redress to all mankind.

> Ring out a slowly dying cause,
>> And ancient forms of party strife;
>> Ring in the nobler modes of life,
> With sweeter manners, purer laws.
>
> Ring out the want, the care, the sin,
>> The faithless coldness of the times:
>> Ring out, ring out my mournful rhymes,
> But ring the fuller minstrel in.
>
> Ring out false pride in place and blood,
>> The civic slander and the spite;
>> Ring in the love of truth and right,
> Ring in the common love of good.
>
> Ring out old shapes of foul disease;
>> Ring out the narrowing lust of gold;
>> Ring out the thousand wars of old,
> Ring in the thousand years of peace.
>
> Ring in the valiant man and free,
>> The larger heart, the kindlier hand;
>> Ring out the darkness of the land,
> Ring in the Christ that is to be.

The peace that had eluded mankind since the dawn of time, the justice that few expected to find outside of Heaven, appears in Tennyson's positivistic paean to be attainable in the here and now. A kind of fellowship that Dante finds only in Paradise is to be brought down to Earth; Plato's imaginary Republic is to be erected and run by enlightened philosopher-citizens. Mankind as a whole is to work his way out of the Cave and into the light of Truth.

It is a grand vision indeed, and Tennyson culminates his poem with a biblical allusion that suggests that God too is on the side of the Victorians: "Ring out the thousand wars of old, / Ring in the thousand years of peace." The allusion is to Revelation 20, where John prophesies the coming of a thousand-year reign of peace, known, traditionally, as the millennium (Latin for thousand). However, theologians since John have differed in their interpretation of Revelation 20: premillennialists claim the millennial kingdom will be established and ruled over by Christ himself, who will return to Earth just before (pre) it begins; amillennialists argue instead that the church age is *itself* the millennium ("a" in Greek is the same as the English "un"), a partly visible, partly invisible kingdom led by the Holy Spirit which indwells the church. Though both of these views can be backed up by Scripture, the Victorians, buoyed up by optimism and faith in the unlimited potential of man, adopted a third view (postmillennialism) that is far harder to reconcile with Revelation: a book which, despite its cryptic nature, clearly teaches that things will get *worse* before Christ returns.

According to postmillennialism—a doctrine that had been partly embraced by American Puritans who fled to the New World from England—humanity would, through advances in science, education, and commerce, propel *itself* into the millennium. Indeed, Christ would not return to Earth until after (post) the humanistic millennium had been built. Tennyson describes the men who will rule this post-millennial kingdom in the epilogue to *In Memoriam*, calling them the Crowning Race:

> Of those that, eye to eye, shall look
>> On knowledge; under whose command
>> Is Earth and Earth's, and in their hand
> Is Nature like an open book;
>
> No longer half-akin to brute,
>> For all we thought and loved and did,
>> And hoped, and suffered, is but seed
> Of what in them is flower and fruit. (129–36)

Proper technology would enable us to control nature, while proper education would allow us to control ourselves. And by means of this double purgation of man and nature, Paradise would rise up in our midst.

So Tennyson describes the great secular saints to come, and then ends with a beautiful tribute to his deceased friend:

> Whereof the man that with me trod
>> This planet was a noble type
>> Appearing ere the time was ripe,
> That friend of mine who lives in God,
>
> That God, which ever lives and loves,
>> One God, one law, one element,
>> And one far-off divine event,
> To which the whole creation moves. (137–44)

Hallam, Tennyson makes clear, was meant to be a member of the Crowning Race, but was born too soon to see or hasten its advent. But all will be well, for Hallam is now one with the great Victorian God who draws all things together. The closing stanza is meant to echo the closing lines of *Paradiso*, suggesting Dante's God will bring to completion in Victorian England the plans he initiated before the foundation of the world.

The Totalitarian Nightmare

Such was the Victorian dream of a new Golden Age, a dream so powerful and seductive that it even influenced atheistic thinkers like Karl Marx, who wrote his *Das Kapital* in the reading room of the British Museum. While denying any form of divine direction, Marx firmly believed that history was moving unstoppably toward a millennium of pure communism in which church and state would disappear (the lyrics to John Lennon's haunting "Imagine" celebrate just such a secular New Jerusalem). Alas, throughout the bloody, war-torn twentieth century, Marx's radical secularization of Victorian positivism manifested itself in totalitarian regimes from both the right (fascism) and the left (communism): regimes in which the force of history, the iron laws of economics, evolutionary genetics, and/or the state itself took the place of God. Would-be utopias metamorphosed into horrific, anti-humanistic dystopias; rather than bring Heaven to Earth, Earth was transformed into a living Hell marked not by cities of shimmering glass but by Auschwitz and the Gulag.

From Nazi Germany to Stalinist Russia, from Mao's China to the Cambodia of the Khmer Rouge, man's attempts to fashion a perfect society have more often than not led to unspeakable atrocities. Neither the horrors of Virgil's Tartarus nor the fiery punishments of Dante's inferno can possibly compare to the physical and psychological torment inflicted by modern totalitarian rulers on their own people. Ironically, what seemed on the surface to be an optimistic view of man—human beings are not inherently sinful, but victims of bad education and a corrupt social order—has led directly to mass extermination. Once the secular humanist rulers of the totalitarian anthill accepted as their destiny the mass reeducation of the people, it became only logical that all people who were too far corrupted to *be* reeducated (gypsies, Jews, landlords, intellectuals, aristocrats, and so forth) would have to be liquidated. Only once the incorrigibles were purged out of the state could the true remolding of humanity begin. With these "devils" out of the way, those who remained could fulfill their destiny and become the new "angels" of a new and eternal kingdom.

H. G. Wells, one of the great architects and champions of Victorian positivism (see his novels, *A Modern Utopia* and *Men Like Gods*), was also one of the first writers to envision a dystopic future in which technology robs, rather than apotheosizes, the soul of man (*The Time Machine, When the Sleeper Wakes*). Such events as Word War I, the Russian Revolution, the Stalinist purges, and the Final Solution led a score of twentieth-century writers to expand on Wells's dystopic vision through a series of novels that combine political speculation with realistic detail. In such novels as Yevgeny Zamyatin's *We*, Arthur Koestler's *Darkness at Noon*, and George Orwell's *1984*, readers encounter totalitarian societies in which individual freedom and personality have been eradicated by a monolithic state-run bureaucracy. Dante and Milton at their most terrible pale before a single line in *1984*, when the new secularized Grand Inquisitor informs the hero that his goal is not to kill him but to change him.

In Aldous Huxley's *Brave New World*, a different kind of Hell on Earth is pictured, one that illustrates the dangers inherent not in totalitarianism but in democracy and the free market. Huxley's citizens of utopia have the peace and plenty they desire, but their lives are devoid of all meaning and purpose; what little pleasure they know is artificial and drug-induced. If Orwell embodies the pain of Dante's sinners, Huxley embodies their utter futility.

C. S. Lewis also tried his hand at the genre of dystopia. In the third book of his science-fiction trilogy (*That Hideous Strength*), he introduces us to the National Institute of Co-ordinated Experiments (N.I.C.E. for short), a secret society of controllers whose goal it is to establish an efficient, "scientific" omni-competent state. At the core of N.I.C.E. is not just the Victorian desire to conquer nature but a disgust for the physical itself. The crowning achievement of their anti-humanistic science is the artificial preservation of the bodiless human head of a criminal, a repellent object to which the atheistic leaders of N.I.C.E. pay religious homage. In actuality, the Head is itself controlled by demons whose hatred of organic life, of individuality, and of human emotion is boundless. Their image of a perfect world is the moon: dead, cold, dark, and sterile.

With a creative genius born out of his thorough knowledge of Greco-Roman and medieval-renaissance literature, Lewis cleverly suggests that the dystopias built by secular humanist totalitarians are, in fact, profoundly spiritual. The demons of Dante, Milton, and the Bible turn out to be the true controllers, the watchers who watch the watchers. Concealed behind the language of science and the machinery of technology, the devils channel and manipulate the dark side of positivism to further their own humanity-hating agenda. In the end, the dark spirituality of N.I.C.E. is defeated, but it can only be brought down with the help of Dante's sympathetic universe. In a thrilling climax patterned partly on Revelation, the Intelligences of the spheres descend and shed their influence on England: an influence that strengthens the good characters but rends to pieces the controllers of N.I.C.E. It is an ending that would likely have pleased Plato and Virgil as much as Dante and Milton.

To Heaven and Back

Before closing this study of the Western world's long fascination with Heaven and Hell, I cannot help but highlight one of the great ironies of the last half century. Although scientific progress has played a major role in diluting modern man's traditional faith in a literal Heaven, advances in medicine have recently, and unintentionally, afforded new and exciting "proof" for the existence of the afterlife. Due to improved resuscitation techniques, a growing number of people around the world have been brought back to life after being declared clinically dead: an event known variously as a life-after-life or near-death experience. Those who experience such miraculous resuscitations tell stories that are remarkably similar in plot and imagery.

As a parallel to my opening tale of Orpheus, I will end not by offering a generic account of the typical near-death experience, but by sharing the personal narrative of a friend of mine who journeyed to Heaven and back— a narrative that is, in its own way, as exciting and poetic as the journey of Plato's philosopher, Dante's ascent to the empyrean, or Milton's recreation of the throne room of God.

One moment Dorothy was in pain; the next moment there was release. Her soul floated upward to the ceiling, and she could see and hear everything the medical doctors were doing to her now-deceased body. Eventually she found herself traveling at amazing speed through a pitch black tunnel, but the darkness was like comforting velvet. Though she had no body, she felt as if her feet were bare, perhaps because she was soon to tread on holy ground. As she drew near to the light at the end of the tunnel, Dorothy began to feel timid and afraid. Immediately, a living friend appeared to her in the tunnel, a figure whom she later learned was an angel who took the form of her friend to comfort her fears.

Reassured of her safety, she left the tunnel and entered a room of dazzling light. The light, Dorothy explained to me, was around her and in her and through her, but she was not herself the light. Slowly, a figure emerged out of the light whom she recognized as Jesus. Together they surveyed all the events of her life. As they reviewed each of her choices, she was told what the better choice would have been, all the while being assured that she was totally loved, forgiven, and accepted. In the room, there was neither time nor space, past nor future: only an eternal present. While there, she felt as if she possessed (directly and intuitively) all the knowledge of the universe, or at least all the knowledge she would ever need. Alas, when she crossed back into our ever-shifting world of time and space, that knowledge was hidden from her as if by a veil, and she now has to struggle to grasp even a small part of that wisdom that was hers for the moment and that will one day be hers again.

When they finished reviewing her life, Jesus raised his hand, palm forward. She knew that if she touched his hand, she would stay there forever, but she knew as well that it was his desire that she should return to earth.

Dorothy obeyed.

Bibliography

Though I have chosen to focus on primary texts in this bibliography, I have listed a number of secondary sources that have passed the test of time, are accessible for non-academics, and/or have influenced my own views on the subject of Heaven and Hell in the Western poetic tradition. When it comes to a subject like Heaven and Hell, it is best to go right to the poets: their tales of the nether regions and the heavenly places are far more direct and memorable than any work of non-fiction criticism could ever be. Just give yourself over to the poets and let them be your guides to Heaven and Hell. For each section, I have first described the books in paragraph form and then provided a formal bibliography.

General

For the details, first consult my glossary; then, if you are hungry for more, purchase a good mythological handbook: Edith Hamilton's *Mythology*, Bulfinch's *Mythology*, Michael Grant's *Myths of the Greeks and Romans*, and Robert Graves' *The Greek Myths* are all excellent, with Graves' work being the most detailed. Particularly helpful when you want to locate a single river or character in Hades are Betty Radice's *Who's Who in the Ancient World* and *Benet's Reader's Encyclopedia*. Every lover of literature really *must* have Benet's on his shelf!

Numerous popular books have been published over the last decade on the subjects of Heaven, Hell, demons, and (especially) angels, most of them richly illustrated. Two of my favorites, that combine pictorial and "coffee table" value with some good commentary, are Malcolm Godwin's *Angels: An Endangered Species* and Alice K. Turner's *The History of Hell*.

Lisa Miller's *Heaven: Our Enduring Fascination with the Afterlife* is one of the finest recent studies to look at Heaven from the point of view of various religions. A more historical survey of the topic can be found in Alan Segal's *Life After Death*. For a more philosophical-theological approach that is strong on Dante see Jeffrey Burton Russell's *A History of Heaven*. Alister McGrath's *A Brief History of Heaven* offers a readable history of the Christian view of Heaven. For a very wide-ranging reader that covers East as well as West, see Carol and Philip Zaleski's *The Book of Heaven*. The books in this paragraph are a bit on the academic side but are still accessible.

I must also add that The Teaching Company offers a number of excellent audio/video lecture series that expand on many of the works treated in this book. These series cannot be found in bookstores, but must be ordered online (www.teach12.com) or by phone (1-800-TEACH12). For that reason I have not listed them in the formal bibliography. Of especial interest are four separate courses by Elizabeth Vandiver on the *Iliad, Odyssey, Aeneid*, and *Greek Mythology*. Also see courses on Dante's *Divine Comedy, The Life and Writings of John Milton*, and *Plato, Socrates, and the Dialogues*. There are also several fine courses on the Bible (both Old and New Testaments) available; my own *Life and Writings of C. S. Lewis* will interest those who enjoy chapter 23 of this book.

Benet's Reader's Encyclopedia, 5th ed. New York: Collins, 2008.

Bulfinch, Thomas. *Mythology*. New York: Seven Treasures, 2009.

Godwin, Malcolm. *Angels: An Endangered Species*. New York: Simon and Schuster, 1990.

Grant, Michael. *Myths of the Greeks and Romans*. New York: Plume, 1995.

Graves, Robert. *The Greek Myths*. New York: Viking, 2011.

Hamilton, Edith. *Mythology*. Boston: Back Bay, 1998.

McGrath, Alister. *A Brief History of Heaven*. Oxford: Blackwell, 2003.

Miller, Lisa. *Heaven: Our Enduring Fascination with the Afterlife*. New York: Harper, 2010.

Radice, Betty. *Who's Who in the Ancient World*. Harmondsworth, UK: Penguin, 1973.

Russell, Jeffrey Burton. *A History of Heaven*. Princeton, NJ: Princeton University Press, 1998.

Segal, Alan. *Life After Death: A History of the Afterlife in Western Religion*. New York: Doubleday, 2004.

Turner, Alice K. *The History of Hell*. New York: Harcourt Brace, 1993.

Zaleski, Carol, and Philip Zaleski, editors. *The Book of Heaven: An Anthology of Writings from Ancient to Modern Times*. London: Oxford University Press, 2000.

Chapters 1–2, 13:
Ancient Greeks and Hebrews; New Testament

For these chapters, your best bet is one of the handbooks listed above, though I'd encourage you to go right to the ancient sources themselves: particularly Hesiod's *Theogeny* and Ovid's *Metamorphoses*. A good overview of Greek religion can be found in W. K. C. Guthrie's *The Greeks and Their*

Gods. C. M. Bowra's *The Greek Experience* has some good relevant chapters. If you can get a hold of *The Presocratics*, it has an excellent chapter on early Greek religious thought. You might also consult Sir James Frazer's *Golden Bough* on the myths and rituals of ancient civilizations; Joseph Campbell is also helpful in this area.

For information on Sheol and Gehenna (Old Testament), a good study Bible and/or Bible dictionary is really all you need. Study Bibles abound these days; my favorite (one that is stuffed with every possible kind of information) is the *NIV Study Bible*. The more recent *ESV Study Bible* is also excellent. Bible dictionaries and encyclopedias come in every shape and size; a good one for the layman is the *Holman Illustrated Bible Dictionary*. For a study of the words used in the Bible, you can do no better than *Vine's Complete Expository Dictionary of Old and New Testament Words*.

All the above books apply as well for those interested in New Testament views of Heaven, Hell, the last judgment, and the resurrection of the dead. Any standard systematic theology textbook will include several chapters on these issues: one example (out of many) is Shirley C. Guthrie, Jr.'s *Christian Doctrine*. Randy Alcorn's *Heaven* sifts through every Bible verse on the afterlife to offer an exhaustive study of Heaven that seeks to replace the common view of an insubstantial Heaven with a more biblical view of what he calls "a resurrected life in a resurrected body, with the resurrected Christ on a resurrected Earth." I highly recommend it. Those interested in the Christian debate over eternal torment in Hell vs. annihilation may consult *Four Views on Hell* and Robert Peterson and Edward Fudge's *Two Views of Hell: A Biblical and Theological Dialogue*.

Alcorn, Randy. *Heaven.* Carol Stream, IL: Tyndale, 2004.
Bowra, C. M. *The Greek Experience.* New York: Mentor, 1957.
Campbell, Joseph. *The Power of Myth.* New York: Anchor, 1991.
ESV Study Bible. Wheaton, IL: Crossway Bibles, 2008.
Frazer, James. *The Golden Bough.* Reprint. London: Penguin, 1998.
Fudge, Edward, and Robert Peterson. *Two Views of Hell: A Biblical and Theological Dialogue.* Downers Grove, IL: InterVarsity, 2000.
Guthrie, Shirley C. *Christian Doctrine.* Rev. ed. Louisville: John Knox, 1994.
Guthrie, W. K. C. *The Greeks and Their Gods.* New York: Methuen, 1950.
Hayes, Zachary J., et al. *Four Views on Hell.* Grand Rapids: Zondervan, 1996.
Hesiod and Theognis. Translated by Dorothea Wender. London: Penguin, 1973.
Holman Illustrated Bible Dictionary. Nashville: Holman, 1998.
NIV Study Bible. Grand Rapids: Zondervan, 1985.
Ovid. *Metamorphoses.* Translated by Mary K. Innes. London: Penguin, 1955.
Vine's Complete Expository Dictionary of Old and New Testament Words. Nashville: Thomas Nelson, 1985.
Wheelwright, Philip. *The Presocratics.* New York: Odyssey, 1966.

Chapter 3: Homer (*Odyssey* XI)

There are many good translations of the *Odyssey*. Believe it or not, I prefer to use the prose translation of E. V. and D. C. H. Rieu. If you want a verse translation, the ones by Robert Fitzgerald and Richmond Lattimore are both good; a more recent translation by Robert Fagles is also excellent. If you wish also to consult the *Iliad*, you *must* read the epic translation of Richmond Lattimore, though I also do approve highly of Robert Fagles' slightly easier rendering. All you really need is Homer's text, but you may wish to consult Peter V. Jones's *Homer's Odyssey: A Companion to the Translation of Richmond Lattimore* for a line-by-line analysis of the poem. My own *From Achilles to Christ* offers close readings of the *Iliad*, *Odyssey*, and *Aeneid* from the perspective of a Christian humanist worldview. Two other books that take a similar approach to classical and Christian material are John Mark Reynolds's *When Athens Met Jerusalem* and Peter Leithart's *Heroes of the City of Man*.

The Iliad. Translated by Robert Fagles. New York: Penguin, 1998.

The Iliad. Translated by Richmond Lattimore. Chicago: University of Chicago Press, 1961.

Jones, Peter V. *Homer's Odyssey: A Companion to the Translation of Richmond Lattimore*. Edwardsville, IL: Southern Illinois University Press, 1988.

Leithart, Peter. *Heroes of the City of Man: A Christian Guide to Select Ancient Literature*. Moscow, ID: Canon, 1999.

Markos, Louis. *From Achilles to Christ: Why Christians Should Read the Pagan Classics*. Downers Grove, IL: InterVarsity, 2007.

The Odes of Pindar. Translated by Richmond Lattimore. Chicago: University of Chicago Press, 1947.

The Odyssey. Translated by Robert Fagles. New York: Penguin, 1996.

The Odyssey. Translated by Robert Fitzgerald. New York: Farrar, Straus and Giroux, 1998.

The Odyssey. Translated by Richmond Lattimore. New York: Harper Perennial, 2007.

The Odyssey. Translated by E. V. Rieu and Revised by D. C. H. Rieu. London: Penguin, 2003.

Reynolds, John Mark. *When Athens Met Jerusalem: An Introduction to Classical and Christian Thought*. Downers Grove, IL: InterVarsity, 2009.

Chapters 4–5: Plato

Let me state right off that Plato's works are vastly easier to understand than are most of the critical works written to explain them. Plato's dialogues are remarkably direct and vivid and must be read first hand. I would advise you to read the complete *Phaedo*, the last several pages of the *Apology*, the

Allegory of the Cave and the Myth of Er in the *Republic* (Book VII and the closing pages of Book X), Socrates' speech toward the end of the *Symposium*, the myth of the Charioteer in *Phaedrus*, and the closing myth of *Gorgias*. For Plato's myth of the creation of the world by the divine Demiurge, consult his *Timaeus* (which strongly influenced the medieval view of the cosmos); for his myth of Atlantis, read *Critias*. In general, stick with the Penguin editions of all these works (which offer helpful annotations), though Richard W. Sterling and William C. Scott's translation of *The Republic* is excellent and very readable. Benjamin Jowett's translations of Plato's works are legendary and are still very readable. Please make sure to avoid Alan Bloom's translation of *The Republic*; though I'm a fan of his *Closing of the American Mind*, his translations of Plato (and those of his school) are unreadable and at times quite ugly. I'd encourage you to buy Plato's works separately in paperback rather than buying one giant volume in hard back; you're more likely to *read* them (maybe even take them on a trip) if you buy them individually.

For a classic study of Plato's view of the universe, see F. M. Cornford's *Plato's Cosmology*. G. M. A. Grube's *Plato's Thought* and A. E. Taylor's *Platonism and its Influence* are also very helpful, but, again, let Plato be your guide.

On the pre-existence of the soul, my texts were Origen's *On First Principles* and Betty J. Eadie's *Embraced by the Light*. Wordsworth's "Ode: Intimations of Immortality from Recollections of Early Childhood" can be found in any collection of British poetry.

Cornford, F. M. *Plato's Cosmology: The Timaeus of Plato*. Indianapolis: Bobbs-Merrill, nd.

Eadie, Betty J. *Embraced by the Light*. New York: Bantam, 1992.

Gorgias. Translated by W. C. Helmbold. Indianapolis: Bobbs-Merrill, 1952.

Grube, G. M. A. *Plato's Thought*. Indianapolis: Hackett, 1980.

The Last Days of Socrates. Translated by Hugh Tredennick. London: Penguin, 1969.

On First Principles. Translated by G. W. Butterworth. New York: Harper & Row, 1966.

Phaedrus. Translated by Walter Hamilton. London: Penguin, 1973.

Republic. Translated by Richard W. Sterling and William C. Scott. New York: Norton, 1996.

Symposium. Translated by Walter Hamilton. London: Penguin, 1951.

Taylor, A. E. *Platonism and its Influence*. New York: Cooper Square, 1963.

Timaeus and Critias. Translated by Desmond Lee. London: Penguin, 1977.

Chapters 6–7: Virgil (*Aeneid* VI)

The best translation of the *Aeneid*, to my mind, remains the one by Robert Fitzgerald; it has epic drive and is a pleasure to read. It also has an excellent glossary of names. The translation by Allen Mandelbaum is slightly more accurate than the one by Fitzgerald, but I find it a tad dull compared to Fitzgerald's more rousing style. Virgil's "Fourth Eclogue" can be found in *The Eclogues and Georgics of Virgil*, translated by the former poet laureate of Britain, C. Day Lewis; it is from his translation I quote in chapter 9.

Two books on Virgil that I have found helpful are Brooks Otis's *Virgil: A Study in Civilized Poetry* and Michael Putnam's *The Poetry of the Aeneid*. For a multitude of perspectives, consult *Reading Vergil's Aeneid*, edited by Christine Perkell. This book evolved out of a 1994 NEH-sponsored summer institute on the *Aeneid* held at Emory University; I myself attended the institute. Domenico Comparetti's *Vergil in the Middle Ages* offers a classic, detailed study of how Virgil was read and "Christianized" throughout the Middle Ages (especially by Dante). Also see chapters on Virgil in *From Achilles to Christ* and *Heroes of the City of Man*.

Many translations of Cicero's "Dream of Scipio" are available. My copy is anthologized in *Cicero: Nine Orations and the Dream of Scipio*.

Aeneid. Translated by Robert Fitzgerald. New York: Vintage, 1984.
Aeneid. Translated by Allen Mandelbaum. New York: Bantam, 1961.
Comparetti, Domenico. *Vergil in the Middle Ages*. Translated by E. F. M. Benecke. Princeton, NJ: Princeton University Press, 1997.
The Eclogues and Georgics. Translated by C. Day Lewis. New York: Anchor, 1964.
Nine Orations and the Dream of Scipio. Translated by Palmer Bovie. New York: Mentor, 1967.
Otis, Brooks. *Virgil: A Study in Civilized Poetry*. Norman, OK: University of Oklahoma Press, 1995.
Perkell, Christine. *Reading Vergil's Aeneid: An Interpretive Guide*. Norman, OK: University of Oklahoma Press, 1999.
Putnam, Michael. *The Poetry of the Aeneid*. Cornell, NY: Cornell University Press, 1989.

Chapters 8–12, 14–17: Dante (*Divine Comedy*)

Many great translators have turned their sights to Dante, but I still think that the best English version of the *Divine Comedy* (*Inferno, Purgatory, Paradise*) is by John Ciardi. (In 2003, the New American Library published a one-volume edition that includes the full *Comedy*.) In addition to his excellent and powerful translation, Ciardi supplies a wealth of notes that help make the work come alive; he even teaches us how to pronounce all the Italian names properly. Indeed, Ciardi is all you need to understand Dante, for his notes draw together much of the best criticism. The introductions and afterwords to all three editions are particularly good.

Allen Mandelbaum has also translated the *Comedy*; as with his *Aeneid*, it tends to be more accurate, but again, lacks the power of Ciardi. Dorothy Sayers (of Lord Peter Wimsey fame) has also translated Dante; though her translation is not as good as Ciardi's (particularly because she chooses to maintain the full terza rima rhyme scheme), her notes are worth perusing. The poet Robert Pinsky has translated *Inferno*, but his translation, though it has a strong colloquial feel, is a bit pedestrian; I prefer the recent translation of Dante by Anthony Esolen. Robert and Jean Hollander have also produced fine translations of the *Comedy*. Dante's *La Vita Nuova* is available in a good edition from Penguin, translated and with an excellent introduction by Barbara Reynolds, who was responsible for finishing Sayers's translation of *Paradise* after her death. Reynolds has also written an excellent biography of Dante.

Ciardi is really the only guide you need to Dante, but if you would like to consult some other works, two of the most accessible are Allan Gilbert's *Dante and his Comedy* and *Dante: A Collection of Critical Essays*, edited by John Freccero. Peter Leithart's *Ascent to Love* is a very helpful guide with an approach similar to my own. I would strongly encourage you to purchase *The Doré Illustrations for Dante's Divine Comedy*, which is available in an inexpensive but well-made edition from Dover Press; the illustrations are powerful and remain in the mind. I have enjoyed the psychological, Jungian reading of the *Comedy* in Helen M. Luke's delightful *Dark Wood to White Rose*.

My descriptions in chapter 8 of the medieval model of the cosmos— a model which reverberates beneath the writings of Plato, Virgil, Dante, and Milton, and which continued to shape European thought well into the eighteenth century—are indebted to three excellent books. For the quickest and easiest overview of the model, consult E. M. W. Tillyard's *The Elizabethan World Picture*. For a more in-depth look that challenges its reader to take the medievals and their model seriously, I strongly encourage you to purchase C. S. Lewis's *The Discarded Image*. For the most exhaustive look at the model (a scholarly yet still accessible tome) take a stab at Arthur O. Lovejoy's *The Great Chain of Being*. Those who love not only the medieval cosmological model but C. S. Lewis's *Chronicles of Narnia* must read Michael Ward's *Planet Narnia*, which compares the seven Chronicles to each of the seven planets of the medieval model.

Fans of C. S. Lewis will appreciate Jerry Walls's trilogy of the afterlife in which he studies, from the point of view of an evangelical Protestant philosopher, the nature of Hell, Purgatory, and Paradise. In his book on Purgatory, he makes a strong case, partly based on analyzing the views of C. S. Lewis, that Protestants can (and perhaps should) accept the reality of Purgatory.

The Divine Comedy. Translated by John Ciardi. New York: New American Library, 2003.
The Divine Comedy: Hell. Translated by Dorothy Sayers. London: Penguin, 1959.
The Divine Comedy: Paradise. Translated by Dorothy Sayers. London: Penguin, 1962.
The Divine Comedy: Purgatory. Translated by Dorothy Sayers. London: Penguin, 1959.
The Doré Illustrations for Dante's Divine Comedy. New York: Dover, 1976.
Freccero, John. *Dante: A Collection of Critical Essays.* Englewood Cliffs, NJ: Prentice-Hall, 1965.
Gilbert, Allan. *Dante and his Comedy.* New York: New York University Press, 1963.
Inferno. Translated by John Ciardi. New York: Mentor, 1954.
Inferno. Translated by Anthony Esolen. New York: Modern Library, 2003.
Inferno. Translated by Robert and Jean Hollander. New York: Anchor, 2002.
Inferno. Translated by Allen Mandelbaum. New York: Bantam, 1982.
Inferno. Translated by Robert Pinsky. New York: Farrar, Straus, and Giroux, 1996.
Leithart, Peter. *Ascent to Love: A Guide to Dante's Divine Comedy.* Moscow, ID: Canon, 2001.
Lewis, C. S. *The Discarded Image.* Cambridge: Cambridge University Press, 1964.
Lovejoy, Arthur O. *The Great Chain of Being.* New York: Harper & Row, 1936.
Luke, Helen M. *Dark Wood to White Rose: Journey and Transformation in Dante's Divine Comedy.* New York: Parabola, 1989.
Paradise. Translated by Anthony Esolen. New York: Modern Library, 2007.
Paradiso. Translated by John Ciardi. New York: Mentor, 1970.
Paradiso. Translated by Robert and Jean Hollander. New York: Anchor, 2007.
Paradiso. Translated by Allen Mandelbaum. New York: Bantam, 1986.
Purgatorio. Translated by John Ciardi. New York: Mentor, 1961.
Purgatorio. Translated by Robert and Jean Hollander. New York: Anchor, 2004.
Purgatorio. Translated by Allen Mandelbaum. New York: Bantam, 1984.
Purgatory. Translated by Anthony Esolen. New York: Modern Library, 2004.
Reynolds, Barbara. *Dante: The Poet, the Political Thinker, the Man.* Emeryville, CA: Shoemaker & Hoard, 2006.
Tillyard, E. M. W. *The Elizabethan World Picture.* New York: Vintage, nd.
La Vita Nuova. Translated by Barbara Reynolds. New York: Penguin, 1969.
Walls, Jerry. *Heaven: The Logic of Eternal Joy.* Oxford: Oxford University Press, 2002.
———. *Hell: The Logic of Damnation.* Notre Dame: University of Notre Dame Press, 1992.
———. *Purgatory: The Logic of Total Transformation.* Oxford: Oxford University Press, 2011.
Ward, Michael. *Planet Narnia: The Seven Heavens and the Imagination of C. S. Lewis.* Oxford: Oxford University Press, 2008.

Chapters 18–19: Milton (*Paradise Lost*)

When it comes to Milton, we are blessed to have the Norton Critical Edition of *Paradise Lost*. This remarkable work offers copious annotations of the poem, a dozen or so excellent critical studies, and a wealth of other verse and prose writings by Milton that are relevant to *Paradise Lost*. This single edition is all you need to usher you into the brave new world of Milton's great epic. I would, however, strongly urge you to also purchase C. S. Lewis's *A Preface to Paradise Lost*. This highly readable and thought-provoking work attempts to reclaim Milton from all those post-Romantic critics who would make Satan out to be the hero (see chapter 21). Lewis helps us to understand *Paradise Lost* from the perspective of Milton's time and culture and of his theological and aesthetic goals. A modern response to Lewis's study can be found in Stanley Fish's challenging and powerfully argued *Surprised by Sin: The Reader in Paradise Lost*. Doré's illustrations of *Paradise Lost* are available from Dover Press.

The Doré Illustrations for Milton's Paradise Lost. New York: Dover, 1993.
Fish, Stanley. *Surprised by Sin: The Reader in Paradise Lost*. 2nd ed. Cambridge: Harvard University Press, 1998.
Lewis, C. S. *A Preface to Paradise Lost*. Oxford: Oxford University Press, 1961.
Paradise Lost. Edited by Scott Elledge. New York: Norton, 1993.

Chapter 20: John Bunyan and John Donne

The best anthology of seventeenth-century poetry and prose, one that includes generous helpings of Donne's poetry, devotions, and sermons and a hefty selection from *Pilgrim's Progress*, is *Seventeenth-Century Prose and Poetry*. There are numerous editions of *Pilgrim's Progress* out there (more expensive ones may include William Blake's beautiful illustrations); almost any will do, though you will want to check if the edition modernizes the spelling and whether or not it includes all the biblical references. My personal favorite is the inexpensive but well-annotated version put out by Barnes & Noble Classics. Lovers of Donne's poetry must purchase the Norton Critical Edition of *John Donne's Poetry*. Another Norton Critical Edition of interest is *George Herbert and the Seventeenth-Century Religious Poets*. Both of these editions include a dozen or so critical essays and full bibliographies and are highly recommended. For an excellent biography of Donne, see John Stubbs's *John Donne*.

George Herbert and the Seventeenth-Century Religious Poets. Edited by Mario A. Di Cesare. New York: Norton, 1978.
John Donne's Poetry. 2nd ed. Edited by Arthur L. Clements. New York: Norton, 1992.
Pilgrim's Progress. Edited by David Hawkes. New York: Barnes & Noble Classics, 2005.
Stubbs, John. *John Donne: The Reformed Soul*. New York: Norton, 2008.
Witherspoon, Alexander, and Frank Warnke. *Seventeenth-Century Prose and Poetry*. 2nd ed. New York: Harcourt Brace Jovanovich, 1982.

Chapters 21–22: The Romantics:
Blake, Wordsworth, Coleridge, Byron, Shelley, Keats

There are at least two fine collections of Romantic Poetry that contain all the poems referred to in chapters 21 and 22. The first is ye olde reliable *Norton Anthology of English Literature*, Volume 2 and *English Romantic Poetry and Prose*. There are excellent Norton Critical Editions of *Shelley's Poetry and Prose*, *Byron's Poetry*, and, best of all, *Blake's Poetry and Designs*. The best one-volume edition of Keats is *John Keats: Complete Poetry*. Penguin has put out a good one-volume edition of Coleridge. An older, but handy collection of Wordsworth's poetry can be found in *Wordsworth: Selected Poetry*; Norton has put out the best edition of Wordsworth's poetic autobiography, *The Prelude: 1799, 1805, 1850*.

Those wishing to explore William Blake's artwork are encouraged to purchase Kathleen Raine's richly illustrated *William Blake*. A readable, well-illustrated biography has been written by Peter Ackroyd, *Blake: A Biography*. Two other critical studies of the Romantics will be of general interest to readers of this book: Douglas Bush's *Mythology and the Romantic Tradition in English Poetry*; M. H. Abrams' *Natural Supernaturalism*. I discuss the Romantic inward turn at length in my *The Eye of the Beholder*.

Abrams, M. H. *Natural Supernaturalism: Tradition and Revolution in Romantic Literature*. New York: Norton, 1971.

Ackroyd, Peter. *Blake: A Biography*. New York: Ballantine, 1995.

Blake's Poetry and Designs. Edited by Mary Lynn Johnson and John E. Grant. New York: Norton, 1979.

Bush, Douglas. *Mythology and the Romantic Tradition in English Poetry*. New York: Norton, 1963.

Byron's Poetry. Edited by Frank D. McConnell. New York: Norton, 1978.

English Romantic Poetry and Prose. Edited by Russell Noyes. Oxford: Oxford University Press, 1956.

John Keats: Complete Poetry. Edited by Jack Stillinger. Cambridge: Belknap, 1978.

Markos, Louis. *The Eye of the Beholder: How to See the World like a Romantic Poet*. Hamden, CT: Winged Lion, 2011.

Norton Anthology of English Literature. Volume 2. 8th ed. Edited by Stephen Greenblatt et al. New York: Norton, 2006.

The Prelude: 1799, 1805, 1850. Edited by Jonathan Wordsworth et al. New York: Norton, 1979.

Raine, Kathleen. *William Blake*. London: Thames and Hudson, 1970.

Samuel Taylor Coleridge: The Complete Poems. Edited by William Keach. London: Penguin, 1997.

Shelley's Poetry and Prose. Edited by Donald H. Reiman and Sharon B. Powers. New York: Norton, 1977.

Wordsworth: Selected Poetry. Edited by Mark Van Doren. New York: Modern Library, 1950.

Chapter 23: C. S. Lewis

C. S. Lewis's works are available from various publishers in many editions, most notably Macmillan, Harcourt Brace, Harper San Francisco, and Zondervan. I have only specified below the editions from which I quoted in chapter 23. Those wishing to get a full understanding of Lewis's view of Heaven and Hell should read *The Great Divorce*, *The Screwtape Letters*, *The Pilgrim's Regress*, the closing chapters of *The Problem of Pain*, and "The Weight of Glory" and "Transpositions" (both of which are anthologized in *The Weight of Glory and Other Addresses*). To a certain extent, all of his fiction has to do with Heaven; the most powerful visions are to be found in the closing chapter of *Perelandra*, as well as in three of his Chronicles of Narnia: *The Voyage of the Dawn Treader*, *The Silver Chair*, and *The Last Battle*. The best of the many biographies remains George Sayer's *Jack: A Life of C. S. Lewis*. My series with The Teaching Company, *The Life and Writings of C. S. Lewis*, includes an extensive bibliography. I also devote a chapter to Lewis's views of Heaven and Hell in both my *Lewis Agonistes* and *Apologetics for the 21st Century*.

Lewis, C. S. *The Great Divorce*. New York: Macmillan, 1946.
———. *The Screwtape Letters*. New York: Macmillan, 1982.
Markos, Louis. *Apologetics for the 21st Century*. Wheaton, IL: Crossway, 2010.
———. *Lewis Agonistes: How C. S. Lewis Can Train us to Wrestle with the Modern and Postmodern World*. Nashville: Broadman & Holman, 2003.
Sayer, George. *Jack: A Life of C. S. Lewis*. London: Hodder & Stoughton, 1997.

Chapter 24: Utopia and Dystopia

The most accessible anthologies of Victorian literature are the *Norton Anthology of English Literature*, Volume 2 and *Victorian Poetry and Prose*. There is also an excellent Norton Critical Edition of *Tennyson's Poetry*. Three classic studies that have some bearing on the issues of religion and the building of utopia are Max Weber's *The Protestant Ethic & the Spirit of Capitalism*, Peter L. Berger's *The Sacred Canopy: Elements of a Sociological Theory of Religion*, and Carl L. Becker's *The Heavenly City of the Eighteenth-Century Philosophers*. I discuss the Victorian spirit of progress with an emphasis on Tennyson's poetry in my *Pressing Forward*. Doré's illustrations of London are available from Dover Press.

Fictional works that concern themselves with building utopia and/ or dystopia are legion. Here is a list of some of the major books (most are available in numerous editions, and so I have not included them in the bibliography below): Plato's *Republic*, Machiavelli's *The Prince*, Thomas More's *Utopia*, Jonathan Swift's *Gulliver's Travels*, Edward Bellamy's *Looking Backward*, H. G. Wells's *The Sleeper Wakes*, *The Time Machine*, *A Modern Utopia*, *Men Like Gods*, and *The Shape of Things to Come*, Jack London's *The Iron Heel*, George Orwell's *1984* and *Animal Farm*, Aldous Huxley's *Brave New World*, Yevgeny Zamyatin's *We*, C. S. Lewis's *That Hideous Strength* and *Abolition of Man*, and Arthur Koestler's *Darkness at Noon*. I have been strongly influenced by Neil Postman's legendary thesis (in *Amusing Ourselves to Death*) that *Brave New World* has turned out to be more prophetic than *1984*.

The seminal study of near death experiences is Raymond Moody's *Life After Life*. Roy Abraham Varghese has provided the most updated information on the subject in *There is Life After Death* (includes a foreword by Moody). Dinesh D'Souza's *Life After Death: The Evidence* is also well worth reading. In recent years, personal accounts of people who have been to Heaven and back (or even Hell and back) have abounded. The three that, to my mind at least, have the strongest ring of truth are Don Piper's *90 Minutes in Heaven*, Todd Burpo's *Heaven is for Real*, and Bill Wiese's *23 Minutes in Hell*. William P. Young's controversial *The Shack* presents its readers with what is essentially a story of a life after life experience.

Becker, Carl L. *The Heavenly City of the Eighteenth-Century Philosophers*. New Haven, CT: Yale University Press, 1932.

Berger, Peter L. *The Sacred Canopy: Elements of a Sociological Theory of Religion*. New York: Anchor, 1969.

Burpo, Todd. *Heaven is for Real*. Nashville: Thomas Nelson, 2010.

Doré's Illustrations of London. New York: Dover, 2004.

D'Souza, Dinesh. *Life After Death: The Evidence*. Washington, DC: Regnery, 2009.

Markos, Louis. *Pressing Forward: Alfred, Lord Tennyson and the Victorian Age*. Naples, FL: Sapientia, 2007.

Moody, Raymond. *Life After Life*. New York: Bantam, 1975.

Norton Anthology of English Literature. Vol. 2. 8th ed. Edited by Stephen Greenblatt, et al. New York: Norton, 2006.

Piper, Don. *90 Minutes in Heaven*. Grand Rapids: Revell, 2004.

Postman, Neil. *Amusing Ourselves to Death: Public Discourse in the Age of Show Business*. New York: Penguin, 1985.

Tennyson's Poetry. 2nd ed. Edited by Robert W. Hill, Jr. New York: Norton, 1999.

Varghese, Roy Abraham. *There is Life After Death: Compelling Reports from Those Who Have Glimpsed the Afterlife*. Franklin Lakes, NJ: Career, 2010.

Victorian Poetry and Prose. Edited by Lionel Trilling and Harold Bloom. Oxford: Oxford University Press, 1973.

Weber, Max. *The Protestant Ethic & the Spirit of Capitalism*. Reprint. London: Penguin, 2002.

Wiese, Bill. *23 Minutes in Hell*. Lake Mary, FL: Charisma House, 2006.

Young, William P. *The Shack*. Newbury Park, CA: Windblown Media, 2007.

Timeline

c. 1200 B.C.	Mythical journeys of Odysseus and Aeneas
late 8th c.	Homer composes *Odyssey*
399	Socrates delivers his Apology
early 4th c.	Plato at work on his dialogues
c. 250	Septuagint (Greek translation of Old Testament)
c.51	Cicero writes "The Dream of Scipio"
30–19	Virgil writes *Aeneid*
1st c. A.D.	Books of the New Testament written
1300	Year of Dante's journey
1633	*Holy Sonnets* (John Donne)
1667	*Paradise Lost* (John Milton)
1678	*Pilgrim's Progress* (John Bunyan)
1790	*Marriage of Heaven and Hell* (William Blake)
1817	*Manfred* (Lord Byron)
1820	*Prometheus Unbound* (Percy Bysshe Shelley)
1850	*In Memoriam* (Alfred, Lord Tennyson)
1905	*A Modern Utopia* (H. G. Wells)
1932	*Brave New World* (Aldous Huxley)
1946	*The Great Divorce* (C. S. Lewis)
1949	*1984* (George Orwell)

Glossary

Though this glossary is quite extensive, I have chosen to leave out two lists of terms that do not have direct bearing on Heaven and Hell: the numerous examples of virtue and vice that appear in Dante's *Purgatorio* and the names of the numerous saints with whom Dante speaks in *Paradiso*. I have also not given separate citations for all the devils and angels listed in *Paradise Lost* or the nine orders of angels that appear in Dante's *Paradiso*, but have listed their names in the citations for "angels" and "devils." Finally, separate citations will not be given for the various incarnations of the Byronic hero.

Abaddon: Hebrew for destruction, this is another name for Sheol.

Acheron: The main river of Hades into which Phlegethon, Styx, and Cocytus run. Its name means sorrow. Charon carries both Aeneas and Dante over the river Acheron into Hades.

Aeacus: Judge of the dead who rules together with Minos and Rhadamanthus.

Aeneas: Hero of the *Aeneid* who descends into the underworld to meet his father, Anchises.

Agamemnon: Leader of the Greek forces that attacked Troy, who, upon returning home, was killed by his wife and her lover. Odysseus speaks with him in the underworld; Plato, in the Myth of Er, has Agamemnon request to return as an eagle.

Ajax (Greek: *Aias*): Hero of the Trojan war, who, after Odysseus tricks him out of the armor of the dead Achilles, takes his own life. Odysseus meets him in Hades, but Ajax will not speak to him. Socrates (in *Apology*) expresses a wish to meet Ajax in Elysium and compare their stories of injustice. In Plato's Myth of Er, Ajax chooses to return as a lion.

Anchises: Father of Aeneas who dies in *Aeneid* III but then meets with Aeneas in the Elysian Fields where he explains to him the theology of the underworld and shows him the march of Roman heroes to come.

Angels: Spiritual beings directly created by God before the world began. Very few angels are named in Scripture (Michael and Gabriel); Milton names several more of them (Raphael, Uriel, Abdiel, etc.). In medieval thought, there were nine orders of angels that correspond to the nine circles (or spheres) of Heaven; in descending order (beginning with the primum mobile) they are: seraphim, cherubim, thrones, dominations, virtues, powers, principalities, archangels, angels. Each of the angels acts as the intelligence of its appropriate sphere, causing it to spin; earth, which is motionless, has no angel, though Dante suggests the earth is controlled by Dame Fortune and her wheel. As the spheres spin, the angels sing, producing together a celestial song known as the music of the spheres (by some accounts, the music is produced by the spinning of the spheres themselves). Our earthly ears have grown deaf to the music. In the religion of Pythagoras, the soul cannot find release from reincarnation until it comes in tune with the music of the spheres.

Apollyon: A devil (probably Satan himself) who tries to tempt Christian (in *Pilgrim's Progress*) to forsake his journey and follow him instead. Apollyon is the Greek word for destruction.

Asphodel: A Greek plant with white and yellow clusters; it blooms on the grass of the Elysian Fields.

Atropos: Fate of the future who eventually cuts the thread of our life.

Byronic hero: A distinctly Romantic hero patterned after the Satan of *Paradise Lost* (whom the Romantics transformed into the hero). The Byronic hero is a man who has committed a taboo sin or acquired forbidden knowledge and, by so doing, has been cut off from humanity. He is a man of grandeur and power, at times almost super-human, but he is forced (mostly by his own sense of guilt and alienation) to live on the margins of society. Examples of Byronic heroes include Prometheus, Cain, Oedipus, Faust, the Wandering Jew, Mephistopheles, Heathcliff, Dr. Frankenstein,

Dracula, Don Juan, Dr. Jekyll, Captain Nemo, and Hamlet. Byron's *Manfred*, Shelley's *Prometheus Unbound*, and Coleridge's *Rime of the Ancient Mariner* all feature Byronic heroes. Byron and Shelley were themselves Byronic heroes.

Cacciaguida: Dante's great-great-grandfather who dwells in the sphere of Mars with the other martyrs of the church (he died fighting in the Crusades). Cacciaguida plays the same role for Dante as Anchises does for Aeneas: he reveals to him both the pain and the glory that is to come.

Caduceus: The magic wand of Hermes (Latin: Mercury) with which he hypnotizes dead souls and leads them to Hades. His wand, with its intertwining serpents, is used as a symbol for the medical profession.

Castor and Pollux: Twin sons of Leda (and brothers of Helen of Troy) who, out of love for each other, agreed to spend alternate days in Hades and on the earth. Castor and Pollux (Polydeuces in Greek) are known to help sailors at sea; the constellation Gemini (the Twins) is named for them.

Celestial City: Bunyan's allegorical name for Heaven/the New Jerusalem in *Pilgrim's Progress*. To get there one must pass through the river Jordan (a symbol for death).

Centaur: In Greek mythology, these half-men, half-horse beasts are known for their lust and violence. In Dante's *Inferno*, they guard those in the first sub-level of circle seven (violence against others). Whenever these sinners try to rise out of the boiling blood of Phlegethon, the centaurs shoot them with fiery arrows. Dante identifies Chiron as a good centaur, and, in Greek mythology, he was reputed to be the wise tutor of such heroes as Jason and Hercules.

Cerberus: The three-headed dog who guards Hades. As one of his labors, Hercules descended into Hades and captured him. Dante has Cerberus guard the third level of Hell, where the gluttons are punished.

Charon: The ferryman of the dead who carries sinners over the river Acheron into Hades.

Crystalline Sphere: A tenth heavenly sphere that does not appear in Dante but which Milton places between the fixed stars and the primum mobile.

City of Dis: Dante's name for lower Hell where the sins of violence and and deceit are punished. The gates to the City are guarded by the rebellious angels.

Clotho: Fate of the present who spins the thread of our life.

Cocytus: River in Hades whose name means wailing. According to Plato's *Phaedo*, Cocytus is the name of Styx when it plunges into Tartarus; it carries in its stream those guilty of manslaughter. In Dante's *Inferno*, Cocytus is a frozen ice cap, in the midst of which Satan is buried up to his waste. In the ice of Cocytus are punished the traitors.

Creusa: Wife of Aeneas who dies at Troy (*Aeneid* II).

Cumae: Ancient Greek city on eastern coast of Italy (near modern-day Naples) that houses the doorway to Hades in *Aeneid* VI. During Virgil's time, Roman tourists would visit Cumae's underground caves.

Danaids: The daughters of Danaus who murdered their husbands on their wedding night and are punished in Tartarus by carrying water in leaky buckets.

Devils: Former angels who, along with Satan, rebelled against God. They not only punish sinners in Hell but tempt those still living on the earth. In *Paradise Lost*, Milton names his devils after the false, idolatrous gods of the pagan nations (particularly those which are named in the Old Testament). They include Belial, Moloch, Beelzebub, Ashtaroth, Osiris, and Dagon.

Diana of the Crossroads: see *Hecate*.

Dido: Queen of Carthage and lover of Aeneas, whom Aeneas spurns in *Aeneid* IV. In response Dido kills herself. When the two lovers meet in Hades, Dido refuses to speak to the repentant Aeneas.

Dionysus: The god of the grape whose death and rebirth mimicked the seasonal cycle.

Dystopia: see *Utopia*.

Eleusinian Mysteries: A secret religious cult that worshipped both Persephone and Dionysus. Their rites were guarded so jealously that we know little of their actual practices.

Elysian Fields: Also known as Elysium, the land where dead heroes go. It is placed sometimes on the Isle of the Blessed and sometimes in Hades itself. Great poets and philosophers are always found there; in the more Roman versions of Cicero, Virgil, and Dante, heroes who fought and died for their country abound. In *Aeneid* VI, all in Elysium have done something that has gained them fame (*fama*); those who have not done something great by which to be remembered eventually return to the earth in new bodies. Dante's limbo (the abode of the virtuous pagans) is modeled after pagan notions of Elysium.

Empyrean: Paradise itself that lies outside time and space; the dwelling place of God and the saints.

Eunoë: Greek for "good memory," this is a river invented by Dante for his *Purgatorio*. Once the souls reach Eden, they must first drink from Lethe, which washes away the memory of sin, and then from Eunoë, which strengthens the memory of their good deeds.

Fates: Name for the three goddesses who control our lots in life: Lachesis, Clotho, and Atropos. In Greek, they are called the Moirai; in Latin, the Parcae. According to Plato's Myth of Er, the fates only assist us in choosing our lots; it is we who bear responsibility for what we choose.

Farinata: Heretic whom Dante speaks with in the sixth circle of the inferno.

Fixed Stars (Latin: *Stellatum*): Eighth circle of the heavens that houses the great constellations.

Francesca: An adulterous lover who, along with Paolo, is punished in the second circle of Dante's inferno (lust). The tale she tells to Dante and Virgil is a moving one and causes Dante to faint with pity.

Furies: Hideous Greek goddesses with snakes for hair; they live under the earth (often in Hades) and torment those guilty of taboo crimes; their names are Tisiphone, Allecto, and Megeara. They are often linked to the Gorgons

(Medusa, Euryale, Stheno), whose look can turn men to stone. Both Odysseus and Dante fear they will be shown the Gorgon's face in Hades.

Ganymede: A beautiful Greek youth who was taken up to Olympus to be Zeus's cup-bearer.

Gehenna: A variant of the Valley of Hinnom where idolatrous Jews sacrificed their children to Moloch. In late Hebrew writings and at the time of Christ, Gehenna became a representation of Hell, where the fire never goes out and the worm never dies.

Geryon: In Dante's *Inferno*, the guardian of the eighth circle (which punishes fraud). Geryon looks like a noble man from the waist up, but from the waist down he is hairy and reptilian and boasts a scorpion's tail: as such he embodies in himself the two-faced nature of fraud. Geryon has wings and he carries Dante and Virgil on his back down the waterfall that leads to the eighth circle.

Golden Bough: A magical branch that Aeneas plucks and uses as a skeleton key to gain entrance into Hades. He is told that only if he is chosen for this task will he be able to remove the branch. The Golden Bough is also linked to the rites of Diana of the Crossroads.

Great Marriage: The crowning event of human history (described in the concluding chapters of Revelation) when Christ (the Lamb or Bridegroom) will wed himself to his church (the Bride).

Griffin: A mythical creature that is half eagle and half lion. In Dante's *Purgatorio*, the griffin represents the dual nature of Christ: man (lion of Judah) and God (the eagle soars toward Heaven).

Guelphs and Ghibbelines: Two factions (the former supporting the Pope, the latter the Holy Roman Emperor) that fought for supremacy in medieval Italy (especially Florence, the city of Dante). The Guelphs eventually won, but then split into White Guelphs (Dante's party) and Black Guelphs. When the Whites took Florence in 1300 (the dramatic year of Dante's journey), Dante gained much political power, but when the Blacks returned a year later, Dante was exiled for the remainder of his life.

Hades (Pluto, Dis, Erebus, Orcus): The realm of the dead in Greek mythology; a dark, gloomy place of bloodless shades. Also the name of the Lord of the dead and brother of Zeus and Poseidon.

Harrowing of Hell: The belief that Jesus, after his crucifixion but before his resurrection, descended into the underworld, broke down the doors of Hell, and took with him all those Jews who had trusted in the prophecies of his coming. The harrowing of Hell, which is implied but not stated in Scripture, is a frequent subject of Orthodox icons and explains why Dante and Virgil are able to enter into Hell so easily.

Hecate: An ancient goddess of the underworld who became linked with the virgin Diana (Artemis in Greek) of the Crossroads: a triple goddess who was believed to exist in the underworld (as Hecate), on the earth (as Diana), and in the sky (as the moon). In ancient times, Diana would be served by the King of the Wood, who won his role by plucking the Golden Bough and killing his predecessor (see Sir James Frazer's *Golden Bough*).

Hercules (Greek: *Heracles*): Greek hero who visited the underworld (one of his labors was to capture Cerberus) and who, at his death, was apotheosized and lives on Olympus with his immortal wife, Hebe. According to *Odyssey* XI, however, his wraith lives in Hades, where it still inspires fear.

Hyperboria: A utopian land of peace and plenty located "behind the North wind" (its Greek derivation).

Isle of the Blessed (or *Happy Isles*): Location of the Elysian Fields.

Ixion: A Greek villain punished in Tartarus by being bound to an ever-turning wheel.

Jacob's Ladder: In Genesis 28, Jacob, while fleeing from his brother Esau, dreams of a ladder (or stairway) that stretches from Heaven to earth and upon which the angels are descending and ascending. Dante uses the image in his description of the sphere of Saturn. Milton borrows the image when he speaks of a prelapsarian stairway that stretches from Eden to Heaven. The causeway from Hell to earth that sin and death build after the fall of Adam and Eve may be seen as a perversion of Jacob's ladder.

Jupiter: Sixth circle of the heavens; it produces tin on the earth and causes men to be jovial; it brings good fortune and halcyon days. In Dante's *Paradiso* it houses the just leaders.

Karma: see *Samsara*.

Lachesis: Fate of the past who chooses the lot.

Lethe: The river of forgetfulness from which souls (in classic mythology) drink and thus forget their past lives. In Plato, this drink prepares them to assume new bodies and a new identity. Dante moves Lethe to the top of Purgatory; once the saints have been purged of all sin, they drink from Lethe and thus forget even the memory of sin. Milton puts it back in Hell; there it taunts sinners who would like to drink from it (and thus forget their torments) but cannot.

Limbo: The area in Hades/Sheol where the righteous saints of the Old Testament were held until Jesus rescued them during the harrowing of Hell. In Dante's *Inferno*, limbo is the first circle of Hell where the virtuous pagans live; their only punishment is to be devoid of all hope. Dante patterned his limbo on pagan visions of the Elysian Fields. In *Paradise Lost*, the Protestant Milton transforms Dante's limbo into a Limbo of Vanities, a "windy sea of land" where all of man's foolish dreams of glory and all his vain superstitions are blown. For Milton, these vanities include Catholic indulgences, monastic orders, and papal bulls. In *Pilgrim's Progress*, Bunyan fashions his own limbo of vanity, but his is an earthly, temporal place called Vanity Fair, a market where all commodities (from food to religion) are sold.

Malebolgia: Italian name for the eighth circle of Hell (fraud); it means "evil ditches" or "evil pockets," for each sub-group of eight is punished in a different ditch.

Mars: Fifth circle of the heavens; it produces iron on the earth and causes men to be martial. In Dante's *Paradiso* it houses the great warriors and martyrs.

Maya: see *Monism*.

Mercury: Second circle of the heavens; it produces quicksilver on the earth and causes men to be mercurial and seekers of profit. In Dante's *Paradiso* it houses those who sought personal ambition.

Millennium: Latin for thousand, this word (which first appears in the Latin translation of Revelation 20) is used to signify a long, utopian reign of peace and plenty. For John, it is Christ who will establish and rule over the millennial kingdom; for the optimistic Victorians, it was man who would build and run it.

Minos: Legendary King of Crete, reputed to be perfectly just. He is always placed in the Elysian Fields where he rules as judge of the dead. In Dante's *Inferno*, Minos is given a tail (surely taken from the Minotaur), which he twists in knots to indicate the number of the level where the sinner is to reside.

Minotaur: Legendary half-man, half-bull beast of Crete. In Dante's *Inferno*, it guards level seven (violence) and embodies in itself the nature of violence (by which men transform themselves into beasts).

Moksha: see *Samsara*.

Monism: A mostly Eastern concept that holds that all is one and that physical matter is finally an illusion (or maya). Though Plato shares much in common with Eastern notions of reincarnation, and though he does view our physical world as a lesser imitation of a more real, unseen world, he tended to stay clear of the abyss of monism. The Pre-Socratic philosopher, Parmenides, was responsible for establishing a Western school of monism.

Moon: First circle of the heavens; it produces silver on the earth and causes lunacy and wandering. In Dante's *Paradiso* it houses those inconstant to vows.

Musaeus: Mythical Greek singer and poet, generally to be found in the Elysian Fields.

Music of the Spheres: see *Angels*.

Mystic Rose: The true dwelling of all the souls in Dante's *Paradiso*. The rose lies in the empyrean; God is at its center and the rose itself spirals outward in concentric circles (like a rose window in a cathedral or a stadium). Each soul has a station in the rose. The angels, like bees, fly back and forth between God and the souls. Half of the rose holds those who trusted in Christ to come (the righteous Jews); the other half holds those who trusted in Christ risen (the church). It is one of Dante's most beautiful images.

Near-Death Experience: An episode in which a patient is pronounced clinically dead and then is brought back to life (usually by medical means). Recently, many patients who have experienced such episodes have claimed to have been taken bodily to Heaven (or, sometimes, Hell) and then returned. The more popular phrase for such episodes is "life after life."

Nekuia: Word used by critics of the *Odyssey* to refer to Odysseus's descent into the underworld and his interrogation of the dead; also used to denote the epic convention that Homer began.

Nirvana: see *Samsara*.

Ocean: A mighty body of water that the ancient Greeks believed circled the rim of the world.

Odysseus (Latin: *Ulysses*): Hero of Homer's *Odyssey*; the first epic hero to descend to the underworld. In Plato's Myth of Er, he requests to come back as an ordinary man. Roman writers treat him less kindly. He is often cursed in the *Aeneid* and Dante places him in Hell as an evil counselor (where he tells Dante and Virgil the tale of his final, fatal voyage).

Olympus: The abode of the Greek gods; also the tallest mountain in Greece.

Orc and Urizen: In the mythology of William Blake, Orc and Urizen represent contrary forces. Urizen ("you reason") is an old, jealous, restrictive, vengeful God who crushes all freedom and creativity; Blake linked him to Jehovah, the Old Testament God of the thou shalt not. Orc (Orcus is a Roman name for Hades) is a young, fiery, revolutionary God; his is the energy both of revolution and creativity, an unleashed, unstoppable power. Whereas the eighteenth-century Age of Reason had privileged Urizen, the Romantic Blake sought to sing the power and potential of Orc. Milton's God and Satan represented for Blake the forces of Urizen and Orc.

Orpheus: Greek hero who descended into Hades to rescue his dead wife, Eurydice. He was told he could lead her out if he did not look back at her, but, at the last moment, he turned to see if she was still there, and she was pulled back into Hades forever. A later cult sprang up that took Orpheus as its titular head. Orphism, the little we know of it, taught the need for the soul to be purified through punishment in Hades. The influence of Orphism is felt in Plato's *Phaedo* and in *Aeneid* VI. In all accounts of the underworld, Orpheus is placed in the Elysian Fields.

Palinurus: Friend of Aeneas who dies in *Aeneid* V and who meets with Aeneas in Hades.

Pandemonium: Satan's capital in *Paradise Lost*; the word (coined by Milton) means "all demons."

Persephone (Latin: *Proserpine*): The daughter of Demeter (Latin: Ceres) who was kidnapped by Hades and became the Queen of the dead. Her annual return to earth provided the mythic origin for the seasonal cycle.

Phlegethon: River in Hades whose name means burning. Plato conceives of it as a river of lava that flows into Tartarus and that carries the souls of those who committed offenses against their families but then repented of it. In Dante's *Inferno*, Phlegethon is actually a river of boiling blood; in it are punished those who committed violence against their neighbors.

Phlegyas: In *Aeneid* VI, one of the sinners who dwells in Tartarus, where he warns all to show justice and piety. Dante transforms him into a blood-thirsty, demonic soul who carries souls over Styx in his boat.

Pirithous: see *Theseus*.

Positivism: The belief, prevalent in the Victorian Age, that, through science, technology, and enlightened government, man could propel himself into an ideal, perfect world of peace, equality, and plenty.

Pre-Existence: The doctrine (propagated by Plato) that our soul existed in Heaven before entering our body.

Primum Mobile ("first mover"): Ninth circle of the heavens. The primum mobile spins out of love for God; it then passes its motion down to the planets below, thus setting the times and days of earth.

Resurrection Body: In sharp contrast to the Platonic notion of the immortality of the soul, the Bible teaches that, in the afterlife, we will not be bodiless souls but will possess glorified bodies like the one Jesus "wore" after his resurrection. Paul describes this body in 1 Corinthians 15.

Rhadamanthus: Brother of Minos, with whom he judges the dead.

Ripheus: A mythical Trojan whom Virgil (in *Aeneid* II) hails as the most just of his people. Though he died a pagan and should have thus appeared in Dante's limbo (with the virtuous pagans), Dante actually meets him in the sphere of Jupiter. To explain this anomaly, Dante explains that Ripheus was given a vision of Christ to come, believed in that vision, and thus was saved. For Dante, Ripheus is a symbol of the power and mystery of God's grace. Dante offers a similar story to explain the salvation of Trajan, a Roman emperor who died a pagan.

Samsara: Hindu word for the wheel of reincarnations a soul must go through before it can reach nirvana or moksha (a state of bliss that is beyond pain and pleasure). Our actions in each life determine our karma, which, in turn, determines the state of our next incarnation. Many of Plato's teachings embody elements of these Eastern concepts.

Satan: Once an archangel of light (named Lucifer) Satan rebelled against God and was cast out of Heaven along with all those angels who took his side (a third of the angels by Milton's reckoning). Satan's rebellion is alluded to in scattered verses of Scripture (see, for example, the following two cryptic passages: Isa 14:12–15 and Ezek 28:11–19); Milton collected these bits, added in his own imagination, and gave the "definitive" account of the rebellion in *Paradise Lost*. Though in most discussions of temptation and of Hell, Satan is a mobile figure, Dante has him imprisoned in ice in the lowest pit of Hell, where he guards his fellow traitors; presumably, it is Satan's lesser devils that meddle in earthly souls and affairs. Satan in Hebrew means "accuser" (the role he plays in Job); devil in Greek means the same thing.

Saturn: Seventh circle of the heavens; it produces lead on the earth and causes men to be saturnine; it brings plague and bad times. In Dante's *Paradiso* it houses the great contemplatives.

Septuagint: The Greek translation of the Old Testament (c. 250 B.C.).

Sheol: The abode of the dead in the Old Testament; generally translated as grave, pit, or Hell. In the Septuagint, Sheol is translated Hades, and it shares some similarities with the Greek concept of Hades.

Sibyl: Aeneas's guide through the underworld. The Sibyl was a prophetess, a sort-of Italian version of the oracle of Delphi. The Sibyl would write her prophecies on leaves that would then blow away (thus Aeneas asks her to speak her prophecies orally). Once, legend has it, she tried to sell nine books of prophecy to a Roman Tyrant (Tarquin the Proud); when he refused, she burned three, then another three, then sold him the remaining three for the original price. There were actually several Sibyls in Italy, but the Cumaean one was the most famous. Medieval Christians often linked the Sibyls to Old Testament prophecies of Christ; Michelangelo includes them on the ceiling of the Sistine Chapel.

Sin and Death: In *Paradise Lost*, sin is born out of the head of Satan (as Athena was from the head of Zeus). Satan then rapes her, and she begets death; death then rapes her as well and causes her to give birth to a brood of dogs that eat out her insides. The two are the guardians of the gate of Hell.

Sirena: During his second night on the mountain of Purgatory, Dante dreams of Sirena, a witch who lures souls into avarice. She is patterned after the sirens of *Odyssey* XII, whose beautiful voices lure sailors toward the rocks.

Sisyphus: A Greek villain punished in Tartarus by being forced to forever push a rock up a hill that forever rolls back down. Camus hailed Sisyphus as a model of the modern existential man.

Stoicism: A philosophical school that began in Greece and spread to Rome where it found its fullest expression in the works of Seneca and Marcus Aurelius. Virgil was strongly influenced by the stoic notion that all nature is controlled by Spirit or Mind and that man's soul is a spark of divine fire; these notions are expressed in Anchises' first speech to Aeneas in *Aeneid* VI.

Styx: One of the rivers of Hades; when the gods swear by Styx, they must keep their promise. Plato has the river Styx plunge into Tartarus where it becomes Cocytus. In Dante's *Inferno*, Phlegyas carries sinners over Styx on his boat; in the river are punished the souls of the wrathful and the sullen. The adjectival form of Styx (stygian) is often used to connote a dark, gloomy place.

Sun: Fourth circle of the heavens; it produces gold on the earth and causes men to be wise and liberal. In Dante's *Paradiso* it houses the great Doctors of the Church.

Tantalus: A Greek villain punished in Tartarus by being submerged in a lake up to his chin. Whenever he reaches down to drink, the water drains away; whenever he reaches up to take some grapes from the vines, a wind blows them out of his reach.

Tartarus: A pit beneath Hades where the rebellious Titans were chained by Zeus and where infamous sinners like Tantalus are punished.

Theseus: Greek hero and legendary King of Athens who killed the Minotaur of Crete. Later, with the help of Pirithous, he descended into Hades to carry away Persephone. He was caught and punished, but was later rescued by his friend Hercules.

Tiresias: The blind prophet of Thebes (he appears in both *Oedipus* and *Antigone*) with whom Odysseus speaks in the underworld.

Tityus: An evil Titan punished in Tartarus by being stretched out over nine acres and having a vulture eat away at his innards.

Topheth: Another name for Gehenna.

Triptolemus: According to Plato's *Apology* (and only there), one of the judges of Elysium.

Utopia: Though derived from the Greek for "no-place," many in the Victorian age believed that, through the blessings of science, social planning, and universal education, man could propel himself into an ideal world of peace, plenty, and equality (essentially a Heaven on earth). The idea of utopia has always been with us (Plato's *Republic*, Thomas More's *Utopia*, Jonathan

Swift's *Gulliver's Travels*, etc.), but only in the Victorian age did it seem fully achievable. Unfortunately, in the twentieth century, when various totalitarian governments from the right and left tried to build utopia, they ended up creating instead a monolithic state where freedom and individuality were crushed (a dystopia or Hell on earth).

Utopian Socialism: A Victorian movement that sought to establish ideal communities in which all labor would be shared and complete equality would be the rule. Many utopian socialists actually put their theories into practice and established communities (some in America). The leading figures of the movement are Charles Fourier, Robert Owen, and Saint-Simon.

Venus: Third circle of the heavens; it produces copper on the earth and causes men to be amorous. In Dante's *Paradiso* it houses the lovers.

Who's Who

Aquinas, St. Thomas (1225–74) Medieval Catholic theologian whose *Summa Theologica* influenced greatly Dante's design for *The Divine Comedy*.

Aristotle (384–322 B.C.) Greek philosopher who studied in Athens under Plato and wrote treatises on nearly every area of human thought. He was one of the main thinkers who helped shape the view of the universe that eventually passed down to Dante and Milton.

Blake, William (1757–1827) British Romantic poet whose *Marriage of Heaven and Hell* presents a Gnostic vision of the afterlife in which perception determines reality.

Bunyan, John (1628–88) English preacher and writer who spent long years in jail for his puritan beliefs and his refusal to abide by the Church of England. During one of his stays in prison, he wrote *Pilgrim's Progress*, one of the most read books after the Bible.

Byron, George Gordon, Lord (1788–1824) British poet who helped develop a character-type that would come to be known as the Byronic hero.

Cato, Marcus Porcius ("the Younger," 95–46 B.C.) Roman statesman (and great-grandson of Cato the Elder) who was considered one of the last embodiments of the traditional virtues of the Roman Republic. When Julius Caesar came to power, Cato committed suicide. Dante makes him the guardian of Purgatory, presumably because he loved freedom so much he was willing to die for it.

Cicero, Marcus Tullius (106–43 B.C.) Roman orator, statesman, and author who was a defender of the traditional values of the Roman republic. His *On *the Republic* (which only survives in part) was modeled on Plato's *Republic*; it ends with a powerful vision of Heaven and the cosmos ("The Dream of Scipio") that influenced Dante.

Coleridge, Samuel Taylor (1772–1834) British poet, essayist, and literary theorist; a major figure of British Romanticism. He is the author of *The Rime of the Ancient Mariner*.

Dante Alighieri (1265–1321) Italian poet whose *Divine Comedy* both offers a survey of the entire medieval Catholic universe and sums up all previous writings on the afterlife.

Donne, John (1572–1630) English poet of secular and sacred works who went from being a man-about-town to the Dean of St. Paul's Cathedral. His *Holy Sonnets* and his *Devotions upon Emergent Occasions* (written during a near-fatal illness) are classic devotional works.

Frazer, Sir James (1854–1941) British cultural anthropologist whose masterwork, *The Golden Bough*, initiated an entire school of myth criticism. He greatly influenced Carl Jung and all critics who tend to read visions of the afterlife in archetypal terms. His book makes a fine companion to *Aeneid* VI.

Hesiod (eighth century B.C.) Greek poet whose *Theogeny* describes the creation of the world, the defeat of the Titans and their imprisonment in Tartarus, and the relationship between all the gods.

Homer (eighth century B.C.) Greek epic poet and author of the *Iliad* and *Odyssey*. His decision to send Odysseus on a journey through the underworld (Book XI) influenced all epic poets that followed him.

Huxley, Aldous (1894–1963) English essayist and novelist; author of *Brave New World*.

John, St. (first century A.D.) One of the twelve apostles of Christ who went on to write not only a gospel account of the life of Christ but a strange and cryptic vision of the future that has baffled theologians for 2000 years. In his Apocalypse (Latin: Revelation), John presents us not only with an account of the end-of-the-world and the final judgment but several sublime visions of Heaven and the New Jerusalem. Some believe that Revelation was written by a different John.

224

Keats, John (1795–1821) British Romantic poet whose *Hyperion* sought to recast Greek mythology in such a way as to make the Titans the heroes and the Olympians the oppressors. *Prometheus Unbound*, written by fellow Romantic Percy Shelley, embodies a similar vision.

Lewis, C. S. (1898–1963) British novelist, essayist, literary theorist, and Christian apologist whose *Great Divorce* offers a vision of Heaven and Hell that contrasts sharply with that of Blake's *Marriage of Heaven and Hell*. Lewis's *Screwtape Letters* also offers much insight into the nature of Satan and temptation. As a theorist, Lewis helped to defend the worldviews of Dante and Milton from their modernist detractors.

Longinus (first century A.D.) Anonymous Greek literary critic who wrote *On the Sublime*.

George MacDonald (1824–1905) Scottish minister and author of children's stories, many of which possess great mythopoeic power. He was a powerful influence on C. S. Lewis (both spiritually and aesthetically); in Lewis's *Great Divorce*, MacDonald plays the Virgilean role of guide to Lewis's pilgrim.

Marx, Karl (1818–83) German philosopher, economist, and political activist who shared the Victorian faith that man will eventually propel himself into a utopian state.

Milton, John (1608–74) British poet and author of *Paradise Lost* whose epic retelling of the fall of Satan is accepted by many as an addendum to the Bible! As a radical Protestant revolutionary, Milton's visions of the afterlife have a different tone than do those of the medieval Catholic Dante.

Nietzsche, Friedrich (1844–1900) German philosopher and essayist. Blake, in his *Marriage of Heaven and Hell*, anticipates by a century Nietzsche's concept of religion as a slave ethic.

Orwell, George (pen name of Eric Blair, 1903–50) British essayist and novelist; the author of *1984*.

Ovid (43 B.C.–A.D. 17) Roman poet born a generation after Virgil whose *Metamorphoses* embodies the teachings of Pythagoras. He had a profound influence on all British poets (especially Milton), and Dante consciously tries to outdo his gift for describing strange transformations.

Paul, St. (died c. A.D. 64) A learned Pharisee and scholar who, after his conversion to Christianity, became the first great missionary. He was responsible for writing much of the New Testament. At one point in his ministry, Paul had a vision in which he was taken up to the third Heaven. Paul is one of our greatest sources for the Christian belief in the resurrection body.

Plato (c. 427–c. 348 B.C.) Greek philosopher and founder of the Academy. In such works as *Republic*, *The Apology of Socrates*, and *Phaedo*, he lays out both the geography and theology of the afterlife.

Pythagoras (sixth century B.C.) Greek philosopher, mathematician, and religious leader whose musings on the nature of the soul and of the universe and whose teachings on reincarnation had a profound impact on Plato and Virgil's visions of the afterlife.

Shelley, Percy Bysshe (1792–1822) British Romantic poet who helped carry the ideals of Plato into the Romantic era and who shared Byron's vision of the Byronic hero.

Tennyson, Alfred, Lord (1809–92) The most representative poet of his age, Tennyson (in such works as *In Memoriam* and "Locksley Hall") embodied to the full the Victorian faith in progress.

Virgil (70–19 B.C.; full name: Publius Vergilius Maro) Roman epic poet who sent his hero, Aeneas, on an influential journey through the underworld. Virgil was considered by most early Christians to be a proto-Christian, a claim based partly on the messianic implications of his Fourth Eclogue; for this reason (and many others), Dante chose him to be his guide through the underworld.

Wells, Herbert George (1866–1946) English novelist and advocate of social reform who embodied fully the Victorian spirit of progress and expressed that spirit in a series of utopian novels that bespoke a glorious future. Oddly, Wells was also one of the first to write dystopic novels.

Wordsworth, William (1770–1850) British Romantic poet who planned to write an epic called *The Recluse*; in his prospectus for this work he proclaimed (in Miltonic fashion) that he would both sink lower than Erebus and ascend higher than Jehovah's throne.

Index of Names

(Index does not include names from Bibliography or Appendices)

Printed in Great Britain
by Amazon

51451898R00147